# Dialogues
# with the Master

# Dialogues
# with the Master

**Paul Twitchell**

**Illuminated Way
Publishing Inc.**
PO Box 28130
Crystal, MN 55428

**Dialogues with the Master**

Copyright © 1970 ECKANKAR.

The terms ECKANKAR, ECK, EK, MAHANTA, SOUL TRAVEL, VAIRAGI, and ᴧᴧᴧᴓ, among others, are trademarks of ECKANKAR, P.O. Box 27300, Minneapolis, MN 55427 U.S.A.

Printed in U.S.A.
ISBN: 0-914766-78-3
Ninth Printing—1987

Cover design by Lois Stanfield

*Dedicated to*

Mrs. Neva Thomas
for her love
and devotion to ECK

# CONTENTS

|  | Page |
|---|---|
| Introduction | 7 |
| A Dialogue On God-Realization | 9 |
| Channels To God | 13 |
| Impersonal Love | 17 |
| Love For The Eck Master | 21 |
| The True Meaning Of Love | 27 |
| The Paradox Of The Universe | 31 |
| The Spiritual Power | 37 |
| Mind-Control | 45 |
| God's Love | 53 |
| The Keystone Of God | 55 |
| Spiritual Conflicts | 63 |
| Who Is The Master? | 69 |
| The Voice Of The Master | 75 |
| Self-Surrender | 83 |
| Influences Of The Astral World | 89 |
| The Cosmic Worlds | 97 |
| The Feeling Of God | 107 |
| Unconditional Love | 113 |
| Practical Wisdom | 119 |
| The Experience Of Spiritual Wealth | 123 |

The Heart Center ........................................................................129

The Will Power ..........................................................................133

The True Reality .......................................................................137

The Desire Of Soul ...................................................................139

The Pure Mind ..........................................................................143

Becoming God ...........................................................................149

The Divine Consciousness .......................................................155

What Is Life? .............................................................................161

A Talk With Rami Nuri ............................................................165

The Lord Sohang Speaks .........................................................173

A Discourse By Gopal Das ......................................................181

The Face Of God .......................................................................191

The SUGMAD Speaks ..............................................................197

The Process Of Death ..............................................................203

Generating Power ....................................................................211

Seven Principles of Consciousness .......................................217

Maya, The Queen Of Illusion .................................................221

The Mind And Its Functions ..................................................229

# INTRODUCTION

DIALOGUES WITH THE MASTER are a series of spiritual discourses which were taken down when Rebazar Tarzs, the ageless emissary for ECKANKAR in the world today, appeared to me nightly in his light body for practically one year and dictated them.

This occurred while living in the nation's capital. I had been in India for a month or so prior to his first appearance. During this visit I was fortunate to meet him in Darjeeling as explained in my book "An Introduction to ECKANKAR."

Rebazar Tarzs lives in a small hut in the wild and remote Hindu Kush mountains on the Kashmir-Afghanistan border. He leaves his physical body there and appears in light form, the Nuri Sarup, to many throughout the world who have some line with ECK. It is said that he was a young man when Columbus discovered America, but to the eye he looks to be in his early forties.

The DIALOGUES in this book are as close as possible to the original words he spoke during his nightly visits to give me advanced training in the secret science of ECK-ANKAR. He concluded his series of talks that year by taking me on the spiritual journey recorded in my book "The Tiger's Fang."

How one accepts these DIALOGUES depends on his attitude and the training which has gone into his spiritual unfoldment during his past incarnations spent in this world.

It is the greatest spiritual adventure of one's life to have an ECK Master like Rebazar Tarzs as a Guru. I have been more than blessed.

PAUL TWITCHELL

7

# A DIALOGUE ON GOD-REALIZATION

Rebazar Tarzs aroused me out of a sound sleep about 1:30 a.m., and motioned for me to go to the writing desk and take a pencil to write. I resisted a little, but he ignored it completely and settled down on the edge of the bed to stare silently at the ceiling. In a few minutes he started talking.

R.T.: "I want you to take down the following words as part of a discourse to give the world. You will act as a channel for this message. Are you ready?"

P.: "Yes. But please go slow."

R.T.: "Man is an individual being. Each person is a cosmic world to himself and, therefore, must consider himself in two lights: his relationship to the outer world, commonly called the objective; and his relationship to the inner world, known as the subjective.

"Because man is complex and deeply involved in his cosmic mechanics, it is a psychological fact that he must go deep into his nature to analyze himself through introspection and spiritual techniques.

"The psychologists and psychiatrists furnish us many ways of introspection and self-analysis by which we can learn to adjust ourselves. But to what? To what must we adjust ourselves? The negative way intellectual man shows us? Or to God which IT gives us? The answer is we must adjust ourselves to God. For it is THE ECK, which should control our lives.

"The mind, which is under the influence of the senses, rules our outer lives in an egotistical way. But man, directed by the Light of Soul, gives us a life of joyous well-being.

9

This is a spiritual truth, for the Soul receives Its guidance from God, the All-Knowing!

"You who have reached this step upon the divine path have been blessed in your lives by the eleventh-hour appearance of such a teaching. You know it as ECKANKAR, The Ancient Science of Soul Travel.

"The living ECK Master is a messenger of God. He simplifies all introspective techniques and puts the spiritual power at work in our lives and directs the mind to the Soul.

"These acts being performed, then the traveler leaves the task to us to follow his commandments. After progression on the path, he takes us through the spiritual worlds, inside ourselves, where Soul treads the familiar homeward path.

"Here great wisdom is revealed through self-knowledge. But this is not the consummation of the search. At this phase of his spiritual quest every seeker of God knows that he must go beyond the revelations of self-knowledge and wisdom.

"To ascend these aspects of God means that we, as seekers, must learn the subtle art of catching and holding the ECK power so that it always flows through us.

"An explanation of this statement lies in a remoteness of expression beyond the horizon of language. It can hardly be focused into crystallized thought. It is one of the deepest secrets of God-realization which comes only after we have passed the phase of self-knowledge and wisdom, and beyond the next step, in our part as actors in the divine drama of life. This last step is that anguish of Soul for the life of the great reality, and the struggle to reach the Master in thought, deed and love!

"This step, or phase, may be described as our conscious, constant control of the pace and rhythm of the God-Power flowing through us!

"Intuitively we know what this means. We must strike

or find within, a certain pacing for our individual vibrations in order to get the maximum benefit from the spiritual in our daily lives.

"We must adjust the subjective self to the spiritual rhythm by which the ECK Master wants Soul to function in the cosmic worlds inside.

"Learning this art is decidedly an individual undertaking. So the Master wisely allows us to learn to adjust ourselves so he can take over completely after our attunement to the great cosmic current.

"Our individual vibrational harmony with the sound-current is what makes us differ from one another. This sense of inner rhythmic attunement takes time to acquire, but once we gain it, we have the key to inner assurance and permanent peace of Soul. Always we will have a sense of security thereafter, for we have the conscious awareness that the Master has our lives in his hands.

"When our minds are so attuned that we can surrender to the Master, a cord of love is established between us. This is similar to the cord of love between a mother and her infant. This is the way we become a vibratory channel for God to pour ITS love into the world.

"This attunement is like a small built-in metronome ticking away quietly inside us, becoming obtrusive, or inharmonious, only when we lose the beat, or get out of tune.

"Undoubtedly, this is the reason why the Master teaches us the science of the cosmic sound-current. Our inner spiritual rhythm reflects itself to the outer world and smooths the path. Not only our path but others', too.

"Then what is the inner pace which we must live by individually? Nobody can tell us. But we know that through the practice of the Master's teachings of the sound-current, we become attuned to our individual Soul vibration.

"So as we progress in our daily contemplations in the sound-current, our lives come under the guidance of God,

11

and eventually we become the conscious co-workers of the universe!

"As we learn to live by the Light of God in this world of complexities, we will be an inspiration to others and of service to all humanity!"

# CHANNELS TO GOD

Rebazar Tarzs aroused me from a light sleep and went across to the table where he seated himself in the chair, throwing one leg over the other in his customary pose. He smiled gently and began talking.

R.T.: "I desire to speak to you this evening about the channels to God."

P.: "I am awake and ready."

R.T.: "Today man is in the midst of the greatest spiritual evolution known in the history of world civilizations.

"Civilization, too, is on the brink of a world change. But this change is for the good of all mankind. It will open the channels to God in such a wide stream that I doubt if man will know or recognize them. He has not in the past.

"Civilization itself is only a toy to the spiritual giants who have walked this earth, spreading their Light through their individual channels to God. And what would you say the channel to God might be?

"To answer this question directly is hardly possible. So we must take an approach to it first through the intellect. Man's individual self always has been a battleground for the elemental forces of good and evil, positive and negative forces to fight out their quarrels.

"Recognizing this fact in the earliest period of man's history, we find priestcraft springing up to coincide with the civilizations of the world. They were formed only to gain control of the minds of the masses and to deal with moral and ethical problems of mankind.

"Rules and laws were made, but in the same instance those priestly sects (like the Brahmans of India) put the worst kind of restrictions upon their own people. The early Christian Church was adopted by the Romans as a state religion in place of their old form called Pantheism. The popularity of Christianity gave the Roman State control of the masses of people in that once mighty empire.

"Now to tell you what this all means is to say that out of every religion in the world comes a reform in the philosophy being taught, to give the people the true essence of the highest teachings of God.

"The esoteric side of religion was not taught the masses in those early days of world civilization. Where a religion was the philosophy of the state (as in early India) it was used to protect and to give the people such codes as making the cow sacred under the law of Manu, so the poor would neither butcher their own nor steal a neighbor's animal without punishment. The authorities were wise in their dealings with primitive minds for the families of India usually owned one cow per family, and this animal was their only means of getting staple food for their meager diets.

"Out of this outer ritual and ceremonies intended to fascinate and hold the minds of the people, grew the great teachings of religions, and the revealing of the secrets of the esoteric side of philosophy and religion.

"These are called the Mystery Schools. But why this name? Because in these groups, gathered under the guiding hand of a Master or teacher of the spiritual truths, the mysteries of nature are revealed. Out of the great religions have come varied mystery groups of modern times.

"Each Mystery School has its own spiritual leader, who either established it or has been responsible for its growth. The paths always have been the same. Buddha sought to find the answer to his spiritual problems, but he had little thought of establishing an esoteric philosophy which would reform Hinduism and erect a line of gurus, who would inherit his spiritual mantle.

"Each school of religious philosophy has a line of gurus, who give to the world the teachings through their own enlightenment. Each Master inherits the spiritual mantle from his successor. His experience in the spiritual world is the basis upon which the Master selects him for succession. Often he is chosen at birth as the Dalai Lama of Tibet. Jesus was known at his birth (to those who could see by the spiritual eye) and a line of mystic teachers followed in his footsteps to establish Christianity.

"To see how the hand of God guides mankind through every period of world civilization, study the history of religion. The best example is the Bible, whose prophets were of a distinct line of some of the great teachers.

"You ask how does this affect either you or me personally? I will tell you this. All seekers eventually come to a Mystery School where the teacher takes charge of their spiritual welfare.

"Each school comes under one of the three divisions of the profound mysteries: (1) The Solar Mysteries; (2) The Lunar Mysteries; (3) The Mystery of Nature. And, of course, there is one more: the Universal Mysteries.

"You are initiated into one of the mysteries in some ceremony peculiar to that Mystery School. To paraphrase an old saying, 'That as water seeks its level, so does nature provide a way that every seeker of God finds his Master'. He will be the one to teach him best in whatever Mystery School he is best fitted for by individual nature.

"The first three Mystery Schools are a preparation for the greater Mystery School, the Universal Mysteries, but this does not mean that the teachers are any less qualified than those of the higher school. No, indeed, all teach the highest philosophy of God-consciousness, and the teachers are travelers, who can help with the most difficult spiritual problems that bother the individual.

"No teaching in the Mystery Schools is orthodox; however, the great Divine Law sees that we are moved into that particular niche which will take care of our spiritual welfare at that particular time.

"When the devotee is ready to go farther into the mysteries of cosmic awareness, God will see that he is moved into that Mystery School which will give him the greatest guidance to his spiritual needs."

P.: "But this is puzzling. Where does ECKANKAR belong in the Order of Mystery Schools?"

R.T.: "When one has transcended all Mystery Schools, or all initiations of the lower orders, throughout one's incarnations of life on this plane, then his next step is to enter into the highest teachings which is ECKANKAR.

"This is given only by the Mahanta, the Living ECK Master. You must understand, know, and believe"

# IMPERSONAL LOVE

Rebazar Tarzs was waiting when I came in late this evening. He was sitting in his customary position in the easy chair, contemplating. He opened his eyes and looked at me.

R.T.: "I promised to return and verify my revelations at the river yesterday. Do you believe in me now?"

P.: "Yes. Of course!"

R.T.: "Then I can reveal more to you. Do you smell the fragrance of sandalwood? I can give off perfumes at any time. Are you not filled with the bliss of God? There, let me touch you. See? I have given you the cosmic Light. What do you see?"

P.: "Waves of Light coming in like breakers on a beach. I feel them so strongly! They are overwhelming me!"

R.T.: "You can stand more of the cosmic vibrations than most people. You hold your strength and vibrations within your aura. That is the secret of love. You learned that a long time ago, in your past life. I taught you that a long time ago. Remember? About one hundred years ago in Tibet.

"The principle of love and the interpretation of love are entirely different. The interpretation of love as taught openly is wrong. I have explained this to you again and again. I wish you would get it straight in your mind and stop letting people mix up your thoughts. Love is everything and everybody — that is the principle. But the interpretation is in the discrimination of its use. This is a dangerous subject to give to the

17

masses. Therefore, a master must teach openly 'Love thy neighbor as thyself' without any hesitation.

"However, there is really a limitation on loving everybody, as all gurus know. Very contradictory, isn't it?

"Since we know that we cannot love everybody equally, then we can love warmly only a certain number, but according to the Law we must give impersonal love to all."

P.: "What do you mean by 'impersonal love'?"

R.T.: "You must choose to love only those who will be faithful in returning a love to you, and who will not use your love for a selfish purpose. This is the use of discrimination in your love for your fellow man.

"Why do I say 'Use your love'? Because you must remember that the spiritual life in itself is in a sense compared to the economic life. You must direct your efforts where they will do the most good for the individual concerned, or for yourself in advancement on the spiritual path.

"When you discover that any one will take advantage of your love, then use discretion and withdraw. Leave him to learn his own lesson. No amount of love that any one can give him is going to help. However, you must obey the Law and give all impersonal love. Hold nothing against any one. Be neutral in your attitude towards all.

"Sometimes a teacher withdraws his love so as not to let some disciple take advantage of his love, and returns impersonal love, which means pure love.

"Warm love (which is the fiery love) draws warm love in return, but it brings problems as all gurus know. Therefore, they watch to see upon whom they can bestow their warm love.

"This is one reason why each guru will limit himself to a certain number of initiates during his earthly sojourn. He picks those who need him and will not abuse his love, which he pours upon them. This does not mean he cannot love all, which he does, in pure love. But he simply can not do his spiritual mission physically with a group who cannot respond to his needs.

"Every ECK Master has a spiritual destiny to the world. He can be one with the world, or one with himself. It depends upon his task. If he desires fifty — or a million — disciples for his purpose in life, he will collect that number to use as his channels.

"What determines this is the spiritual duty given him by the spiritual hierarchy for this world. However, it is left up to him to make his choice of spiritual workers and select only those who will help carry out his assignment.

"Pure love, or God love, is another discourse. This is when the traveler can give only the highest love to those who are fortunate to come under his guiding hand. He diffuses love rays to those who are made channels for pure love and they act as physical and subjective transformers to allow this love to touch everything with which they come in contact. Jesus said, 'Ye are the Light of the world', meaning that all who could receive the Light, or Love, became his reflecting mirrors to bring joy to the world.

"If you give love indiscriminately, the world will soon teach you that it is wrong. The lessons you learn will be far greater than you think, and soon the Law will show that it is best to love only those who love you. Love them with every fiber of your heart.

"But above all, love the SUGMAD! Have faith in ITS word, and love that which belongs to you. So much for this.

"I have given you a forecast of what is to come in your life. You will go over the world to do certain jobs for the SUGMAD. Everything will be arranged for you.

"One of your trips will be to South America, to the vicinity of Quito, where will be found one of the seven spiritual cities of the world. These are kept secret from the profane masses.

"I will not say anything further except that your conscious mind will not reveal anything beyond its own limitations. Always go beyond your conscious mind. Go straight to the SUGMAD for the answers to a problem.

"I have given you many secrets of ECK, but keep them to yourself until the time comes to reveal them to the world."

## LOVE FOR THE ECK MASTER

Rebazar Tarzs was sitting in the chair in my bedroom when I looked up from a book. He smiled and stroked his chin.

R.T.: "I never cease to think of you!"

P.: "That is wonderful! But why?"

R.T.: "Because of your spiritual breath. Your aura shines brightly and those who can see know that it portrays the breath of a good Soul. The spiritual power is maturing in you and you have given it an outlet to materialize in the outer world. My love pours through you into the earth plane."

P.: "Well, I am amazed! I didn't know this!"

R.T.: "Of course not. Most of the spiritually advanced Souls do not know they have evolved to a high state. It is only those who are so concerned about their Souls and talk so much about their advancement who are really undeveloped. They only pretend.

"I need you, as you need me. This is not unusual to say, for all travelers need ones like you while on earth. This is a necessity for we must draw upon the love of man for our existence."

P.: "What is that? I have always understood that a traveler did not need love from the human being. That he could exist with the bliss of God alone!"

R.T.: "Now look here. I tell you that this is getting into some truly deep secrets. In a way that is correct, but those who live to themselves, existing in the bliss of God alone, cannot do so for long, or they will come to the unbalancing of their minds and bodies! While in this body serving out a duty upon the earth, whether we be a Master or a common laborer, we must balance the spiritual forces between ourselves and all other things — be it a tree, house, dog, or human being!

"What does this have to do with a traveler being self-sufficient unto himself? That he can dwell in cosmic con-

21

sciousness whenever he desires? Or is this a belief of man based upon false knowledge?

"Now I tell you. This is true to the extent that as long as the traveler is in human form, he must adhere strictly to the laws of the earth plane. Remember the saying by John Donne, in his Devotion 17, 'No man is an island unto himself'. While I am here in human form I must act according to the laws of nature. One example: Is not everything born of the female species?

"Yes. Every man can live beyond the laws of the earth plane, but he needs the help of his fellow man to do so!

"Now you ask why does a Master need the love of a human being in order to exist?

"Simply this, I tell you. In the material world we need the good fellowship of every individual to exist. But if we have the love of each individual with whom we are in relationship daily, then our inner powers are lifted and a channel of love is open to God, through and by the efforts of others!

"There is the example of the mother and infant. A mother can love her infant dearly, but if that infant is so bad (in crying and other departments of its tiny life) fatigue and depression overcome her and soon she loses her patience. And if this continues for weeks, the cord of love may be broken between herself and the infant. She cannot grow spiritually. If the case is vice versa, she is lifted in her love by the love of the infant, and her family, neighbors and friends; and even though she is dwelling in cosmic consciousness now, with the love of those around her, she is lifted still higher into the God-like state."

P.: "This is confusing to me. Why does a Master need human love?"

R.T. laughed.: "You were told the other night that the ECK Master is sent always to the earth by the spiritual hierarchy for a spiritual mission, and that he could select those whom he desired to help him in this important and valuable work. But while doing this he also selects those who are capable of giving great love!

"Esoterically, it is this. Each human being is like an

22

electric battery giving off etheric love-currents. The love-currents of a group of disciples, given off individually, will become a great Current which has a two-fold purpose. First, it gives the Master an opportunity to use this Current to do his work in this world, through love, with the advantage of a wide channel of love. The greater the number of disciples, the greater becomes the Master's work. For example, that is why I said that in the world in this life I would need as many as a million or more initiates. A wide channel is needed for the work I must do here on earth.

"Secondly, as the traveler pours out his love upon his disciples, it is returned to him, and his circle becomes, in comparison, something like a secured family circle.

"So while doing his work in the world he is buffeted often by the Kal or negative forces. And if his work (as it does often) becomes so strenuous that he cannot have time for his retirement periods with God, he may become one-sided and could lose spiritual ground, as Moses did.

"The love of his disciples builds a strong aura for him, and often he can draw upon this love to help him, for it is actually the drawing upon the love of the SUGMAD.

"I depend upon your love to give me assistance, and take me through the maze of details so my mind will be free for God.

"Mark those last eight words! 'So my mind will be free for God'. I can ascend to God any time I desire, but unless my disciples have a pure, constant love for me while in this body doing my spiritual work, the task is more of a strain upon me!

"The love of the Master's followers builds an aura for him and themselves. This is true of a church or spiritual organization which always builds an aura of this kind for itself, and has a peculiar power to inhibit or keep out any outside influences. Inside this aura the Master works easily and readily, but once there are quarrels and dissension among his followers, he soon learns that he must withdraw to himself and depend mainly upon a few, in order to fulfill his spiritual destiny in this world.

"A teacher who blunders in any relationship with his followers soon will lose his faithful ones, and eventually he is surrounded by ignorant, stupid ones who ruin his work and wear him out with their mistakes.

"A few Masters, who have come to earth to teach, have done just that. Jesus trusted too much. His followers did not give him the great love required of his spiritual stature. As a result, his spiritual efforts were diminished gradually and he became a victim of his own mistakes, like the parable of the talents.

"If you believe that you can exist completely without giving love or receiving human love while living on this earth plane, then you are mistaken. Neither can a teacher, nor any other highly developed Soul. However, at the same time you must be extremely careful to whom you give your love. I say this without hesitation that you cannot give love to all!

"Remember that the spiritual world has two streams of current, the spiritual and the negative. There are many minor currents within these, but for brevity we will consider only the two.

"An ECK Master seldom puts faith, trust, or love in any man who is submerged completely in the negative current. He will not waste time to be bothered, unless that Soul is actually a highly developed one lost in it. Then, perhaps. Or if directed by the spiritual hierarchy to help this one Soul. The effort takes his strength and spiritual initiative, and maybe too much association with such a Soul he could become unbalanced in that direction. And the higher you are, the harder it is to get back on the path after a fall from Grace.

"Be indifferent, and do not love these people. They will pull you down to their level of negation. Do not open your psychic channels to them or their negative forces will reach out like tentacles and fasten onto your etheric body.

"It is so hard to make one understand the real intricate points of the spiritual body of man, and its needs, productions and functions. It is so simple and really so very unwise of anyone to say that the Master will take care of him. That is a lazy man's way of saying it. And it is cited often by the lazy devotee that God is taking care of him — and he will give you many examples, but they mean nothing. Tell me. How will God take care of anyone who is too lazy to pray or contemplate, or too busy to do either of these?

"Now it stands to reason that if the Master does not get time for contemplation during his daily life, because of the demands of his spiritual duties, he could slip from the Grace of God. But if he has the love of his devotees, he can be held to those heights of God from which he has to work in order to fulfill his mission, and could go on indefinitely without daily contemplation. However, the love of the devotees must be universal and without selfish cause; otherwise, the ECK Master cannot work freely with spiritual success.

"An example of this is: A class in a school for Yogis experimented in prayer for the return of the astral form of a long-deceased Indian Saint. Their prayers were successful but the Saint admonished them, saying that he had been called back for an unworthy cause. He would have to stay in that form until its time-span was past, and would be kept from his regular spiritual duty upon his respective plane. In earth years that astral life span might have been twenty-five years or more.

"You see, a Master generally cannot dissolve his human form at will to leave this earth. First, because of the spiritual duty he must perform; and next, because of the pull of the prayers of those devotees who have their own interest at heart. As it is, he must stay here until his duty is fulfilled and his human life span is finished.

"That is why I need your love, as well as that of the ECK devotees in a universal way.

"You would find agreement on one thing. Each person is positive he knows what he does. But each knows something different and what I tell you is entirely of the secrets which come only from Fifth Plane knowledge, and is divine wisdom. Too many receive their wisdom and answers from the astral or through the earth ethers and believe them to be the higher wisdom.

"I leave you on this last note. Always remember: I need

25

you as much as you need me — so love me! That love for the traveler always will be returned one hundredfold if it comes from a loving heart.

"Soon I will give you the purpose of your life here on the earth plane and your spiritual duty. Goodnight!"

# THE TRUE MEANING OF LOVE

Rebazar Tarzs stepped through the door into the room and stood by the bed looking down for a long time. Finally, he went to the chair and seated himself. His eyes were brilliant, glowing darkly in the half-light. He laughed silently and joyously.

R.T.: "Love is the profound Current of Life. Everything has its center in love on every existing plane. The spiritual science is based upon love, but not the love which we know in this world. It is not even the love which we seek for the bliss of God. This is an illusion of the mind. That love is said to be the highest love of all! But this is not true. The God love, or the love of all, is not the highest love of the universe."

P.: "I am amazed to hear this from you, Master. What is the highest love in the universe?"

R.T.: "Many who have come to this earth to teach man, have left the conception of God in many forms to be worshipped. As we might designate the reality, it is not a law, a principle, a man, nor a being, nor the stream of life which flows through every living organism in the living worlds.

"All of this is abstract. We go farther back than that. We go to the complete Fountainhead of that stream of life permeating all the planes of existence. Out of this Current flows the great stream of atoms, molecules and protons to give us the total substance of consciousness.

"This is the Source of all — Absolute! The name we give to this deity is the SUGMAD. Nameless in form and ideal is this great Ruler of all the cosmic worlds and universes. IT controls all and gives life to every living atom that moves through the millions of worlds. All is under this magnificent Soul. ITS voice is the Living WORD. ITS body is the Light of the worlds.

27

"Then we come back to the question: 'Whom or what do we love, as human beings?'

"Do we love profoundly the great Soul, the SUGMAD? I tell you yes! But we cannot love IT as the All-embracing Deity, for this is too great a strain on the imagination of those who have hardly gone past the astral world and even for those in the mental plane. It staggers the human mind not yet trained in the universal concepts of the spiritual science.

"So then we draw the lines finer to what we must love. We will tighten our understanding to bring the mental conception to two aspects of God. These are Light and Sound. These two-fold elements of the Great One are manifested in the highest state on earth by the form of a living traveler.

"I pause here to say that not all teachers of the Truth are travelers. There are evolutions of teachers who eventually become Masters. The Masters will evolve to saints and after this, become angels or heavenly spirits. Ultimately they merge into the body of God and remain in ITS presence. They may become the spiritual travelers, to return to the spiritual stream of life as the highest form of consciousness, which is taken into the consciousness of a Being somewhere, be it on a planet other than the earth.

"For your knowledge, the graduated Masters (or travelers if you wish to use this term) often go to other planets like Clarion, Venus, or those where higher evolved Souls are living, to help carry on the work of God throughout the universal worlds. Hence, we can think and believe in the flying saucers or other phenomenon from those worlds beyond.

"Light and Sound, the basic elements in the body of ECK-ANKAR, are blended into a single form and called 'God' for the sake of those without imagination. This is what we love at this step of our development. Call it God, Reality, the SUGMAD, or whatever you desire for the sake of identification.

"The Light is the conveyor of the Word. Breaking this up into an illustration of what it means simply — I tell you that the Light is the reflection of the universal atoms, and the Sound is the movement of those atoms in space.

The stream of atoms passing out of the Supreme Being is one great force of positive (or love) atoms. But after passing into the lower worlds — below the Second Grand Division, they break into two streams — the positive and negative, for these are needed to keep balance in the lower worlds.

"The seeker should look for the ECK Master (the incarnation of the Supreme Being) or a Satguru, one who has reached the top of the Second Grand Division; and invoke his help, and receive instructions from one of these supreme guides as to the manner of his devotion and procedure to love God.

"Now I tell you. We have learned what to love and the procedure to love. Next, we must know how to live in order to love.

"The knowledge of maintaining life comes through the balance of the attitude towards love. Since we dwell constantly in the great stream of life, we must be taught to balance ourselves within it. Man cannot escape the negative forces nor the positive forces, so he must make the effort to have a well-adjusted outlook on the middle path.

"Hence, the teachings of the great Masters of the world who were neither fanatics, nor weaklings, but strong-willed in God, seeing their own weaknesses and strength; pitting and balancing good and evil in their lives in the two streams of consciousness flowing through their worlds, the subjective and objective.

"Buddha portrayed this in his wonderful teachings to mankind. 'Travel the middle path', he said. Now, herein, on the middle path, the consciousness of man eventually becomes the impersonal atom of pure intelligence, and the seeker is no longer himself.

"His consciousness is not the angry, cascading stream of negativism, but in pure balance with the positive, like some broad, placid river. The usual phrases, protesting or fearful, that went through his mind, are no longer tormenting him, and in their place are large, serene thoughts which come floating along the river of consciousness like nobly colored barges.

"He discovers within himself no noticeable pieces of wisdom, as a follower of the spiritual path, but feels wise — as the Master, not the agitated slave — of experience.

"It is this special attitude of balancing the mind, in contemplation, to dwell upon the two-fold aspect of the Great One, Light and Sound, that shows where love can be placed. For Light and Sound blended is the traveler within one. Love then the Master! I am only the symbol of that part of the Great One, and to love the Inner Master is to love the highest form of all love. When man can do this, he is no longer a bird in the cage of negativeness, but rises out of that into the positive stream of life and balances his consciousness, or inner self, while living out his life-span upon this earth.

"There. I have given you the true meaning of love, and what it is that man should love! Have I made myself clear?"

# THE PARADOX OF THE UNIVERSE

R.T.: "I love you as my son."

P.: "I am humble in your presence. You are my father and Soul."

R.T.: "Indeed, I am. I am the Soul of every man, yet I am not the Soul of every man. Again, I say that I am your Master, and still I am not your Master. I permeate all things, and yet I do not. This is the great paradox of life. You ask how this can be. This is the great question which puzzles every Soul who struggles to know himself and God. I am, but yet I am not!

"To answer your question I must ask you, who am I?

"Your reply is that I am the living ECK Master, and life is embodied within me. True, so far as it goes objectively. But again I say it is not true.

"Life as we live it upon earth consists of a series of paradoxical questions. If we live in God, why do we go through these awful periods of questioning ourselves? There is a definite answer. It can be given in one word. Attachment. Attachment to what? Attachment to all things which have been given to us in our objective and subjective lives. But most of all, that of our mental baggage. We carry a lot of mental baggage, you know. We come into this world with it. I think in your constitution there is a line which goes like this, 'All men are born free and equal'. That is wrong, for upon rebirth we come into the word unequal, carrying useless baggage.

"An example of this is: We hardly think for ourselves. We are surrounded on all sides by the printed word, the spoken word and the very ethers are filled with streams of negativeness from human radios. So it is little wonder that we can have an original thought on God.

"However, as man travels along the road homeward to God, he eventually comes to the gate of the first cosmic world. Here he is halted, for there are tests which he must pass before going through that gate, be it consciously in the hands of the Master, or by some means having wandered there alone. Yes, many Souls have wandered here during the sleep of their human body, and never knew what was taking place in their objective world when the tests were taken.

"These tests are a series of apparent setbacks in men's subjective world. Everything he does or thinks seems to go against him. His best friends criticize him and desert him, the world turns against him and his family. All his possessions flee from him. He stands alone in the inner worlds on the very edge of time where the divine force carried him, and he is left alone to face God.

"Here he looks out over that awful gulf of vast chaos in the outer space where time is limitless and nothing but himself alone. What can he do? Where can he turn?

"Before he can pass through the gate into the land ruled by the Lord of the first world, several things will happen to him. He must rid himself of that baggage which is carried within his Soul. Doubt will seize him and for days, weeks and maybe years he will shake outwardly with terror. The Kal force will tear him apart and disbelief will rattle all the faith he had in the Master, who has never left his side. All sensitivity within him is flayed like the threshing of grain. Soul is whipped to a finer tone to face the task before it.

"And you ask what is this task which the devotee must face before he is ready to comprehend the great paradox of God.

"The great task before you is to face the Lord of the first world. This is not an easy task in the spiritual life you have taken up. This is the beginning of the path to journey to the far-flung planes of the inner cosmic worlds. But some day you will be able to cross and recross the borders of all planes with the charged words, and the presence of the Master. However, first you must pass the test with each Lord of each world.

"Many have wandered across the border of the first plane and have come face to face with this great deity by chance, or purposely by divine guidance, and mistaken him for God. They have changed so radically in their basic nature by this encounter that their minds were unbalanced and they were caused to believe their place in the scheme of God's creation was divine leadership. You, yourself, have seen these misguided ones who teach wrongly and lead their followers off the path of God instead of toward it.

"Should these misdirected Souls be initiates under the Master, then due preparation for their care and encounter has been made.

"Now let us get down to the heart of the explanation of this encounter. First, we must learn what must be done in order to pass over the border and have this rendezvous with the deity of the first world, known to us as Jot Niranjan. You do not go by chance. All preparation is done by the Master who will contact the deity just as you do on the earth plane by making an appointment with whomever you desire to seek and keep the appointment.

"The rest is simple. Our minds and hearts must undergo a purification with the Master's help. We must put aside everything and have complete trust in the Master. We must bring to a halt the shaking of the mind by terror. All attachment must be dropped from our minds, with only one thing left. This is the love for the Inner Master — Light and Sound.

"Our expression will be this. It will seem that I have left you but my presence is there, everywhere. You are met and escorted down a highway filled with people on a pilgrimage to a great castle in the distant mountains. Your escort is an angelic being in a white robe. He takes you into the castle and down a long hall into the presence of a mighty being, seated Yoga-fashion, on a dais. He will be a Light rather than a being, a Light greater than that of a thousand suns, so blinding, you can not look into it.

"By now you are without feeling or thought. A great humming sound, similar to the roar of thunder is heard, and a voice speaks from out of the Light. 'I am IT, whom you know as God, but I am not God. I am in every man, but I am not in every man. My love is you, but not in you. When you have solved this riddle, come back again.'

"Now I tell you this. This is the great riddle of life for every devotee to solve before becoming fit for the highest stages of spiritual life.

"The ECK is wordless. When IT came into being, IT was called the Word, or Nam of God, and the whole world is an expression of IT. IT appeared in the form of Light and Sound. That Sound or Voice spoke to the devotee, and seemed to come out of the Light telling that IT is God and so every man is an expression of IT. But all the same IT is not God made into expressions, for IT is the center of all expressions and from IT must flow creation, as such all creation never existed in IT.

"Mark those last six words. Creation does not exist in you either, nor in me, but we have the power of creation. Understand?

"IT is unconcerned about the world around IT for the world continues to function as does a machine after the switch is thrown on to make it run. All IT must do is watch over it.

"IT is the highest and the lowest. Those whose inner vision is open will see all creation in IT (meaning the play of the divine drama) and IT in all creation. This means ITS hand is in all things. You know now IT is detached or unconcerned as though the whole creation never existed in IT.

"For your understanding, I am the great Deity of the First World as well as the Lord of all worlds inside. I never left your side, though it seems so. Yet I am a man while on earth subject to the laws of the earth's nature. This applies to my existence on all planes. But in the Atma-Sarup, or Soul body, I transcend all laws of all planes. I am then everything

34

and in all things, but unconcerned about any living thing in this universe, or throughout the cosmic worlds. As the living deity on each plane, I must be concerned about life on each plane.

"But why am I unconcerned about the whole? Because all is in its proper place, and the activity of the living atom is in divine order, even to the minute chirping of the cricket. Therefore, I look upon all as the Whole moving as the Whole, or unity, throughout time and space, out of and returning to the divine Fountainhead.

"I am detached and unconcerned about man because man as an individual Soul will return to his home some day. If it takes a million years for a Soul to learn where lies Its true home, why should I worry? For as God I know all things, yet as man I am compelled to show you the path by which you are to travel to reach my door.

"So you see I am the Master, and yet not the Master. I am the highest and the lowest, and no man can resist my love, for it is like the love of the father towards his child. Every Soul who has reached perfection can say what I have just said. So they be the same, but we are few who have found perfection. And this much I can say, that after I have passed into the worlds beyond the Second Grand Division I am the Absolute, the Complete and the Whole.

"To those who reach the sacred borders of the first world and knock on the door of the Lord, and feel the terrors of the stepping off into the unknown of the spiritual world, I say to have courage and faith in the Master; but if you have no master, put it to God, for I am also God. For after all, it is only myself whom you face and I am gentle and loving toward all my children.

"After I cleanse and purify your heart you can face me and unlock the great mystery of the universe.

"Eventually everyone of you will reach this stage of the path, and must face the great test of God's love.

"So I tell you to have courage, faith, and love regardless of the world outside shaking about your head.

"Once you have solved this riddle, never again will you be a part of the masses. You will not act in a conventional manner, be orthodox, nor be a part of this world except to live out your life span and do your duty in your spiritual work to mankind."

# THE SPIRITUAL POWER

Shortly before 1:00 a.m. I cut off the night light and tried to sleep, but found it impossible, for Rebazar Tarzs' voice seemed to keep talking from somewhere about the room — in my head, in my heart, but I could not locate it. I had not seen nor heard him earlier that evening. Finally, I got up and turned on the light to look at the clock. The time was 1:45 a.m. Then I saw him sitting in the chair, smiling.

P.: "How am I going to get any rest?"

R.T.: "You do not ever rest when the call comes. Look at me! Do I get to sleep or rest with the whole world at my feet asking for something?"

P.: "Yes but I am not divine, nor have I the powers that you have."

R.T.: "Ah, but you are wrong there. Every man has the powers, if he would but recognize and allow the ECK Power within himself to be used by the ECK Master.

"Now let us get down to some specifics. What is this cosmic power within you? Do you know or understand what it means? I rather doubt that hardly a man actually knows of what the spiritual power consists, and how it works upon this plane.

"Now let me tell you this. The teachers of truth all teach us about the God-Power within; it has many names: God, Universal Power, the Christ Power and others. They all agree upon this strange, mystical power which flows through the myriad worlds, and which man can control if he is aware of it.

"At the very beginning, I say this to you. The spiritual power is different! It is the highest power in God's whole creation. This power is that stream of God-Current flowing through you, as one often thinks of it, but different from anything that you can imagine in your mind. It is above and

37

beyond any thought or conception of the belief of the teachers of occult science, or truths!

"Let me try to define this power to you. It is this. It is the ancient power which man had in those days when this earth was inhabited by spiritual giants . . . the magnificent stream of God-Power flowing through those who really are imbued with the mighty Deity of the highest plane. It is the actual contact with the Source of the highest stream of God-Consciousness pouring out of the divine Fountainhead.

"Furthermore, only the ECK Master can awaken and bestow the power in a devotee. He can make channels for the power of any of his followers, any or all of them. It makes little difference to the ECK Master.

"Now, when I tell you that the power is within you and extending all feasible help, the words should not be taken lightly.

"I do not bestow such words upon too many, for it is well known what they might do with this power. But if you recall that while sitting in my little place in the Hindu Kush Mountains, I told you these words: 'You need never again fear anything, for I am with you always, and the ECK power is always working through you.'

"You now begin to understand what was meant by such a statement. For once I grant this power to any of my devotees it gives them the greatest of spiritual strength, understanding, and discrimination.

"Look here. I tell you this. All devotees who receive the power from my hands usually will have a great struggle, and fight within themselves at the beginning. For it takes a period of time between when the actual power is given, and the body and mind of the devotee actually are fitted properly for the use of it as a channel. If I have time (as in my own ashram), the devotee gradually is conditioned to accept this power to work through him, as one learns to control his body under the circumstances of accepting bolts of electricity. As in your case, when time was short and I had to condition you quickly, all sorts of troubles broke loose within you and you seemingly fought against everything and everybody and were often

38

moody, in deep depression, and uncertain of yourself. It was only the period when the power was cleansing your body of all finiteness to make it fit as a channel which the Master could use in his work.

"Now we get down to what the spiritual power actually is. It is the highest power working through the chela to do the Master's cause. The power comes from the Master who uses the chela for every possible reason for furthering his spiritual mission on earth.

"The devotee has surrendered himself completely to the Master and lets himself be of service. He is no longer his own, but now works for the universal cause. He is what I call a conscious co-worker of the universe. He is at the call of the Master, even though most of the time he does not know consciously what he is doing, nor why he has done certain things in his life; his world seems topsy-turvy at times and many things he does just do not make sense to him.

"Let me describe briefly what the cosmic power consists of in a scientific nature. It is the process by which the spiritual activity is progressing, always from no-activity to activity and back again. It is a perpetual progress; and in this universe we can see it in all stages, graphically spread out in all its development.

"If I explain it from the earth plane, it will be easier to understand. Let us start with the ether, a term invented by scientists to describe the basis for observed activity in what is an all-permeating substance existing in space and in solid matter alike, flowing through both with equal facility. Some mistakenly call this 'God'. This is really disintegrated matter, often called the positive force, while as matter it is the negative force which when dissolved returns to the ether.

"In order to understand the process of the cosmic power more clearly let us start with the ether, with the matter stuff, with those finely divided particles which can be divided no further. They represent the atoms, which are broken down into neutrons, electrons, and protons. They fill all space and we call that area the sky, horizon, space, or any other term that designates nothing.

"These particles are the essence of the ECK power, that original pure Current which flows out of the Fountainhead of God, from the highest plane of the cosmic worlds.

"Now to get down to some basic facts about creation. When you think a strong thought, this causes a whirlpool in the ethers within the aura, or perhaps outside the aura. If this process is generated from the superior beings, in the worlds, at the command of the Lord of the Universe, then we actually can see a process of the whirling of the great spiral nebula in the heavens, spinning, coiling upon itself, integrating, forming a mass of matter at its center. There are new universes in the process of creation constantly, through this means of creating. Thus we get somewhat into the ways of creation. Remember all of God is the Whole and it is thus hard to take portions of IT, or IT and discuss IT clearly.

"The spiritual power will start the creation of the whirlpool within the individual, and this little spiral nebula goes out into space, touching another, and there their two thoughts come together in harmony or otherwise.

"This ether is called the 'ECK' by the Adepts of the Order of Vairagi. It was well known to the ancient mystics, who gave us great knowledge but now most of this lies in the field of science, and the mystic is a forgotten man!

"The ECK is our primal substance, consisting of primitive atoms, being mainly hydrogen, which are descending constantly from the higher worlds, breaking off from the spiritual Current and completely passing through the sun and earth in a spiral motion. This is the spiritual stream from the Fountainhead of God. When it descends below the Second Grand Division it becomes a two-fold stream, of positive and negative, or Prit and Kal, forces.

"The spiraling motion of the atoms always is toward the center of the earth. This is the ECK Power flowing through man. That is, if man has been awakened to accept this within himself, and use as the power of God.

"Therefore, man controls this to the extent of his understanding and knowledge of its mechanics. The greater his

40

knowledge, the more his control of the power and its use for universal benefits.

"The principal use of the power is for growth. This gets us back to the realm of science again; and to explain we must go deeper into the elemental causes of nature. Einstein, Edison, Mozart, Bach, Shakespeare, Schweitzer, Tagore, and others got very deep into this study and unknowingly contacted and made great use of the power. In fact, every genius whom God has let walk upon this earth has made use of the power in fulfilling his obligation to raise the masses to greater spiritual heights.

"Now I tell you that those who have eyes to see will know that huge clouds of hydrogen occupy the vast reaches of space. Often these clouds lie closely to the earth's surface, and within them are electro-magnetic fields which when stirred by a powerful thought force established by a prayer group, a master-mind, or through the Lords of this world, start causes which must have effect somewhere, somehow, even though they might be the creation of new worlds. This is often the beginning (or causes) of wars, great prosperity periods, and other cycles of mankind. Oh, yes, the thought or mind-power is so established upon this earth plane that it will be ages before the ECK Masters will be able to clear it out through education of the races for true spirituality. You know occult powers in the past have destroyed many continents and land areas.

"Activity in the ECK force manifests both gravity and the electro-magnetic fields. The inflow of the primal substance is gravity and the whirling motion that causes the inflow is an electro-magnetic field. Now I tell you this. Since we are concerned with the cosmic power on the earthplane, let us think of it in its lowest form. This is for understanding only. All teachers of the so-called Truth are emphasizing love and hate. They teach only the ethical nature of God.

"The power is so far above this that normal man has little concept of what it is. Here is how it operates through man, who is in constant, conscious control of it. The power is embodied within him by the Master and always is working out

God's cause, always on a universal scale, and not for any individual purpose.

"Cords of Light or Love (for Love is really Light in the worlds beyond and hatred is darkness) are attached between the Mahanta and his chela, and wherever that disciple goes or whatever he does, is determined by the Master. Therefore, the chela is simply a channel whereby the traveler's Light is being spread throughout the universe. The power operates in a clockwise spiral motion through the devotee to whatever he touches, either physically, mentally, or spiritually. This is the creative force pouring through man, developing growth, and everything he touches leaves the Master's Light.

"It is like working through an electro-magnetic field which when powerful enough permits the creative forces to operate, but when weakened allows the Kal, or negative forces (which spiral counter-clockwise) to take over and destroy.

"Now man is composed principally of hydrogen and oxygen, and therefore considered an electro-magnetic field. Especially is this so when you can see your fellowman through the spiritual eyes. Therefore, the power readily can work through each individual, because of this fact. That is, if the Master would open the channel in the devotee for the power to flow fully through him.

"Now should you be given the power and discover the complete use of it, master it, and solve the final secret of all creation, the primal force that causes creation, you can do anything with the power. Knowing how to cause creation, you can reach immortality, or live in the state of constant life. Some call this existing in the bliss of God. Note this carefully — not God, nor one with God, but in the bliss of God. Yes, there is a difference. Of course, there are arguments over this point. But once you attain this step you will know the difference.

"The Vedantists call it consciousness, existence, and bliss absolute. This is the result of the complete control of the cosmic power. Few have attained this in the cosmic worlds, but many will tell you that they have reached this God-like state and even passed beyond it. This is only lip service. They are pretending.

"At this point let me say briefly that the use of the will power is necessary in your spiritual life with the power. The willing of the power into your life, for the use of God's cause is right. The willing of the cosmic consciousness and holding it is compulsory. By all means do so, but only if a Master is watching over you.

"Furthermore, let me say this. Growth is life. But growth is more difficult in the denser forms of matter. In the dense life (as minerals) it is slower and harder to reach the higher forms of consciousness.

"We could get into very deep secrets beyond the horizons of intellectual thinking of man, but you must understand that science and religion are related fields. Effected are the results of everything we see upon this earth. Now, if you could know what happens if you are a follower of the Pranic system of Yoga, you would not use it. I will tell you briefly, for it is correlated with the power and its use. The arousing of the chakras within you only arouses an astral motion which sets off the whirling of the Prit, or creative force, within you. But these are not the highest forms of creation, because you have touched only a lower power. You must go all the way to the JOT or thousand-petalled lotus, for results in the use of the ECK Power, and sometimes this takes years, if you are using the Pranic system. Therefore, you only arouse the lowest forms by the use of this system.

"Try taking a short cut to God. Look within for the Light and listen for a Sound. If I have bestowed you with the use of the ECK Power there is little effort needed in reaching these two aspects of the great Deity Sat Nam, and the Master will escort you to the plane in the inner world to broaden your understanding and give you wisdom. Why waste your time going through exercises which may take a life time to reach a certain goal and then learn there is an easier way?

"You wonder why the Kal force is so much greater than the Love force on this earth plane. It is very simple, but I do not attempt to discuss it here. However, I say this to you, that when you become proficient in your understanding of the negative (or disintegrating forces) you will learn of the deepest secrets of all universal worlds. Then and then only can you become one with God, and learn to live in me forever. Contradictory, isn't it? But for your understanding, the negative (or Kal) power is a much maligned subject and must some day be corrected for the knowledge of the races.

"You do not understand what I have told you? Do not become too deeply involved in your thoughts on what I have said, because as told to you in the beginning, the power is always with you and flowing over your head.

"Have faith in my word. Some day you will see, understand, know, and digest everything that I have told you. That is all for now. Goodnight!"

# MIND-CONTROL

I opened my eyes to find Rebazar Tarzs standing near the bed; he smiled quietly and began to speak.

R.T.: "You must spend most of your time in thought or contemplation upon any problem before you. Once you have reached the solution of the problem stick to your decision, for that solution will not be an ordinary conclusion. It will be the decision which I have given you!

"Never crowd your mind with trivials or unnecessary thoughts, with reading too much, too many plans, nor trying to do too much physically. Remember this: Keep your mind clear, unhurried, and filled with my radiant form. Never let anything take your mind off me, never be pushed into anything because of anyone's strong personality or force-fulness. If some one seems stronger-willed than you, think of me and I will come to your aid.

"Going after God requires you to have every mental faculty filled with ambition for IT. Keep your mind completely filled with thoughts on God, but only upon IT, ITSELF, not on any aspect of God. I am your Master and your God; therefore, keep your mind on me!

"For example, electricity is a spiritual aspect, which was brought into use openly for the comfort and growth of mankind, but it is not God. It is only a part of God as the body with its arms and legs. We could live without either, though not as conveniently as with them. Such is the nature of God. We live in God completely, not just with God. Therefore, how can you have time to think of anything else but God?

"I told you once that if I should go to a movie or read a book, it would take my mind off God. Why should I do any-

45

thing that would break that continuity of the ECK-Power flowing through me?

"Let me quote a line from Macaulay: 'When he drew the sword, he threw away the scabbard. He knew the essence of war is violence, and that moderation is imbecility!'

"So it must be with God. You must go to God with the same intensity that the warrior goes into battle, your mind completely on the divine goal, determined that you are going to have God in your life.

"Now, just how are you going to meet this problem of holding your mind on God completely at all times? I will tell you. It is so simple that it is considered one of the elementary aspects in the training of the aspirant, yet no teacher knows enough to tell it to you. It is a secret, yet not a secret—so fully your own self that hardly any seeker discovers it of his own accord.

"Call it mind-control. This is the basic element in this aspect. I call it 'guarding the mind of God'. Nothing startling, but the step which hardly any of you can take until a Master gives you the Light and Sound.

"I have seen thousands pass through the lower stages on the spiritual path, then come to this gate upon the path and flounder, perhaps for a whole life time, because there was no traveler to teach them nor open the gate of the mind. It is really the doorway to the first plane.

"Now let us get down to the finer points on mind-control. These are the controls which we must handle objectively.

"Civilization teaches us not to strike a fellowman or scold him because we are offended by his behavior. Gandhi summed this up nicely when he stated that the desire to strike your fellowman is as bad as the actual deed. This is true because you have set up a cause which does not have its manifestation on the physical plane, and frustration is born within the mind. The man becomes a neurotic and his life pattern is disturbed.

"What we are trying to stop is the setting up of a cause. I tell you that only the living ECK Master can take care of this

46

basic problem. I, being the SUGMAD Sarup, the Living Master, will see that this does not happen to you, but I need your cooperation.

"Briefly, let us study two principles of the earth plane which are so prominent in the Cabala. I consider them strong basic mind laws with which we must be concerned in order to learn and understand mind-control.

"One of these laws is: 'Nothing can exist except in relation to its opposite'. This is an age old principle of the positive and negative. The positive is the outgoing, the God force; and the negative is the inert, receptive force.

"For example, laughter must have its opposite, tears; and neither can the universe have complete joy without sorrow. Therefore, this universe is not static, but is a constant dynamic state. There is nothing eternal on this plane but change itself. This is where God arrives in our lives, for behind the change lies the eternal, the unchanging which the outer eye cannot see. As long as anything exists on the mental and physical plane, it is due to be in constant change.

"Now, the second principle is, 'That the positive is forever transforming into the negative and correspondingly, the negative is forever in the process of becoming the positive'. This I have told you when discussing the spiritual power.

"Each power needs the other in this world. Without one the other could not exist. So you see, that is why the truth as now being taught is wrong for the citizens of the earth plane. The teachings need to be revitalized and reformed to show the world how to take advantage of the two forces, not to put a strain upon the individual aspirant to hold to one constantly, when it is almost an impossibility unless he is trained by the ECK Master. Therefore, do not despair if the cycle strikes in a low depression at one time, and then later turns to the higher, and vice-versa.

"The law of physics tells us that only one thing at a time can occupy space. This is taken up in the Bible in the First Psalm which says, 'A double-minded man is unstable'. Therefore, why should you have your mind on anything but God?

"Briefly, let us discuss the mind. It is like a cavern on a

47

tunnel through which there constantly passes a stream of whirling, spiraling atoms, broken down into electrons, protons, and neutrons. They are like a mass of people, sometimes crowding and pushing through the tunnel to get through — now slow, now fast or tumbling over one another or drifting through, now stopping — and with all the effort possible, you cannot get them out.

"These atoms are thought-atoms. You cannot see them but they strike images within the brain and these images become pictures or symbols which react on the emotions, or the sensory body.

"After initiation, the ECK Master settles his radiant body in the Tisra Til to guard the gate of the mental world inside man. He is the guardian of this stream of consciousness that pours constantly through the brain of the individual, and as long as the aspirant is in contact with him, this flow of mind play is purified. But when he begins to miss his spiritual practices, or becomes fanatic in his behavior toward the Master, or watches the objective senses more (such as allowing himself to become more concerned with another devotee's behavior, or duty to the Master), then the play of the opposite becomes stronger in the aspirant.

"One might be seized with great depression and stay there while the Master stands aside watching sorrowfully, because the devotee does not have the strength nor faith to call upon his help.

"Now I tell you this. One of the basic reasons for the traveler being in earth form is so that the human mind (which is held in on all sides by self-made fences) can see, understand, and grasp enough of a view of the traveler so his mind will be held to a symbol for the inner worlds.

"The 'stream of thought' is one of the most delusive terms which the western world uses. It is delusive because it sounds concrete and yet it is used variously and vaguely. Yes, the writers and teachers of the metaphysical field today talk in vague terms and symbols, and so mysteriously that it is little wonder that the God-seeker is confused, trying to unravel all the true and false knowledge thrown at him. Most of the ancient writings today are arcane, for, although they are basic truths, they need to be presented to the world in a new light.

"The 'stream of thought' is useful, clearly as a term, but is figurative and less precise and stable than any we can use at this point for demonstration. It is the stream of God consciousness flowing through the cavern of the brain. It is the mind consciousness. This indicates the entire area of mental attention from pure consciousness on through the levels of the mind up to and including the highest state of God-awareness. This is where we are concerned. The stream of God-consciousness differs precisely in that it is concerned with only those levels that are rudimentary rather than rational verbalization — those levels beyond the margin of attention. Let us think of this form of consciousness in the form of an iceberg; the whole iceberg and not just the relatively small surface portion. To follow the comparison, the stream of God-consciousness is concerned greatly with what lies below the surface.

"As I said before, this stream of consciousness is made up of molecules, the manifestation of spiritual energy (or ECK Power, as I call it). But these molecules are not solid, for they are nothing but energy and space — just atoms in space, and each atom is nothing but a tiny uncovered sphere of empty space, with nothing in the center but electrons. These electrons are separated from each other by space (which is enormous) compared to the size of an electron. Then, lastly, electrons are held together only by energy, which impels them to circle around their centers, just as the planets circle around the sun, without anything between them except empty space and energy. Each electron is nothing but an empty vortex hole of energy in empty space. Scientists call an electron a particle of energy, meaning a part of energy, not a part of matter.

"Since these electrons are flowing through your aura and your mind, you have the power to control their vibratory rate — this is the feeling or emotional part of yourself.

"The Bible says, 'Be still and know I am God', but we take

49

the wrong concept of this. We do not stop this stream of consciousness but become still in an objective and subjective sense. Just relax. In other words relax completely. The flow of consciousness then takes shape in the mind and the Inner Master takes over. You do this by gazing sweetly into the spiritual eye. This is the beginning of mind-control.

"Now you know what the power flowing through you is, now let us proceed to the technique of controlling it. The process of mind-control is: (1) putting the mind completely on God and keeping it there, (2) letting the traveler have control of the Soul, and (3) by control of the vibrations.

"Now the whole secret of mind-control is in the feelings. Once you get this fixed firmly in your mind you will understand how to control the thoughts passing through your mind. It is determined by the vibratory rate of the mind. Does this sound simple? Then the secret of successful mind-control lies in the control of the vibrations. It begins with the right symbol within. Should you have the image of the Master always before your spiritual eye, there is little or no problem, for this will bring the right mind vibrations.

"For after all, the old law exists in the mind-plane — 'Like attracts like!' So the secret is: I am always with you. But are you always conscious of my presence?

"Further, the ego is the natural enemy of self-control, and must be overcome in order to have full self-control. It is the false self chiefly concerned with protecting itself. It fights against any change, especially the advent of God-Power, or the change of the mind to God thoughts. The seeker has his greatest fight against the ego. Do not try to eliminate the ego but overcome it with a change from itself to the God self, through a process of putting your mind upon me constantly.

"If you are in a bad business or social situation, and remember that I can and will work through you to take care of either (for the sake of furthering my cause) is there any need to worry?

"Mark this point forever in your mind. Every present thought solidifies into a future condition. So, the point is, if you are thinking badly, stop pushing or crowding your

50

thoughts against the door of the mind, for they pile up badly, creating just what you are fearing. But by reversing the thoughts, not letting them momentarily lapse into anything, but keeping your mind on me, the Light and Sound within, then there will be a release of the darkness within, and Light and joy will prevail. Then you will have control of your mind and thoughts.

"Now here is something every disciple is faced with when the change comes for a higher step upon the path — his vibrations are changed with a higher rate of vibrational harmony and there is bound to be a change in his life. But the old vibrations seem to make a last desperate stand to remain with him. New vibrations are established by putting yourself further into my hands. You are pushed into unfamiliar paths, and ruthlessly taken out of the life you have been living. All obstacles which stand in your way to God are torn out of your path.

"During this period, have greater faith in the Master or you may be caught in a vicious circle and stay in it a long time. Just let the Master take over and control your life.

"Now I tell you this. When you are seized with the negative forces or stand in personal danger from any source, turn your thoughts strongly upon me, and give the names of the SUG-MAD or HU, or the name of the Master, or your own word given in the initiation.

"I will come to you willingly, for when my children need help, it is forthcoming instantly. My power is that of God, for I am God, and will not let you suffer. For does a father desire to see his child harmed? No, and I tell you that your mind must be kept on me at all times. Then, and only then, will you become the channel through which the Master's cause can be furthered. Then why do you need mind control, for I speak and act through you to spread my Light to every corner of the world?

"By calling upon God in my name, I will give you anything and everything which is for the benefit of all. Like Jesus, who said he was the Light of the world, I will expand your consciousness at all times by my statement that I am the Light

51

of the Worlds — and the Voice of God. By living in me constantly I will give you all and control over every living cell in your atomic body, which is a part of the structure of this universe.

"I could have explained many of the secrets of the universe, but you cannot go higher than living within me. So be joyous and happy in this knowledge. Give your love to me, and it will be returned a hundredfold!

"This is all for tonight!"

# GOD'S LOVE

I put on some soft music and played it for most of the evening while my mind reflected on Rebazar Tarzs and his work.

This was an evening of experimenting as to what the Tibetan would respond to. I tried several ways of extending my thought power, making a stream into the ether to draw him, but nothing came out of this. Then I thought of the idea of making a rocking motion of my vibrations outward like a mental curve progressing, a sort of imaginary light wave like what you might imagine would be the vibrations of a ringing bell — such as the vibrations moving to and fro, until they swing far out into the universe. These were streams of Light filled with a gigantic expression of joy and good will toward Rebazar Tarzs.

Suddenly, he was standing at the edge of the bed, looking down with a twinkle in his eyes.

R.T.: "So you have learned a secret of getting to me?"

P.: "How did I do it? I am very curious to know what happened!"

R.T.: "You set up a vibration over which I could travel to you. Very few people can do this, purposely or by accident. But I knew that sooner or later your keen mind would find a way of getting to me.

"There are several other ways, which I will discuss with you some time."

P.: "I am ready for your work, Sir. What do I do?"

R.T.: "Nothing except what I tell you and have faith in God so hard that it hurts. Go beyond this! Absolutely know that what I am doing with you is the best for the Universal Cause — and not for your personal self. Do nothing without having your thought in God. What I bring to you is for the benefit of the mission which I must do here on this earth plane. You must understand that I can move all heaven and

53

earth, and therefore a few human beings can be responsive to God's desires."

The Tibetan leaned very close, his eyes about six inches away. His voice was roaring thunder. His eyes became glowing circles, and I felt carried far away.

R.T.: "I tell you this, dear one. I tell you this in no uncertain terms, that you have absolute confidence and faith and knowing in my word. You cannot help it, for it is ingrained in you like the air about us and within us.

"There is no way in which you cannot help but have the greatest knowing and love for my word. So what I tell you is the living truth of God. You cannot go higher, for, since I am God, I bestow upon you this wonderful talent of expressing yourself by the written word. The ECK Power has been awakened within you, and you act as Its channel. Your mind will be expanded beyond anything that was ever expected.

"Do you know what is happening? ECK is taking you over. You are becoming IT, to act, talk, see, understand, know, and express life as IT, the Lord of the Worlds and the Universes.

"Exert yourself humbly in ITS name. For your life will become so different that you will wonder who the lad was that once occupied your physical form. Yes, even your physical features will change.

"So look for the God force, for you are now being used as a channel for the powers that flow down from the highest planes. You are becoming known to us in the inner planes as a Child of the Light."

# THE KEYSTONE OF GOD

Rebazar Tarzs sat silently in the chair all evening, apparently preoccupied, so I went about my chores and prepared for bed. After a while he gave me a steady gaze and started talking.

R.T.: "Why didn't you get up this morning at 8:30 when I called you?"

P.: "I thought another minute wouldn't hurt. But it was 8:45 when next I looked at the clock."

R.T.: "Don't do it again. Be alert and aware! Don't forget for one second of your life that I am with you. Let that be impressed upon the screen of your mind forever! I am developing in you a trait of agility to think on your feet.

"I call tonight's talk the Keystone of God. Do you know what a keystone is? It is that part of the archway which holds the rest of the stones in place. So with man the subconscious is that part of his being which holds him in place in the cosmic world. This is the channel through which man's mind rises to reach God, and vice versa; the way that God descends into man.

"Unfortunately, there is much misinformation about this obscure realm of man's self; misleading claims and statements are made frequently concerning it. The powers of this realm of the mind are great, but they are the lower parts of the powers. As is true of all forces, they can be used either to create or destroy. The peace and strength of our lives can be determined by these forces in the manner they are controlled and directed.

"Now here is where the crux of the teachings lie. The truths of God start in this realm of the inner world. In Vedanta, Hinduism, Yoga, Theosophy and other teachings this is called the mental world, but this is not the true home to which man must return. It is only one of those worlds through which he must pass and under no circumstances stop there to look at the beauty of this realm.

"But alas, this is where all the teachings of God's truths have come to a bottle neck. The teachers have deluded themselves and believe this is the crux of their union with God. The subtle powers of the mind will deceive and delude the seeker unless he has a true Master to show him the way to God.

"Here it is that many deluded ones stop and begin upon a road to establish religious and occult empires, which have almost ruined the course of mankind in his journey homeward.

"Now we raise this question: Whom can we believe? How do we determine whether it is mind-power or actually God-Power which is directing our lives?

"Here is the difference. Let me see if it can be defined in the simplest terms. Mind-power is that power which arises from the mental plane to direct our lives in the course upon this plane from an intellectual viewpoint. For example, Raja Yoga is the teaching of the mental plane. Those who can lean upon their intuitive sense for enlightenment in emergencies, or to direct their lives will believe it is the hand of God handling their affairs. This is not always true, for it is the Lord of the mental world, whom we call Omkar, putting his powers to work.

"In reality, I am the Lord of the Mind World, as the Lord of all planes, but the seeker is using a lower power in my universal body. As God, I can give you any power desired to fulfill your wishes; but as the Master, I advise you to seek only the highest.

"Before going to the ECK Power, let me say that if you are sensitive and can read other's thoughts, then you are using only the mind-power. A teacher who can give this teaching from the mental plane will use great word symbols to strike the imagination and set up mental rapport on this plane with his devotees. He often ties the devotees to his heart through a certain kind of mental magic which is far beyond their conception. Inside, he is normally a person of indifference or impersonal attitude towards others, but outside he radiates warmth and personality, catering to those who can help him most.

"All of the great writers on philosophy have been those who understood the subconscious; for example, Ralph Waldo Emerson. He is one of the foremost advocates of mental science. Of course, so is Buddhism, as well as Vedanta, Christianity, Sufism, Hinduism, and many more which we can name. They do not, in their present form, teach anything beyond the understanding of the mind plane. The advocates of the Sound Current of AUM are the followers of Omkar, the Lord of the Mental World. AUM is the Sound Current of that plane.

"The teachings of these great ethical religions have been used badly by cults which sprang up in America during the latter part of the last century.

"Now, let us get to the ECK power, which is the great power of the Lord of the highest plane — the real God-Power. If you have used this power, the spirit passes through the mental world (and those that follow) into the highest plane. Those who can go beyond the subconscious powers can know and see. This is the basic difference — the mind power is based on faith and belief. The ECK Power is based upon knowing and knowledge. There is a vast difference between these two concepts.

"For example, I can give you any understanding you are capable of desiring. But how broad is your understanding, and how far can you stretch the horizon within yourself? That is the question and the problem — and upon this lies the key to passing beyond the mental plane into the worlds beyond.

"If you rely upon the mental powers to do your daily tasks, this is a sign that your life is being directed by the subconscious powers. But if everything in your life is directed by Spirit, even to the willing of some thing into your life (and this is right at times), then your life is being directed by God.

"Basically, here is the difference between the two. In order to allow the mind powers to work freely in your life, relax the mind to such an extent that the subconscious takes over.

This is really the first step to God. The second is to relax the will and invite the Master to take over all affairs in your life. Then you are using the ECK spirit.

"Now here is something for you to remember. 'What we have left to God will do us a thousand times more good than what we leave to ourselves to do!'

"The basic teaching of the mental scientists is that we are verily a part of all that we have thought. Therefore, we should be careful and discriminating always as to the thoughts and impressions that we entertain seriously and thus make a part of us. Give the subconscious good material and it will give back a good life.

"Now we know several things about the subconscious: (1) That the miracle powers of thought do occur, (2) That subconsciousness thinking conforms to reflective principles, and (3) That subconscious development of ideas and solutions can be fostered and cultivated, (4) That a subtle form of affirmative belief is an essential factor in cultivating the subconscious powers. This is often called auto-suggestion.

"This is the Kal force at work in the creative process as the great geniuses, who during a mental lull have received their greatest ideas. Let us take the difference in composing between Mozart and Beethoven. Mozart was an advocate of billiards and played constantly. He caught snatches and parts of his musical composition during his game, writing them down in a notebook, then worked from that. An aria in the Magic Flute came during a game.

"On the other hand, Beethoven was possessed with the movements as a whole before he thought out the details; and the search for the theme was to reduce an already existing whole to its simplest terms.

"So you see, those who are under mind powers deal with and see only parts of the whole. Those under the Mahanta see the whole and reduce it to a simple premise. This has been your greatest problem, because upon receiving or seeing the whole in your inner world, a technique of reducing the nebula to the atom was lacking. Thus you wrestled at all times with

58

cosmic problems which, if the Master had been with you, would have been handled easily. Nobody could help you with this inner problem until I came, and that was the cause of all your unhappiness and struggle in life. Many others have the same problem, also.

"The Illumination, or Light upon the mental plane, is unstable. It flashes into the mind and is gone again. The devotee struggles to hold it, not knowing that if he would let the traveler tear away the veil, the Light and Sound would come of their own accord, and be steady in his life.

"One of Emerson's thoughts upon the elusive nature of the mental life was, 'Look after your thoughts. They come like a new bird in your tree, and if you turn to your studies, disappear.'

"The subconscious is no exception to the rule. All basic powers must begin with and end in God, regardless of the place from which they arise.

"A calm, contemplative mood is conducive to subconscious activity, suggesting the interaction of the temporal and spiritual. Under pressure the subconscious powers will react to intense mental effort devoted to a particular problem. Belief is the controlling factor, and the distant feeling of getting the prompt, but correct answer. Tremendous thought energies are released and remarkable results are given often to solve the problems, especially among business men in conferences.

"Those who teach upon the mental plane show the two basic rules of the subconscious powers: (1) We must know and believe beyond a doubt that these subconscious powers are in us and (2) That we can and eventually will arouse them and use them. Often it takes days, weeks, and months of right thinking and contemplating to acquire them, but when acquired and made a part of our natural, normal attitude become a priceless possession and the first step to God.

"Now on the mental plane (as in other worlds) we must know at all times where we are in the use of the subtle powers, or we shall wander about aimlessly. The principles are: (1) Take bearings and determine our immediate and ultimate goal, (2) Whether we are proceeding toward them inductively or deductively and in what stage we are, and (3) How far we have proceeded and how we expect to negotiate the remaining distance.

"The greatest point on this stage of the path is that cause and effect relations always should be rooted out and studied carefully. It is not always easy to distinguish between the two. The subtle powers often bring a confusion of cause and effect, and we debate over which comes first. This leads to error in our thinking and often produces unfortunate results.

"For example, many times in your life the worry over a failure was wrong. To a large degree it was the effect rather than the cause of the worry. This set up a vicious cause and effect cycle without you realizing its existence; a process of one feeding upon the other, often continuing until the point of exhaustion or collapse was reached. These conditions can be avoided by turning the problem over to the Mahanta and the ECK power.

"Remember that the subtle forces within man are the same, but the important thing is the manner in which we call upon it. If we speak to it in negative terms it responds in that manner. We impose self-limitations upon ourselves to give the power an opportunity to work through the subconscious mind.

"Thus man has been studying the ancient scriptures which are limited in a way. Job says, 'What I fear has come upon me.' This is an old mentalist teaching. We are far beyond this into the spiritual planes. Job spoke to the stream in a negative way.

"Now let us say then that the subconscious is the repository of our racial instincts, the Karan Sharir, or causal body. This being true, then we are subjected to the influences with the past and present environments, lives, and beliefs. How are we going to overcome them?

"Mentalists say by self-suggestion or the teachings that God is good — Mantram Yoga, or any other type of thought-provoking ideas to clear out the subconscious. This, however, is not the ultimate answer, for you are aware that unless the

Master's Atma-Sarup fills the inner vision all is void. Man must have a visionary symbol, be it that of a dog, cat, or traveler, but it must be placed within the spiritual eye. And the traveler will see that your vibrations are lifted to the highest scale to which you are capable of reaching in your present development, for travel in the inner worlds.

"Basically, the step of the path at this stage is to work out the solution of the inner conflict, instinctive forces, which are a part of the subconscious. Usually, the strife is a part of both the conscious and subconscious mind. If we have a negative belief, it is caused by a sense of personal inadequacy, a belief that we cannot achieve our purposes. It relates not to the task as such, but to the personal factors involved. Usually such beliefs result from fear and its derivatives, doubt and anxiety.

"The knowledge of control of these subtle powers is one of the keys to Godhood. This leads to self-regard of Soul from a mature viewpoint. Call it mature self-regard, if you desire.

"Now the greatest problem here lies in the conflict between the ideal urge and the indifference urge. The seeker who desires to reach God in perfection is being taught wrongly, for he must come to tremendous blows with that instinct which is fearful and anxious about the outcome. This makes his body a battlefield and in the end he will not be as far along on the spiritual path as the aspirant who has just found the Master.

"Resign yourself to me, this I tell you. Do not seek any power but that of the highest and I, the Master, will see that your life is cared for and protected in every stage of the spiritual path.

"You see why at times the Kal force made greater inroads upon your body as a battlefield. He can only touch the lower powers, and this applies to most of his devotees. That is why his teachings are not the highest though he claims them to be. In his way, he is saying only what he knows to be the truth. Therefore, as he sees it, he is being truthful.

"When you come to me then your life is changed, and you are lifted into the highest, if you know what the highest is and desire that!

"Let us stop here. Tomorrow night I am going to tell you

61

why the general teachings of the Orientals are not on sound ground. Goodnight!"

With that, Rebazar Tarzs arose and walked through the door, disappearing into the night!

# SPIRITUAL CONFLICTS

Rebazar Tarzs was gazing steadily at me, while I worked at the desk, late in the evening. After a while I glanced up and noted he had taken a chair.

R.T.: "I have been waiting. Why did you slip off to the movies? There is work to be done."

P.: "Don't I deserve some rest?"

R.T.: "Those who have been called never rest. So never think you are going to dodge any duty by trying to substitute another. That is not possible!

"Now as the ECK Master, there is much to tell you. Very soon I will start dictating a new book to you. This is to be an esoteric story which will surprise the world. It will be a story of spiritual conflicts in man. But there are some other jobs you must do first.

"The forces which hold man together have enough explosive materials to blow him apart if set off properly. Now this is precisely what happens in many cases when we fail to balance ourselves and do not understand the proper spiritual powers within, and are unable to avoid prolonged conflict between the poles in the inner self!

"Heretofore, I have said that the power within man is of one nature, and that it is only how we react to it in order to get results. If we set in motion a negative cause, the result normally is reverted to the lower pole and the results are of a negative nature, and vice versa. Thus materialism is of a negative nature, for it is of the coarser vibrations and atoms. On the other hand, the higher the thought, the finer becomes the vibrations and the atoms by which it is constructed and grows into the higher spiritual forces, near the Fountainhead of God.

"For the purpose of defining the two main conflicts in man (which are commonly called God) meaning the good and evil, or positive and negative, let us give them prosaic labels

63

such as aggressiveness and passiveness, two of the greatest basic qualities possessed by man. These are known in the mystic language as the subjective and objective, higher and lower self, and the positive and negative pole. In Indian terms they are the Prit and Kal. But as long as man lives in the lower worlds he will be torn between them.

"Actual conflict between them may be quite severe but of a relatively short duration, or near exhaustion of the vibrations. This conflict results in blocking the spiritual flow within man, which interferes with his physical and mental vibrations, with the consequential ineffectiveness and frustrations. If continued, it will lead to chronic forms of conflicts with its distressing symptoms of exhaustion, failure, and despair. The effects of stoppage of the spiritual powers flowing through man can be tragic.

"Of course, we know that resignation to the Atma-Sarup of the Master is the answer to all conflicts. But too often there is an over-anxiety to succeed in our drive to reach God and the acute conflict will rage greater within, instead of quieting. This last statement is so true of many seekers normally, we call it over-anxiety.

"If your agressive nature is too demanding for greater effort in the attempt to reach God, while the quality of humility has been violently contending that the efforts of the other is all too strenuous and exhausting, and that the striving should cease, then we must do something about it. If we resign our inner selves to the teacher, then we come to real self-surrender. If this is done completely, the conflict will terminate completely and the Master will bring peace and harmony to the Soul.

"Very often when you cease to strive for perfection, it comes like a thief in the night. With the inner strife and tension subsided, the ECK power begins to work within one, and spiritual and mental effectiveness returns.

"Undoubtedly you ask, should I give up my ambitious strivings for God? No, but such strivings must be continued without tension, anxiety, and conflict — for these are the negative side of man.

"Yet remember that these two natures of man are striving to move you closer to God, for the lessons which they bring daily are only to give you the spiritual efforts behind all events. This is the main reason why Buddha cautioned us to live the balanced life.

"In other words, the aggressiveness in man serves best by means of intense effort to overcome the obstacles to reach God. But the humble side (being the adaptive nature of man) sees to it that our interest is best served by the opposite means, by conserving our energy vibrations through avoiding tasks that are too difficult, or those where we fear we might fail, and adapting and conforming to conditions that appear negative without effort to overcome them.

"Thus when Jesus said, 'Turn the other cheek for thy neighbor to strike', he meant that by resigning or submitting to the insult it would win the victory without the effort of expending energies on physical violence, which might set up karmic ties and open psychic channels which could take several lifetimes to work out. So you see, as the Americans say, 'Why bother?'

"It is like this — the aggressive nature of man is the green light to proceed and continue striving for God. The submissive side is that red light which says stop and take a look, for something needs adjustment.

"Now I tell you this. Here is where the use of subtle discrimination becomes a great art for man. He must use his discretion to determine if the will power is forcing his way when submissiveness would be of greater use on the spiritual path. Millions of people face neurotic problems daily because of the lack of proper spiritual training in the use of discrimination.

"Now let me say here that all instincts in man except the sex urge are striving constantly to preserve and protect him; and ultimately for him to reach God. Of course, the sex urge always is striving to preserve the beauty in the union of man and woman to a higher spiritual consciousness.

"Where the ECK Master steps in to handle all problems of the individual lies in the fact that each drive within the mental

65

field of man is selecting and pursuing the individual's interest as the common end and aim, but in a blind, unreasonable way.

"Thus if you turn yourself over to the Master, all inner life is organized for a single purpose — that is, to follow the will of God. Furthermore, if you have a healthy love for the Inner Master, the awful burden of self-contempt is lifted, and the spiritual journey is easier for traveling.

"Of course, negative belief, or a belief in our own inner inadequacy always arouses this submissive side. Where such belief is intense or prolonged, the submissive gains complete control over the spiritual with disastrous results.

"The advocates of the Eastern philosophies have considered the greatest enemy to our peace of mind to be desire, and so they have taught the necessity of avoiding desire. Thus, on the whole, the Orientals have achieved the peace of mind; yet they have paid a great price for this avoidance of inner conflict. They have conquered the aggressive quality in man, and brought out the submissive side, and therefore, have yielded to their environment without effort or desire to improve their material status. This was the result of the teachings that were brought in by the Moslems who wanted to dominate the masses, and had the Priests to rewrite the scriptures, as in the case of the Holy Bible. (The great problem before the authorities of free India is to re-educate the people to care for themselves, to develop free will, and aggressiveness to make a livelihood.) For this reason, anyone showing spiritual inclination and development has been idolized and given great stature. This is a form of idolatry.

"Most of this has spread to the West and superstition prevails in the Western mind, as well as in the Oriental's. Inner peace has been attained at the terrible price of quenching the instinctive desire to achieve and advance in all worlds. The Hindus have achieved inner peace by destroying the wrong instinct to the inner conflicts.

"The Christians and Jews seek to avoid conflict and attain inner peace by restraining the submissive or negative nature and letting go with the opposite. But they are applying these vital principles wrongly. The Occidental is victimized often by his own anxious negative thoughts which stimulate the submissive side and prevent peace and progress inwardly. We need the Oriental philosophy, infused with the Occidental, but to the extent of restraining the fearful, anxious aspect of our desires in that it inevitably invites conflict with its associated evils. Thus we can maintain objective progress and advancement with peace of mind.

"Intense desire without conflict is essential to our highest performance and can be achieved. Of course, the highest form of desire is to reach God and have a willingness to work for this achievement. This attitude is so challenging and should arouse the best within us. This is where I, the Master, step in, and take your hand to lead you to the highest.

"Furthermore, if you always hold an attitude that God is going to make the neighbor do exactly what is best for him, and you will see his action in this light, your attitude is in a subtle manner transferred to the other, and the Master will move him in accordance to your best plans, if your plans are in harmony with the living ECK Master's cause.

"When we have a bad day, or a distinct slump in our performance, usually it is because we have forgotten the Master and let the weak, negative or submissive phase of ourselves be on the ascendant. If in the opposite stage, it becomes the positive or aggressive side which is on the upgrade, and we are free of any limitations.

"Remember this. Impressions gained through transference often will have a more potent effect than those gained through the spoken word. If we want others to think well not only of our capacities, but ourselves, we must take care of the thoughts we think about ourselves and about them.

"Sadly we are mistaken when we assume that what we think about others, without expressing it, is our private affair, and they will not know. When we are most anxious for others not to know what an innermost thought and feeling might be, they are most likely to sense them, or rather apprehend them through psychic perception. Thoughts charged with an emotional tone of fear or anxiety are especially apt to transfer and those we are most anxious to keep to ourselves.

Therefore, I say to you to cultivate sincerity and good will.

"Let us discuss the perfectionist briefly. He is usually an intelligent, conscientious, striving person, a very desirable type, but one who makes the mistake of pursuing certain virtues to excess. He suffers from nervous tension and frustration through inability to achieve a high degree of perfection for what he has undertaken. He is patient and forgiving of others, but for himself severe, and an unrelenting taskmaster.

"He tries too hard and this he needs to realize—he will attain a higher degree of perfection when he learns to relax his effort and remove from it the tension and anxiety that results from conflict and exhaustion. Sometimes by practicing total indifference to the Light it will come.

"But by practicing the presence of the Master, you will integrate your powers for a higher step upon the path.

"Only I can help you. Nothing else can, and you can learn to feel my presence unmistakenly if you proceed in absolute faith. For I am always with you. Thus your task is to recognize my presence and my guidance.

"Goodnight!"

With that, Rebazar Tarzs seemed to rise into the air and disappear into the light from the lamp, as if the yellow rays themselves were his body.

# WHO IS THE MASTER?

The Tibetan's presence kept growing in my consciousness this evening, ever letting me know that he was there. Yet I could not see him. After a while he started materializing and his familiar voice spoke.

R.T.: "I need to go to work. Please don't hold back any longer. Are you ready?"

P.: "Yes. Let us start!"

R.T.: "I want you to be absolutely bold in your thinking. Go beyond the farthest horizons in your mind. Be completely dependent upon me, but strike out with great courage to reach that goal you once set for yourself. Very shortly you are going to end this wild work schedule and settle down into a steady routine. You will write on a fixed schedule and have a good income from it.

"At this time you are approaching a complete change in your life. The date set for this is March 25th. Be prepared for this change. It comes on Sunday, and actually this is going to make such an absolute change in you from that day on, hardly any of your friends will recognize you. Everything you do and touch will turn to spiritual gold.

"Within the next few days I want you to slow down on my dictation and let yourself catch up with getting all into the notebooks.

"Before getting into this specific discussion tonight there are a couple of things to take up. (1) Where are you now in your life and goal? (2) How far have you progressed? (3) How are you going to negotiate the rest of the way?

"Now here is where you stand in life. Exactly at the start of a new life, the beginning of acquiring first-hand knowledge of the cosmic worlds, and the first step toward your spiritual mission. This is similar to a young man's first job in life. He takes it with full confidence and faith, trusting in the spirit to carry him through. It is a new freedom, a

69

dependence upon himself, a burst of Light. His horizon has been pushed back and he sees that some day he will be president of the company. So it is with you. Your horizon has been pushed back far, and you see that some day you will be one with God on the other planes, not just the earth plane. Your goal is the voluntary step across the veil into the other world.

"Secondly, your progress is good and will continue outwardly. There is no possible way for you to slide back again. For I have taken over your life, and am handling everything. New vibrations are changing your attitude and constant outlook on life. Your viewpoint is absolutely changed. It will keep changing into the full Light of God until you are living daily in IT.

"Third, how are you going to negotiate the rest of the way? Simply this, by putting your complete faith in me. In fact, it is more than faith—it is a certain subtle knowing that I am taking care of you in every possible way, in the smallest details, even as to your breathing, heartbeat, and flow of blood through your precious body.

"Do you know that your heart is continuing to beat whether awake or asleep? You are absolutely certain of this. Then you know for sure that I, who am responsible for every detail of your life, will handle everything in your life now and up to the time you cross over the borders into the beyond.

"This brings us to the discussion for the evening. Who is the ECK Master? Are you certain that I, standing before you in my Atma Sarup, the radiant form, am the perfect teacher, or is this a delusion of your senses? I tell you this, the perfect teacher is real, and the absolute highest who can reveal only the essence of the Soul. I can give you proficiency in Para Vidya which consists of releasing Soul from the shackles of mind and gaining complete freedom.

"When you have gained self-knowledge, which is Para Vidya, then the Self lives by that law which is beyond the physical senses.

"The living ECK Master is far beyond the Laws of Nature, yet, as a man, knows and sees that Para Vidya, or knowledge

70

of the physical senses, is necessary to the growth of man to reach that stage whereby he comes to me.

"Now we come to the delicate point of who is this being that is the perfect teacher, or the Master? This is the question posed before the masses of seekers today, for they go thither and yon to teachers who have not the eyes to see. The blind lead the blind until they finally bump into me, and there I have waited until the aspirant finally makes his appearance. Soul will seek until it comes to the true Master.

"Now briefly, I tell you this. The Master is the SUGMAD. All ECK Masters will tell you this, and the answer is apt to confuse the seeker. Therefore, we must get to some definite understanding along the path to our objective!

"We know that God is Light and Sound. When we look within at the spiritual eye, usually the Light is the first of the two-fold aspects of the Deity to appear. Then comes the Sound.

"After a while your inner form, the Light body, will go through the Light into clear space, past the moon and sun worlds, to where it seems balanced in the sky, and where you are greeted by my radiant form. Thus you have come to the three-fold aspect of the Deity!

"Light and Sound and Form! In a sense this is the broadening of our understanding of God. It is the trinity. As one might say, the three-fold aspect of God. Therefore, I am Light, Sound and Form, the manifestation of your God-Realization.

"This is far beyond the comprehension of those trained only in Para Vidya, who have much learning in the occult studies, moral ethics, the Upanishads, religions, hymns, and other things of the earth nature. It is beyond that part of the teachings called God-Consciousness. Often it is referred to as the Christ-Consciousness; Hiram Abiff; Supreme Love; Self-Realization; and other names. But here again, is a misconception of understanding. What the scriptures, religions and teachers are giving is only a glimpse of the aspect of God, and not of God Itself. Here we come to the term used in the New Testament, called 'Jesus Christ' which is

71

only another name for the Cosmic Power, and speak of its use of the individual man as the channel in order to give the Light to the world. But the ECK Power, or the Light Itself, is only an aspect of God. And the body of the Mahanta.

"Some mystics misinterpret this as God, but it is not God, although this power is of the highest aspect of God. Next, is that some say the Sound is God; although a higher aspect of the divine than Light, the Sound is not reality itself. Then again, we have reached that aspect which is the radiant Form of the Master in the spiritual vision, which is not God completely, but the ultimate whole made up of Light and Sound, the two-fold aspect of God.

"Have you grasped this so far, what I am telling you? No? Then look at it in this manner. Let me say that every mystic and philosopher has tried to reach the ultimate goal by different paths and failed unless the Master appeared and explained what God is to them. Each has sought always, through various disciplines of introspection, to arrive at a knowledge of the ultimate immutable essence that under-guides the subtle physical worlds. Remember Plato said twenty-three hundred years ago, 'The true lover of knowledge always is striving after being!'

"Now this is where we are at this moment. Let us simplify these vital questions. Who is the Mahanta, the living ECK Master, and Is he God?

"The simplest illustration is this. The only world man knows is that created for him by his senses. If he expunges all the impressions which they translate and memory stores, nothing is left. Hegel said, 'Pure being and nothing is the same'. A state of existence devoid of associations has no meaning. So, paradoxically, what the scientists and the mystics call the world of appearances, the physical world of Light and color, is the world which man has made by his essential nature for his own use.

"What is called the world beyond, the world of reality, or the cosmic world (which is beyond the perception of human eyes) is an invisible structure built upon the Light and Sound, and controlled by the ECK Master.

"In other words, the cosmic worlds are as much of a physical universe to those who live and travel there, as this earth plane is to finite man. However, here the tables of atoms which uphold it are of far finer nature, growing finer on each upward plane until they become like rarified mountain air, which only the trained mountain climber can inhale.

"Now we will think in terms of the three-form eye symbol which makes up the reality called the SUGMAD.

"Let us reduce this to its lowest common denominator by using this example. We see, feel, touch, and hear on the physical plane. These are our most common senses in the physical world. As you develop spiritually, one of the strange things you encounter on the path is that you learn that each body of your being has corresponding senses—such as the astral, causal, mental and other bodies, including Soul. Each of these bodies when reaching the plane to which it corresponds will put in use these senses on that plane through the sight of the spiritual eye.

"Let us say you decide to have a new chair in your room. It comes first in the form of a thought, a movement of inner words saying you would like a chair. Then the chair appears before your physical eye in a store. Perhaps this is not the best illustration, but it will do at the moment.

"This is similar to going within with a strong desire to find the Master. First, you seek the Light, and then the Sound follows, then the Master appears to take your hand and lead you into the worlds beyond. It is not that you will him, but your desire and love are so strong that he could not resist them. Your spiritual senses saw, heard, and touched. Understand?

"Basically, we are made up of the Light and Sound but man hardly has conception great enough to realize this. By this statement we can say God is in everything, penetrating all—and I, the ECK Master, being God, am in all things—yet I am not, for those are only my aspects. My higher self is that radiant form within which comes to you when your desire is so great and intense that a cord of love draws us together, just as love draws men and women to become one in a union of love. So we, too, become one in a spiritual understanding and Light.

"The touch in the inner world is not the physical touch as we know it, but the profound emotion which is the sensation of the mystical. Neither do I touch your hand, but that cosmic hold in the spiritual clasp of our hands is the strongest and noblest tie that one may have.

"Now for the first time you realize what is meant by the perfect Master. I have served my apprenticeship and reached the ultimate perfection, and therefore become God, or the Blessed One of the Universe. Abstraction is no longer the cold, bare symbol which once confronted us, but now takes on reality.

"The other worlds have been shaped, formed and made a place of realities by those who have populated them, regardless of their spiritual growth. The drunkard has made his hell on the astral plane, and the saint his heaven on the Fifth, or Seventh. And you make your world by what you expect of it. Not what you will today, but that which is the ultimate result of all until you reach the Master, and then it depends upon your understanding, love and breadth of spiritual vision.

"Does this answer the question: Who is the ECK Master?

"Many words pour from my lips to explain the spiritual truths, but what counts is the understanding you have of each spoken word. What I say is not as great, nor as important, as what was not said. There is more to be comprehended than the vocalized words.

"I repeat again that faith is the keystone of all spiritual life. Just believe in me and I take care of all. Leave all in my hands.

"Remember this, Paul. You grow according to your understanding. You travel in the inner worlds and see all according to your understanding. You take down my words according to your knowledge and understanding. So you know now why it seems that my sayings are contradictory. I never am, but to you it seems so because you lacked understanding at the time you heard and saw. Goodnight."

# THE VOICE OF THE MASTER

The Tibetan kept calling me but I would not pay attention. I needed sleep more than anything else. Finally, he came over to the bed and shook me awake.

R.T.: "Get up, dear one. I let you alone last night, but tonight there is work to be done. Get to your chair and take the pencil in hand."

P.: "I don't know why you couldn't have selected somebody else to do this job. I need to rest. I am not capable!"

R.T.: "Stop grumbling and get to your chair. Now listen to me. Remember the revelation you had that morning in London? That was when you sat in contemplation, saw the white Light, heard music and then went through a golden moon into a clear field where I was waiting to take your hand.

"You were led up a long road through the fields and forest to where Milarepa sat under a tree. He said to you, 'Go with Rebazar Tarzs today, and tomorrow! Do not leave his side at any time. He will need you at a moment's notice. Discuss this with him in private. You are to tell him that you will come to India, at the proper time, for spiritual development under him, for there is work to do for God's cause.'

"Yes, you remember. From that moment on, you became Spirit Itself. Milarepa had informed you to surrender yourself to ECK Power. When you did this your life started to change, and it was possible to awaken the ECK Power within you. Never again can you make any movement or thought without it being a part of that mental or physical motion.

"People are filled with awe for your wisdom. How you arrive at your conclusions is a mystery. They try to figure out whether you draw for inspiration on the ECK or whether it is by logical comparison and deduction you arrive at your findings.

"Now I want to tell you this by making a statement on the mind, which we studied previously, by saying that states of mind which are shared between the Master and devotee are like thin wires running from the former to the seeker. Actually, they are cords of light. But these states of mind always are in silence. No words pass between the teacher and disciple. There is no need to be, for the pupil readily understands the teacher's desires and carries them out fully without question, often without himself being conscious of doing so.

"The Master rarely tells his disciple what to do. He talks to him mentally for the reason that thought instruction has a greater universality of understanding than verbalization.

"The Master knows that the point at which thought is turned into words often causes great difficulties in those disciples whose instinctive urges and codes of conduct are different. This is why devotees in America have been hard put to reach certain understandings, and why they get into mental qualms and struggles. Because, basically, their code of mentalization and conduct is different from the Oriental's.

"Am I making myself clear? Let me put it this way.

"Man is the same everywhere, of God, and on the inner planes with IT. But his social and ethical nature is different, and this is as true of the Occidentals and Orientals. Now here is where the path stops and forks temporarily—just which way shall we go? I believe in one pattern of conduct because my social, physical and racial background trained my mind in it for years.

"If you would put an orthodox Hindu in a Western home, job and social life, it is doubtful he would like it. Neither would you like the rigid code of the Hindus.

76

"Now down to some basic pattern of this former point.: Some persons whose basic urges and codes of conduct are not in accord, have difficulties in getting out words.

"The projection of the unexpected feeling is obvious. It does not allow feeling to come to the consciousness as a thought for which the devotee must assume responsibility.

The borderline of conscious and unconscious contemplation is a wide, shadowy band which exists at that point of human expression where effects turn into thought. Many devotees suffer from the great difficulty in finding words which would suitably express their thought to make themselves really understand what is wrong, or the problem within themselves.

"This blockage is due principally to the fact that they wish to find words which will express the effect of their thought, yet not reveal anything which will expose the ego.

"Seldom can this be achieved, for few such words exist in any language. But where there is true humility of the devotee toward the Master, then there are few or no words spoken between them. The mental and spiritual vibrations passing between them are greater than words which the tongue can utter.

"This silent exchange is the secret language so often referred to by the adepts. It is one of the most normal procedures between the devotee and Master. An example is that between lovers a glance passing from one to the other will tell more than any sweet spoken words.

"Remember the glance I gave you in the home of Sudar Singh, in Allahabad that evening before the contemplation started? That told of my love for you!

"The Master undertakes a baffling and tedious task when he seeks to reach the emotions immobilized and imprisoned beneath the surface by the aspirant who remains detached and impersonal, yet looks to the guru to give him enlightenment without effort on his part. The ECK Master must attempt gently to probe and pry so the coiled spring of emotion may be loosened and brought into action to let go with love.

"On the other hand, those aspirants who have gone in the opposite direction need to have this spring of emotion tightened to keep them from being overly discriminating.

"This is done through the Voice of Silence, that phase of contemplation passing between the Master and devotee. It is doubtful that a perfect teacher would sit with his devotee and discuss any fault of the aspirant. No, I tell you, hardly ever will a Master tell one what is wrong within, but he will concentrate on the error and bring about the change from the inner outwardly, without pain or difficulty to the devotee, and very often without the conscious knowledge of the aspirant.

"Now this is done through the use of love. Love is the true philosophy of the saints. Not the love you see portrayed about you, but that of the highest. And now I tell you that there are planes beyond the Fifth. But we shall not discuss them yet. From these planes flow the great Current of Love to permeate the worlds below.

"Briefly, I will also tell you that within the last realm of space, we have over ten million worlds upon which life exists. If this is beyond your imagination do not think about it.

"The inability to give love and, through not giving, the failure to receive it, are fundamental factors in the troubles of man. In psychology we say this is the factor in many types of severe neuroses, especially in schizophrenia.

"The tiny infant has an absolute essential and biological need for warmth and attention, in the spiritual as well as the physical sense, and also for affection and love. Denied these, one solution remains to the child for satisfying the instinctive need. This is to find it within itself, and to love itself excessively. During the adolescent years this self-love may lead to self-indulgence and a vicious circle is begun which fosters shyness, antisocial tendencies and sullenness from which the person may not emerge.

"Thus you see, the ECK Master, is faced with the great responsibility of opening the hearts of the devotees. If I should do so without care or caution, the seeker may be thrown off his delicate emotional balance and become a social problem for his fellowman.

"Now the law of the world as we know it is this: If a man's attention is focused upon an object which gives him pleasure, he will have pain if it is removed.

"So you see, this law of nature compels us to place the attention of many on a permanent object so that there will not be an unbalancing of the emotions too greatly through pleasure or pain.

"Let me tell you here that the word detachment is too cold. What is meant in spiritual terms is this—we, as one with all, will have a certain amount of pleasure and pain, but will not let it affect our emotional balance too greatly to throw our minds into the extreme poles of joy or sorrow. The real control is detachment from fear. Once you have gained this important attribute of God, then you can enjoy greater life. Yes, you can have a joy mixed with pain and not be affected to the same extent as previously. Only when fear is in control of those two poles is your life attached to its physical, mental, and spiritual possessions. Give up fear and you need never to give up another thing in your life. Great joys physically, mentally, and spiritually can become yours, balanced by what sorrows there need be in your life!

"Of course, sorrow comes to you. If your parents pass on, your sorrow does not come from death taking them, but from the fact that they must go away. If fear has been cast out of your life, then this emotion is true sorrow, an emotion which belongs in the psychic realm. This is true of a mother who weeps when her daughter is married. Does she weep in sorrow? Perhaps, but mixed with joy!

"Now we come to the point in our study of the devotee's problem often called karma. You remember the questioning period after one contemplation when I said that the Master takes upon himself the devotee's karma? Many of you did not understand nor believe this. Yet it is true, but not as you think. The answer is very simple.

"When the devotee takes the initiation from the Master, there is a subtle exchange of the interplay of thought between them.

"In psychology the system is called transference of the emotional problem to the doctor. These problems are often mental symbols. The fact is, that many diseases or mental conflicts and long-standing problems, even incarnations, are self-limited, and that spiritual strivings are converted into bodily expressions of illness.

"The Master can see easily that all karma falls into one or another set pattern. He knows from a glance the illusion under which the Soul who comes to him is suffering.

"Often magnified, the devotee believes that great karma has been set in store for him to work out, and this illusion weighs his mind down with its chains of guilt and other emotional, negative feelings. It is really the lift of the mind from the lower pole to the opposite.

"Often the Master will let the devotee act out his problem mentally, and by doing so, go through the process of transferring the negative forces to the teacher. Of course, I can dispel these forces at will, but first must take them from the devotee.

"This action works in two ways. First, if the devotee, because of an early denial or repression, has an insatiable desire to be loved, and throws positive love upon my universal body and establishes a cord of love which is overly balanced in the devotee, and adjusts in time to a steadily faithful devotion for the Master, he will have the ability to walk without my support.

80

"Second, often the devotee transfers his negative karma to the Master in the form of hostility and feelings of hatred. In time, the devotee will become a true follower of ECK, giving only the highest devotion and love.

"In a way, this is the method by which I take over the karma of my devotees. But if one has a karma to bear which must be done alone, in order to get across a lesson, I do nothing about it for my own law compels me to stand aside and let the disciple learn without help, until he reaches out to take my love without regret or remorse for the higher step.

"Frankly, it is very important for you to know yourself, as I have always preached. In time the devotee learns to realize the meaning of love and hate (which he finds reflected in his own Soul) in order to be rehabilitated (if I can use this word) himself, in the spiritual world.

"Before leaving off this discussion, let me say that you can be rid of a complex or phobia by forcing it. But the ECK Master must take it and fill its vacuum with love.

"Man is forever in search of love. He never forgets, even subconsciously, the warmth of his mother's body, so he dreams of better luck in his next life through the return to the womb and rebirth.

"Water, therefore, becomes a symbol of rebirth to him. This symbolism is very important through mythology and the ideology of childhood. Thales, the Greek philosopher, said water was the origin and womb of all things.

"In this formula the conception of the individual origin of man in the mother is extended to my universal body. Sometimes the hero of mythology and spiritual endeavor is not born through the uterine waters, but found in or on the water as were Moses and Noah.

"This spiritual conception is taken from the waters of the amniotic fluid which accompanies birth. Many interpretations of the Scriptures have overrated greatly the terms of the use of the water in its pages.

"We know that from its general importance in the process of birth, water is associated symbolically with cleanliness and absolution. People wish to wash away their sins, and cleanliness is next to Godliness. The compulsion to wash our hands nearly always is associated with a karmic need to be rid of some guilt feeling, which usually is hidden and of a lower nature.

"Now in conclusion I say be not dismayed if a Master has little to say to you. Open your ears and listen to the Sound, for it is I who speaks and advises you constantly."

# SELF-SURRENDER

The Tibetan seemed to be annoyed with me today, for he kept telling me to buckle down to work. I had taken it easy all day except for a couple of hours when my job gave trouble. I asked him to come in tonight, which he did, and he seemed to be in a good humor.

R.T.: "You have been loitering. Don't you know better than to get away from the schedule which I have established for you? There is more work than one can ever imagine. Now let us get down to facts.

"The subject of self-surrender is one of the most debated points in all spirituality. In fact, very few of my devotees know what true self-surrender to the Master means."

P.: "I have a mental concept of it."

R.T.: "Ah, there. You give the answer of the typical seeker. As people say, 'You hit the nail on the head'. The majority of seekers have a blurred idea of self-surrender. Some of them have a feeling of self-surrender, and the rest a mental concept.

"Now self-surrender is the real key to spiritual success. If you are looking for any growth on any plane, this is the way. Only by self-surrender do you gain illumination and knowledge of true spirituality.

"To whom do you surrender? To the Inner ECK Master, of course. To him who comes to you in the Atma Sarup, or the radiant form. He is the Mahanta, the true Master.

"Yet you ask, how do I surrender to the Inner Master. This is one of the paradoxical questions facing every seeker. Almost every true seeker of God becomes frantic and desperate to reach the ultimate goal, or for some Light upon the path. Yet this serves only to increase his frustrations.

"There is only one way to find God, but only the daring, the enterprising, and the ambitious will find Him. The way is simple, so much of a primary thing that we are apt to overlook it. Just sit in silence, looking sweetly into the spiritual eye, with 'effortless effort', and the Light will come. After awhile the inner ear is opened for the Sound Current and after this, the radiant form of the Master appears.

"Simple, isn't it? Well, so far it is, but then again we have not yet surrendered to the Master. Yes, we can have the Master in our lives, but not yet be surrendered to him. This is the paradoxical nature of God. To have God, but not have God. You may have the Master in your life, but still again the Master may not have you. If you are thoughtful enough about this puzzle it will be solved easily. Yet how many of you are willing to put thought to the problem? Man would rather sit in a congregation week after week and let somebody tell him what to do. He is lazy, the goat among the sheep, and must have a shepherd. And woe to that shepherd who does not bring the real truth to his flock; who does not give them the adoration of God with the science of Reality, as much as he can truthfully. However, only the Master can give the way to wisdom and understanding!

"The seeker must start with an effort (or at least a settled turn) toward the concentrated love for the Master. This concentrated power is composed of the mind, heart, and will — a consummation fully possible to the seeker when Soul has submitted Itself to the radiant form of the Master. Only then can the perfection of the mind, life and body effectively be fulfilled for the Master's work as an instrument, consecrated, perfected, and grown fit for selfless service. This is done, not by eliminating the lower self, or ego, but by balancing and making the best use of it.

"Now the word concentration is wrongly used by most writers and teachers. I would prefer to use the word attention. It is better in the connotation of what I am trying to get across for your understanding.

"Attention means to have all your faculties gathered upon an object because you desire it to be. Otherwise, concentration means forcing the will to hold the attention upon the objective whether it be for your best interest or not.

"Now this is where the Master's teachings differ from all mysticism and occult philosophies. Your attention is placed upon the Inner Master; that is, you must love him more greatly than anything else. It is as simple as that. Where does a young mother's attention lie? Upon the tiny infant at her side. Every gurgle it makes and every movement keeps her aroused to its welfare. This is the way you should love me!

"The secret of self-surrender is this. Be so completely interested in the Inner ECK Master that nothing else matters! Of course, you go about your duties without thought as to their results, for I take care of all, even to your physical welfare.

"Does not the spirit of the Inner Master take care of the birds, flowers, and all life? So then it should include you, personally, among its children! Remember Jesus spoke of the lilies beside the road, that they toiled not—meaning they were under the care of God!

"This I tell you. That when your attention on the radiant form within will be consummated by the mind, when constantly you see the Divine Self in Itself (meaning the worlds within and the Divine Self) and that It is also in all things and beings and events, then you will be on the full road to self-surrender.

"Furthermore, when you see that Soul is consummated by the heart and all emotion is summed up in the love of IT, or ITSELF, in the universal body and for the universal body, then you have surrendered completely to the Master.

"Of course, this includes the love of the Divine Self in all my beings, powers, and forms in the universe. This love will be consummated by the will, so then you will feel and receive always the ECK Power and accept that alone as your sole motivating force. Then you will have been taken into the universal body as one. This is known to the mystics as the union with God.

"Naturally, there are many steps which move the seeker toward the goal of perfect self-surrender. But only by complete dedication to God's purpose and God ITSELF, do you reach the final stage of this momentous goal.

"The release of your tensions and conflicts is the first step into self-surrender. To turn your life over to the Master is to develop a knowing beyond the perception of the senses. It is when you actually come to know that IT has taken over your life and controls it for the advancement of the Master's cause will you have faith in me. This is beyond any conception in this world of senses. One can never explain nor tell what it is, but must lean upon that intuitive knowing that I am you and you are me.

"It is actually this simple: by becoming the instrument through which the cosmic power flows so readily that you can hear the Sound like the low hum of a motor—sometimes bells, thunder or rolling drums. Then you are in my hands!

"Self-surrender is very simple. You start by faith and let it grow into the knowing. Lean on your creative faculty, as Einstein did. He knew how to set the stage of a theory with a situation carved out of his inner processes.

"He did not sit in silence and see that this was going to be solved by God. No, he started with some point to determine the point of self-surrender to his creative processes.

"First it must be done with desire and the creative faculty —not the imagination but the use of the cosmic power (call it creative force if you wish) to build within what is needed in life to serve the Master. Then let us begin at this point, by the use of our own inner effort and initiative, which is needed to work as in our daily lives. For example, we must not leave everything to the Master. For all (in accordance to the Law) must be done by free will.

"If you set out to write a book, the subject must be selected, materials gathered, and the outline laid down. Following this you must select your chapters, and put them together until there is a continuity like beads running together on a string.

"Giving up to the Master is not letting go of free will, but making use of it for the Divine Plan of God. For like the writing of the book, your interest is given over to the Divine Life. All attention is put upon God, and therefore,

86

you plan according to your instructions received from the wisdom I give you from the inner worlds.

"Now here is where the creative faculty and free will are put to use. Like other faculties on the inner planes each flows through its own channel to the objective faculty.

"If you sit in contemplation to wait for the traveler to come and take you into the cosmic worlds, you will most likely be disappointed. Therefore you must put to use your free will in determining where you would like to go under the Master's guidance, and what might be expected there.

"Normally, if the Master feels that it is right for you to take the journey to the plane of your desires, your will can be fulfilled. On the other hand, it takes the use of your creative faculty to plan and measure out what might be before you. In cosmic worlds everything is in accordance with your experience or your belief.

"I mean by this that if you desired to travel from Chicago to New York City, your astral will-power and creative faculty would be used in getting to your destination. But as a child, who does not believe that anything exists in the world outside its own environment, you would not believe there was a New York City. So it would take all the creative faculty to build an inner image of it. Am I making myself clear?

"You must believe there is a Second or Third and even a Fifth Plane in the cosmic worlds. Use your creative faculty in a positive manner to see or think what is there, and your free will to decide to make the journey. Then use will-power to determine to get there, unless the teacher decrees it otherwise.

"By the use of these three faculties in man (constantly fed by the Divine Power) you in actuality can become the architect of your own free-will to determine whether or not you will follow my choice of course for you. You are the Master of yourself and you are the Master of your life. Only when you harmonize your free will with the Divine Life will your life follow the direction of Soul!

"Your free will determines whether your life will come

to a perfect self-surrender to the teacher. Now, have I made myself clear?

"Now let me tell you this. Fear no one's will-power. You can handle all situations with ease and charm. Meanwhile I will take care of any who try to harm you. Nobody can harm you, for you are under my protection and care and doing my work. Spirit has taken care of you constantly. It will continue to do so! Let's leave off here! Goodnight!"

## INFLUENCES OF THE ASTRAL WORLD

Rebazar Tarzs came into the room tonight while I was working at the desk. He took a seat in his usual place and waited, then started talking.

R.T.: "Let us begin at this point. Tonight I desire to discuss the fallacies in the teachings, and the problems which beset the seekers on the path.

"The greatest dangers facing the aspirant are those influences of the lower astral world. Frankly, I have to step in often to take many newly initiated devotees out of entangled situations in which the lower nature of his psychic channels have involved him.

"This stage of the path has brought the aspirant to the point fairly common in the psychiatric world, but uncommon to the average man. Mostly, man fails to understand that his problem can be solved easily by his fellow man if allowed. But he wants to wrap himself in some mysterious cloak and loudly proclaim that the Master has taken over his life, and therefore all is well. No claim could be made more falsely.

"The seeker has found great advances have come with the recognition of the tremendous significance to him of his ideas and emotions. They are the result of trying to enter into the inner worlds through contemplation without due preparation or without the help of the Master.

"This is true of those who follow the teachings of the Yogis. Now I tell you seriously many of the teachings are dangerous for they have the tendency to unbalance the seeker instead of adjusting him properly.

"Often the ideas and emotions of the seeker are to him reality; grim, terrifying and fascinating. Now with this strange contest going on with himself, the seeker begins to want something. He becomes convinced of some power in possession of himself, and then begins to have a flood of mental pictures as though an album of photographs was unfolding itself. Too often, he is terror-stricken or overwhelmed with fear of the unknown, and there are times when he is certain that he is going to die.

"Then suddenly he sees things in a new light and all takes on a different appearance. He is certain that the Dawn of Creation has come. Communication comes out of the ether which impresses him with the feeling that there is a cosmic struggle between the 'higher and lower selves' going on within.

"Often he feels that he has lived before his present time and life, and at one time he might have been Genghis Khan, Julius Caesar, Alexander the Great, or even Jesus.

"There are times when he reviews the universe in spirit and associates himself with God.

"Now, sooner or later, the seeker comes up against hard set points in his inner world, and it becomes a real world. The drive for God-Realization has stopped and the individual becomes listless, ineffective and often unable to care for himself.

"He shows very little emotional disturbance, no marked thought-pattern and often has a normal reaction. But he drifts towards dissolution and destruction within himself.

"Now I tell you this. Often the seeker at this point tries to save face and refuses to admit defeat or error, and resorts to distortions of belief in order to escape the sense of failure and guilt. Then he voluntarily isolates himself from his fellow man, to live alone with his own world. He is looked upon as neurotic, or queer, and often his ego gives him great joy in this distinction.

"Now we come to the crux of this psychic situation. Only a few individuals can drift towards inner destruction, or build up an effective system of delusional misinterpretation, without at some time or other becoming aware of this danger. It is at this point that they start looking about for help. It can be at this time where the true Master steps forward to give them a lifting hand. If not, he will place them in some position for their understanding and work out certain karmic effects until ready for his true appearance.

"Too often the seeker has dark, negative impressions or pictures at this time which come off the lower astral plane. This is thoroughly characteristic of acute psychic disturbances. They begin with some eruption of the subconscious which is interpreted as a manifestation of the supernatural. The impact of their experience is apt to be a shock to the nervous system. It can destroy the foundations of their inner organization and upset the structure upon which the objective judgments and reasoning processes are based.

"Then the seeker finds himself living completely in the subjective world without divine help. This is a strange new world where accepted standards of value do not apply. There are strange meanings in everything about him and he is certain of only one thing: that things are not real on the physical plane.

"Very often, the mental processes are quickened and ideas and images flash into the mind as if from an outside source, in the form of voices and visions.

"In general, the seeker may have dark, angry images of a cosmic catastrophe about to occur, or that he is the Messiah, and that all the universe is operating from out of his heart— and many times he proclaims this to the world, only to be reviled by the public. More common reactions are deep depressions, feelings of guilt, self-blame, persecution, and acceptance of responsibility which may be thought of as being on a national scale.

"Throughout these periods the seeker will show remarkable frankness, telling apparently everything about himself, even though it is disturbing to him. Often he cannot stop talking!

"In the spiritual world, he classifies people as the drifters, the self-deceivers, the panic-stricken, the reactionaries, and the simple type.

"Here is where we move to another step upon the path. In the world of religion, many people with disorganized minds can point to wide religious experiences. And in many of the so-called religious geniuses and mystics we can hardly fail to recognize features that are definitely psychopathic.

"Now I tell you this. We have advanced to the real challenge on the path of spirituality. How do you determine the constructive experiences of true God-Realization in comparison with that of the destructive experience of the psychic world? This challenge we must seek out and determine.

"Except for the true mystical experience which the Master gives his disciples, as a Grace, most experiences in the inner world are problem-solving experiences. They are attempts to reorganize the full inner-self and marshal its forces to meet personal failure and isolation created by the struggle between the aggressive and the submissive qualities within man!

"Strangely, the sick of Soul rush everywhere but to the Master for the healing of themselves. Search the history of all religious geniuses and see what a struggle they had until finding their own true Master.

"Now I say, 'their own true Master,' but in reality every teacher is the cosmic spirit—every ECK Master who walks the planes, including the earth-world, is this Spirit. It speaks through all. None can escape it, for it is the personification of the cosmic worlds—of time and space!

"Then again, there are some through which I will not speak nor act, for their followers are on the lunatic fringe. These I leave alone until the proper time for them to turn to the lifting of the vision to ask for my heart.

"Thus, here lies the hope for man. In the history of every great follower of God, a similar experience of disturbance is recorded. It is the burning up of the karma and the removal of the dross so that the teacher will be able to make use of Soul and refine it to become the instrument for the cosmic power to work through.

"One great inner conflict is the characterization of alternating moods of elation and depression, of hope and despair, hyper-suggestibility, morbid conscientiousness, and the obsessive fear that the seeker has committed an unpardonable sin.

"The simplest way to be rid of these negative qualities is to lose the fear of them through your faith in the power and mercy of the Master.

"To suffer for your mistakes (or sins, as the scriptures term them) is an archaic symbolism of the kind we find so characteristically among the psychically disturbed seekers in mental hospitals.

"Frankly, this heavy hand of sin is laid upon many who have sex relations either in marriage or out of it. They suffer terribly through the teachings of conventional religious or moral codes. This I say, that they have more faith in the lower powers than in the ECK Power. Let me say here that anything done with love and in the consciousness of the highest ideal is blessed with the cosmic power. And all things have their place in God. But self-condemnation is the worst sin of all. How can you sin when you are me, and I am you? Remember this. You live in the Law unto yourself when you act in faith to the teachings of ECKANKAR!

"Too sadly we find the results of the churches today to be the tragedy of loyalty, the loss of perspective, and the tendency to over-emphasize the petty and trivial and diverse.

"You have seen that those whom Spirit touches and who have inner conflicts are generally those using some unsatisfactory protective devices to quiet and surpass a troublesome conscience, until the tension reaches the breaking point and the solution comes with cataclysmic suddenness.

"Generally, those seeking God will attempt to solve the problems connected with their own personal destiny, loyalties, and values created by their objective life. They constantly are asking, 'Who am I? Why am I here, and where am I going? What is going to happen to me? How can I solve this situation? How can I make atonement for my sins and mistakes?'

"This only means that they are looking for the teacher. The way to reach them is through a staid and unbroken development of the ideal. Cataclysmic experiences, regardless of outcome, are manifestations of Soul's attempt to get rid of attitudes and blocks that stunt growth, and to effect a reorganization of the inner self to accept the Master's help.

"Frankly, the tradition of mystical God-Realization is prominent among those who suffer from the sense of self-division. I mean that the strain of struggling against what they call sinful desires may result in mystical practices, and too often failures, although there are a few who reach unification with God, even without the teacher. So few, indeed, that it is not worth the struggle to try without the Master's help.

"The goals of ECKANKAR should generally be: Serenity, poise, an organized will—that is, from an objective viewpoint. On the subjective side, let Soul become the channel for the ECK Power for my work in this world.

"Saint Teresa, the Spanish mystic of the 16th Century, is an example of the objective features of morbid asceticism, blank despair, and joy, vision, etc. But growing towards the ultimate goal of realization with the Master. In the end, a transformation of the ordinary woman into a fine mystic. She was the intuitive type who arrived at her solution by means of subjective crises. But her system was completely wrong. She could have reached the same goal through a normal life, marriage, children, happiness, and giving to the world her love in doing for others. This among the Catholic Saints is wrong. They could have reached God without terrible strain upon their health.

"Now here is what I am trying to say. The moral code of the church has been too strong in the West. The procedure of the ECK teachings differs from that of the church. The church always has taught that conviction of sin was the first step to salvation. It seems to make the seeker face a fact in his life in the light of the church's teachings, and square accounts within himself.

"I say this is wrong. Simply this is the answer: Stop thinking about your problem. Give it to the ECK and ECK will handle your life better than you can possibly conceive. Once you have relaxed, then I take over and reorganize your inner capacities. Remember—pain and sorrow are only incidental to the process of growth and happiness.

"The struggle of all great people is like this. Even the story of the ECK Master shows us this. Out of it comes poise, beauty and serenity of character.

"Personal failure is often the sense of inner disharmony which extends from the divine discontent. That is, a precondition of effort and growth to the loss of that which makes life worth living for the individual.

"Often this sense of inner disharmony is the sense of moral failure and guilt which appears as the primary cause of difficulty in many seekers.

"The attitude should be one of aspiration, reverence, faith, confidence, and self-reliance outwardly. All this comes from a balanced life in finding satisfactory self-expression in social, vocational and family life in the objective world, and the radiant form of the ECK Master in the subjective world.

"Always the Master knows what is wrong with the seeker. He looks at the aura—it tells the story. But the seeker must tell him frankly what is wrong, or what he supposes is wrong. He must bare all to the Mahanta and let the traveler find or loosen the difficulty.

"Now I say that what is wrong with most of the human race is that they are unorganized in their inner lives. Even in marriage they have no sense of sentiment or responsibility. They are never heroes of tense love dreams, of sacrifices for a woman's love. With them love is merely sex, merely an appetite to be satisfied. Their women are occasional playmates, never some one to work for, make sacrifices for, to live with in companionship.

"They must be with others, never alone, for this makes them uneasy. There is no deep concern for those they meet, no loyalty to anyone or to any ideal. They never mull over the past or future and their emotional lives are too shallow. Their moods are to suit the moment. They never attain to adult nor spiritual development in their lives.

"For your information, there is a difference between detachment and attachment. This I shall explain some time.

"Now strangely enough, those who seek me believe that

they have found the Light (as did Saint Teresa and other Catholic mystics, including Saint Francis, Augustine, Vivekananda and dozens of those we could name)—possibly the whole range of seekers show that they have sought and found the Light, and become transformed. But here lies the fallacy of their greatness. For them the mystical experience merely infused new life and meaning to a dead tradition by connecting it with a vital relationship; but of no important insight. And do you know why? They did not have the Sound Current, and without the Sound Current it is impossible to see the radiant form of the Master. Have I made myself clear?

"Before leaving off let me say this. All those who are suffering to reach the path for my help can have it if only they reach for it. I give my hand to all.'

# THE COSMIC WORLDS

Rebazar Tarzs came late tonight and started right away with his discourse. He seemed to be eager to talk and told me to get seated at the table at once and take a pencil. He paced the floor while talking.

"Let me begin at this point. Those ECK Masters who were explorers of the cosmic worlds have been pioneers for mankind to reach the inner heights. They have left legends which we adore and worship. These greater ones gave us philosophies to study and live by, but much has been perverted and used for individual gain instead of for the universal cause of mankind.

"Their real contribution has been the descriptions of those mystic lands beyond the physical world. What lies on the other side of this earth plane? How many worlds are there? Where do they lie and how much does the physical scientist know about them?

"The scientists look at the heavens from an objective eye and make use of the canopy of air for the purpose of helping mankind in this world. But the mystics start from the inside and travel through the same planes looking at each with a spiritual eye.

"The scientists say there are five layers in the atmosphere, lying upward, and that we are like the primitive savage who stands on the shores of an ocean and wonders how far the water stretches beyond the setting sun.

"They call these regions or layers the troposphere, tropopause, stratosphere, ionosphere, and the unknown. The mystics call them the Astral, Brahmanda, Daswan Dwar, Maha Sunna and Sach Khand; beyond these are other planes called Alakh Lok, Alaya Lok, and Agam Lok.

"The Vedantists call these planes the Astral, Mental, Wisdom, Bliss and God-Plane.

"The difference being, the objective side of these planes is seen only by the physical scientists, and the subjective by the mystics. And of course, the mystics can come and go at will in their spiritual bodies to any place they desire.

"Let us begin with a study of the comparison of these planes as seen by the materialist and spiritual philosophers.

"First comes the troposphere plane, in which we live as the physical world, and which is about five miles thick at the poles and about ten miles thick at the Equator. It is a region of rapid changes in weather and turbulence—a layer of storms here and calm there—and of polar cold and tropical heat; a layer in which the temperature falls steadily about one degree Fahrenheit for every 300 feet until a low of 67 degrees Fahrenheit is reached. Eighty per cent of the air by weight is packed into the troposphere.

"The mystics call this the Astral plane, and it is known as the Anda, the lowest of the heavens, and it lies nearest to the physical world. The lower part of this world is the gross material or the earth planet and its fellow-worlds. Course matter dominates all but a few minds and Souls. This region embraces all the suns and planets known or unknown to astronomy. It extends out into space (without the knowledge of the scientists) far beyond the reach of any telescope. The Masters return to this region again and again to help mankind, who live in the darkness of a negative world.

"The capital of this world is at the top of the Astral region (which is sometimes called Turiya Pad) and named Sahasra dal Kanwal, which means the thousand-petalled lotus, the center which all Yogis strive to reach for spiritual attainment.

"The ruler of this region is Jot Niranjan, the negative power that creates matter in the lower worlds. He is in the center of the power commonly called the thousand-petalled lotus, the great cluster of lights which is the great light that the mystic views when approaching the higher astral planes. This is the actual power house of the physical universe. and what the scientists have been seeking to understand.

They have come to the duality of the atom, turning from its spiritual refinement to gather with the coarser ones to make up the matter experienced by the physical scientists.

"Out of this power house flows the power which has been created and now sustains all the worlds in the universe. Those lights are of all shades and tints, but basically made up of the seven shades of black, red, green, orange, blue, yellow, and white. These flow off into streams of rays throughout the universes, and each has its different aspects to help with the physical life on the planets. For example, green is the individualizing ray which shows the growth of the being in man's aura, as the rays touch each aura in every living thing throughout the worlds.

"Black is the pure color of the darker or negative side while white is opposite. Red is the color of human love; orange the ray of life (called Prana by the Hindus); blue the intellectual ray from which all great thinkers and creative artists receive their inspiration; and yellow the spiritual ray.

"Note the colors worn by any individual. They express somewhat the dominating astral rays in his aura.

"The great astral city lies just below a shining mountain. It is called the City of Light. Here dwell many of the earth's most renowned people, of all ages in history.

"This is the home of Jot Niranjan who lives in a great castle in the shining mountain where I once took you on an inner journey. The Sound here is the bell and conch.

"The astral region is the negative pole of the whole spiritual universe. Life is so long here that many of its inhabitants believe they have reached immortality. All work at some creative occupation.

"This world is often wiped out after several million years, followed by a period of equal darkness; then a new creation is started.

"Now for the second region. The scientists think of this as being a no-man's land lying above the first region, and call it the tropopause. According to the physical eye this region is a thick layer in which the temperature ceases to fall with increasing altitude. It lies many miles above the earth, and has not yet been too well explored by the material scientists.

"The second region is known as Brahmanda which means the egg of Brahmand and refers to the name of its Lord, Brahman. This deity is supposed to be the Supreme Being of all creation by the Yogis. This is the highest world known to practically all faiths, including Christianity.

"If any Yogi or other claims to be a Master, that Brahman is the highest of all creators, and this is the supreme heaven, then he is not a Master. He is only a humble seeker under the Supreme Ruler of this plane.

"This world is the Second Grand Division, the top of the three lower worlds (the physical, lower and upper Astral).

"This is the region of the spiritual-material world, because spirit dominates it. This is the region of the universal mind, whose power is called AUM. Hence the word Omkar, the power of this plane, which is still the negative force. The lower part of this region is called the Home of the Universal Mind. It is from here that all individual minds are derived and to that region all minds must return when they are discarded during the upward flight of spirit.

"The traveler takes you on, for he alone is the guide and knows the path, and is the recognized Lord of all. All other lords, rulers, and peoples on every plane pay homage to him. When you arrive at the gate of this region, the Sound of Omkar is heard continuously, resounding like a great drum. We go on up a hill and open a gate to enter a crooked tunnel, passing on to the other side. Then we cross high and low hills. The vision now seems to be reversed and it is as if we are traveling in reverse. We pass through a fortlike region which is the home of the ruler Omkar, and halt for Soul to become adorned with the attributes of devotion and faith. The seeds of the devotee's karma are burned and destroyed here.

"The color here is that of the beautiful setting sun. Above this region is another part of the world of Omkar where we find deserts, mountains and gardens. Flowers are arranged in artistic designs, and are everywhere. We are intoxicated with joy, wandering through a splendid region of canals and streams, before coming to an ocean over which we cross by bridge to the other side where there are three mountain peaks called Mer, Sumer and Kailash.

"This is the stopping place for the spiritualists and many mystics. The Yogis believe this is their heaven. The miracles of the mind are performed from this plane. For example, here one can stop railway trains, fill dry wells, and heal the sick.

"This world is extremely vast, despite what the scientists think, when compared with the physical universe or the astral world. There are six planes within this plane, and its chief city is a place called Mer Kailash after its three mountain peaks.

"This region is controlled by Brahma, whose chief duty is to control the great power called AUM. The function of AUM, a part of the great Sound Current, is to create, maintain and destroy the universes below it. It is the center of creation of the material and astral worlds. Many of the great scriptures have sprung from this region, including the Vedas. Lord Krishna as well as many other spiritual leaders make their homes here.

"Now for the Third Plane. The physical scientists know this world as the stratosphere which extends for miles into the sky. It is a region of steady, gentle winds, beautiful clouds and steadily rising temperature. In this area is the ozone layer, and beyond that very little physical air.

"The mystics call this region Daswan Dwar. It is filled with a brilliant light. The Soul here bathes itself in the lake of nectar called Mansarover, and joins the swans, the Souls known as Hansas. Soul gives up all its bodies, physical, astral, and causal, and is purified.

"The lord of this region is known as Ramkar. He is the power-supplying station for the lower worlds. Soul light becomes equal to the light and radiance of twelve suns together, and the happiness and bliss experienced by it at this stage are beyond physical description.

"While in this plane man is capable of performing grand miracles such as giving sight to the blind, sometimes raising the dead, and the ability to travel through the ether in his physical body.

"The orange ray controls this world, as the stream of life-giving forces. This is the land of the Hansas who are known on the physical plane as Paramhansas. Very few go beyond this realm. Yet their understanding is wondrous, for they are much in the worlds beyond their world.

"You are taken on by the Master to the top of this region where you hear the sound of violins. Here you cross the Tribeni, a place where three streams meet, hence the Kumba Mehla, a religious fair, held every twelve years in India, which is a reflection of this place in the third heaven. Then the Soul enters the region of Maha Sunna, where it picks up the secret knowledge of all the worlds. This region is very vast in earth miles in circumference, and in the center there is pitch darkness. Four Sound Currents are heard from invisible sources. The jhankar predominates and is indescribable in human words. You are entranced by their sweetness and must be pulled on by the Master. Also here are five egg-shaped regions or worlds, full of a variety of creations and each permeated and governed by a Brahm. Each has its predominating color such as green or yellow, or even white. They are quite vast. In comparison with them the entire universe below appears insignificant.

"He who has gained or attained this region will have increased power and understanding. In proportion this region is vast beyond description in extent, as related to those he has been taken through. But there is increasing difficulty as you go higher, in giving expression to anything relating to the upper regions. The very ideas in those upper regions are beyond the grasp of man's thoughts until man has traveled them, and then he cannot put his words into earthly language.

"Now for the fourth region which the scientists call the ionosphere. The physical air is so thin that there is a constant electrically excited condition which stimulates the atoms. In this condition they are called 'Ions'!

"There are several layers in this region which serve as reflectors of radio or mental waves. One layer reflects long waves, others reflect short waves. Some short waves pass straight through. Mind and radio waves are like light waves; they travel in a straight line. The curvature of the earth would prevent us from transmitting and receiving radio messages, and even psychic impressions, if it were not for the ionosphere. That electrical mirror in the sky reflects waves back to the earth. The earth sends them up again, and so they finally reach their destination. Hence, if you send out a strong desire for something, it goes through the same process and returns to you materialized.

"The mystics call this region the fourth plane, or the land of Sohang, as the mystic Lord of this world, through whom the power flows.

"This divine being lives in a city of great light called Arhirit. He is filled with majestic beauty and grandeur. When Soul sees him Its consciousness is filled with overwhelming joy, and It says to Itself, 'I am That!' This is the meaning of the word Sohang. At this moment of sublime realization you know that you are one with the Supreme. In union with me, the Master! This is why the Vedantists call this plane the Bliss Plane!

"To reach this plane we must cross the pass above the Hansi tunnel and enter the Rukmini tunnel where you see a strange and beautiful structure, where the faculties of the power to hear and the power to see give peace and satisfaction. To our right are bright islands, and to the left are many continents covered with palaces, appearing as if made of pearls, having their roofs covered with rubies and studded with emeralds and diamonds. Only the brave can venture this far. That is why I have told you previously that only the courageous, the adventurous, daring, and enterprising would have God!

"In the distance are the Bhanwar Gupha mountains. The Sohang Sound is heard plainly. The Sound is like that of a keen flute. You see the sun above and find the region most beautiful, sweet and full of Light. Souls living here exist

103

on the Sound Current as their food, and those groups of Hansas who have been so fortunate as to have penetrated this region move along on the roads with their own followers and devotees, trying to reach the regions above.

"There are numerous planes and worlds with a variety of creations, inhabited by millions of devotees living here on the nectar of Nam. Kabir said there are eighty thousand continents in this region, with beautiful homes for their inhabitants.

"The color of this region is blue, for it is spoken often of as the Home of Truth, and is the plane of true miracles, from which all things can happen; but woe to him who misuses this power.

"The scientists say there is nothing beyond their fourth region. They admit something may be there but have found nothing as yet for their physical instruments to record.

"On the mystical side the approach to the fifth region is guarded by a zone of such deep, dense darkness that none but a pure Saint can cross it. Only he who has the Light and Power may tread here and take his disciples with him. Now we come to the gateway of Sach Khand. Here dwells Sat Nam, the Lord of All, above and below. His brilliance is so great that even one hair on his body would radiate a Light equal to that of many millions of suns combined.

"This is the true home of Soul. It is the grand headquarters of all creation and the region of immortality. It is changeless, perfect and deathless. It is called the God-Plane by the Vedantists. It is untouched by dissolution or reconstruction. This is the world of the Saints and where they live.

"The fifth region is the start of Soul into the great worlds of pure Spirit where the citizens are pure Spirit in such countless numbers that no man could estimate them, and there is joy so great that you cannot conceive of it.

"In the fifth region is a fort-like place where is situated the throne of the Lord of the Worlds. You should know him as the true King. Soul is now taken by the Master to a great park where the scenery is indescribable. There is also a huge reservoir here, like those on the earth plane, from which flows the most delicious nectar out through canals to supply distant regions. Golden palaces are set in open fields of silvery light. The landscape is beyond human description, and the beauty of the Saints living here is incomprehensible, the brilliancy of each equal to the combined Light of sixteen suns and moons.

"We have reached the real entrance to the city. The watchers at the gate are Saints who pass us through into the Palace of the Lord and we are greeted by Sat Nam. He is the first definitely limited manifestation of the Supreme One. He is the power, the Light, the great Master Power-Current flowing down and out into all creation, to create and govern and sustain all regions, like a gigantic stream of water.

"This is the Sound Current, or the audible life stream which permeates all systems of the cosmic world. This is the positive pole of the spiritual regions.

"Above the fifth region are worlds beyond description, and the ones living there under the Supreme Being called The SUGMAD, a living force, not a being, nor anything but life itself. Your very imagination begs to be relieved of what lies beyond the fifth plane.

"When you come to face Sat Nam you say 'I am He'! Love is the holy bond that holds all the worlds together. Only a Saint can reach this region and travel into the next worlds above. Then he is called a Param Sant.

"All the Divine Power coming down from the upper regions comes to a perfect manifestation for the first time in Sat Nam, as the first actual or complete personification of the Supreme One. IT is the great Father of all to worship and love with complete devotion. IT is so fathomless and impersonal that we cannot approach IT even in thought. IT sits between the infinite Light and the created universes and so in time, when purged of every imperfection, we approach IT as our Father and receive ITS gracious welcome home.

"While still in the lower regions of the Astral plane and that of Brahm, Soul is liable always to return to earth and to rebirth and death — the 'Wheel of the Eighty-four.' But when it reaches the pure region of Sat Lok, which is

105

the first plane beyond Sach Khand, there is no more returning to earth, except as a Redeemer. Soul becomes a saint Itself; and the mission of his Master is through, as far as the journey goes. But Soul has yet to travel over the most sublime and beautiful part of Its journey. For above Sach Khand there are three other planes of inconceivable splendor. Here the Lord of the Fifth World, Sat Nam, takes over and guides Soul to the end of Its journey.

"First, It becomes united with the very essence of Sat Nam in a mystic sense, and so becomes one with IT, partaking of all ITS attributes. It then advances to the three remaining regions.

"Next is Alakh Lok, presided over by the Alakh Purusha, and after this is Agam Lok, presided over by Agam Purusha. Finally Soul reaches the end of Its journey, the region of the nameless ONE, or the SUGMAD, the supreme LORD of all that exists.

"No words can describe IT. No thought can embrace IT. IT is formless, the All-embracing ONE. IT is the impersonal, infinite ocean of love. From IT flows all life and spirituality, all truth, all reality. IT is all wisdom and love and power. All visible Lords of all regions are ITS manifestation. IT takes forms, many forms, in order that ITS purpose may be carried out in all creations. They are all ITS forms; but none of them expresses ITS totality. IT may take millions of forms, but IT, ITSELF, remains formless, impersonal, All-pervading. IT is universal Spirit, universal Light.

"When Soul reaches here, It is so absorbed in Its joy, lost in Its splendor, that It at once realizes the futility of even attempting to explain."

# THE FEELING OF GOD

The Tibetan came into the room at 11:30 tonight and asked that I start work at once. He began his dictation as soon as I was at the table.

R.T.: "In this discussion I will talk about the broadening of your horizons for the purpose of helping yourself to live in this world, yet not of it.

"I will call this the Feeling of God. It will be about the actual faith and power within you which makes everything you touch spiritually become spiritually successful.

"There are times in your life when you feel that everything is in harmony. You feel that everything you do, regardless of what it might be, is right and is executed perfectly with the greatest ease and facility. All you have to do is make the effort and let nature take its course.

"You cannot describe this feeling. No man can. It is everybody's secret of gaining God, or even the secret of knowing within that all is well with the Divine Reality.

"The first step in seeking to polarize the spiritual activity within one's self is to know absolutely what you are doing, and go after it with a positive feeling of precision and absolute trust in the Master. But this must be done without analyzing it. This depends mainly upon the elements and attitude in the spiritual nature of man.

"Basically, the definition of the God-feeling is this. It is man in perfect attunement with God; man who has become the channel for the God-Power to flow into his world. It is the art of handling the vibrations with perfect control.

"Now there are several principles by which you advance towards the development of the cosmic power. First, it is this. Not only let your breathing act in concert with the air which surrounds you, but let your intelligence also be in harmony with the intelligence which embraces all things.

"Now what does this mean? Let me tell you this. I am saying that you must harmonize yourself inwardly and outwardly. As you are with your breathing so become one with that Divine Self within. How can you become a channel for the ECK Power by being out of harmony physically or mentally or spiritually?

"This is literally impossible. Your breathing is harmonious with the body as long as you are at peace with yourself. As long as you are keeping your mind upon my radiant form there can be only harmony within you!

"I control all things for the spiritual worlds, and for every one of my creatures, including man, even to his environment, situations and circumstances. For example, to control circumstances, the mentalists say a knowledge of certain principles of mind action is required. But I say there is a quicker way of handling this, the control of circumstances, or environment. The repeating of the charged words can dispel any negativism!

"Now we come to the point of utmost importance — that we have a special faculty within the brain, and when you choose to enlarge your spiritual power you deliberately exercise this special faculty over and over with increasing attention and concentration upon my radiant form.

"This spiritual faculty is known to most seekers as the spiritual eye, or the Tisra Til. It is just back of a gland known as the pineal located between the eyes, in front of the brain.

"This is the sixth center of the chakra in the subtle body and is sometimes called the do-dal-kanwal, the two-petalled lotus. It is situated back of the eyes or on a level with the lower part of the eyeballs, but exactly in the center of the brain cavity of the pineal gland. It is the seat of the mind and Soul. This is the center of control over the body. All chakras below this one are subordinate. All forces which are said to govern the body are themselves subordinate to the mind and spirit of man which resides at this center.

"Now for the second law. Growth is attained through an exchange of the old for the new, of the good for the better; it is a conditional or reciprocal action, for each of us is a complete spiritual entity and the completeness makes it possible for man to receive only as he gives. He cannot receive if he clings tenaciously to what he has.

"Let me say this. Difficulties, unharmonious conditions and obstacles indicate that we are refusing higher planes and broader visions. The greater man's ability to know what he requires, the more certain he shall be to discern its presence, to attract the ECK Power and to use it for the benefit of the universal plan.

"Now let me add this point. Nothing can reach you except what is necessary to your growth. This applies to all disciples and seekers. All conditions and experiences that come to you do so for your benefit. Difficulties and obstacles will continue to come until you absorb their wisdom and gather from them the essential of further growth. You gain permanent strength exactly to the extent of the effort required to overcome your difficulties.

"The inexorable requirements of growth demand that you exert the greatest degree of love for what is perfectly in accord with Soul. Your highest happiness will be attained next through your understanding of and conscious cooperation with the cosmic power.

"Now briefly, the mind of man is bound often by the paralyzing forces of the earth plane, which are accepted and acted upon without question. Impressions of fear, worry, disability and inferiority are fed the mind daily. These are sufficient reasons in themselves why man achieves so little upon the spiritual path. This is why the lives of multitudes are so barren of results, when all the time there are the possibilities within themselves that need only the touch of the Master's hand to expand them into spiritual greatness.

"Women have been subjected to these conditions, perhaps even more than men. This is true because of their finer susceptibilities, making them more open to vibrations from other minds, and because the flood of negative and repressive thoughts has been aimed more directly at them.

"Women as well as men are beginning to anchor to their spiritual possibilities. They demand that if life holds any secrets, they shall be disclosed. Modern science is teaching that Light and Sound are singly intensities of motion and this is leading to discoveries of forces within man and woman. All this leads eventually to the radiant form of the Master.

"In order to possess a vitality the whole being of man must be impregnated with love.

"Now for the third and last principle, which is, 'As thy faith is, so be it unto you.'

"Your faith in the Mahanta's concern over your welfare must be so great that it makes contact with the cosmic power, and generates a current of sufficient strength to bring your purpose into manifestation.

"This faith is a product of the emotional body of man. We often call this 'feeling' in the material world. The secret is that we contact the ECK Power through the faculty of emotion within the body. I am not speaking of the faculty of the subjective self but that of Soul.

"By this then we know this faculty is the very Fountainhead of the power within. Why, in the physical self, do the emotions so easily overcome the intellect, and why must we put feeling into our thoughts if we desire results with God? Thought and feeling on the level of Soul are the irresistible combination for a union with God.

"So, to become united with God on any plane, you must know, believe, and feel that your purpose is being accomplished, and that if it is within God's plan it will be done. It is really your predominating attitude that counts.

"This is the essence of the teachings. You must decide if you wish to have the feeling of God, and this is in the phrase: 'The recognition of the creative nature of the ECK Power and your ability to control it for the divine purpose.'

"One point I want to make clear before leaving tonight. There is a difference between Self-Realization and God-Realization. Self-Realization is self-knowledge. It is the Para Vidya, or the spiritual knowledge of the objective world — like the knowledge of the Vedas, worship in church, occult studies, reading of the Holy Scriptures, Astrology, conduct, morals, and ethics.

"God-Realization is the Prada Vidya, meaning beyond the sense-world; it is the knowledge of God. He who has God-Realization is released from the bondage of all things and stands before Sat Nam.

"When the disciple enters the region of Atma Lok, the Fifth Plane world, he is stripped of all materiality and beholds himself as pure spirit. This is Self-Realization.

"Then he advances to the Hukikat Lok, the Ninth Plane where he beholds the most sublime manifestation of the Supreme One, merging himself with the great deity and comes to know God. This is God-Realization!

"A few more things. You are stepping far out of the masses of man. You are picked up and moved into an environment where I can work with you temporarily until the complete change-over comes in you.

"The operation of the law may be looked upon as chance, but this is not true. It is the logical result of the fixed law proceeding with an unerring and inevitable rule of action, and brings results in strict accordance with my nature — results mathematically exact and logically perfect.

"You are the extension of the universal body, saturated

with the universal love atmosphere. The spirit of those who love God is reflected in some subtle way by the places in which they spend much of their time. Places have their own characteristic atmospheres which result from the mental vibrations of those who abide there.

"I will leave off here but my next discussion will be on unconditional love. There lies a mystery and puzzle in this phase of spirituality which you have come to on the cross-roads of your spiritual path."

# UNCONDITIONAL LOVE

The Tibetan took a seat in the chair at his usual time and motioned for me to get out of bed and begin taking his dictation.

R.T.: "Let us get down to the discussion for tonight, which I will call 'Unconditional Love.' This is a subject which I have long been waiting to discuss with you.

"What is the most powerful force in the inner worlds?

"It is the force of love, which we call the ECK Power. Yet it is not what you think it might be, and this I will attempt to prove to you.

"Everything in the mineral world appears to be solid and fixed, while in the vegetable and animal kingdoms the force is in a state of flux, forever changing so rapidly that it is quite apparent to the eye, always being created and re-created. In the atmosphere we find heat, light, and energy. Each plane becomes finer and more spiritual as we pass from the visible to the invisible, from the coarser to the finer, from the low potentiality to the high potentiality. When we reach the last invisible world, inside the self, there is love in its purest and most volatile state.

"The most powerful force in this earth plane is, therefore, the invisible. Likewise, we find that the greatest force in man is also invisible, for the spiritual force, the Divine Power, or Love, is that side of him which is always moving into the higher, the greater.

"The only way in which this force can manifest itself is through the process of thinking. Thinking is the only activity which the spirit possesses, and thought is the only product of thinking. This of course pertains to the earth plane, and to man's individual being.

"Therefore, additions and subtractions are spiritual

113

transactions; reasoning is a spiritual process; ideas are spiritual conceptions; questions are spiritual searchlights; and logic, argument, and philosophy are spiritual machinery.

"If the spiritual process works through the thinking faculty, the power for this motor is the feeling process. In mechanical terms, the motor is the mind, but the fuel is the heart, or subconscious power. One cannot operate without the other to any degree at all.

"Thus every thought combined with feeling brings into action certain physical tissue, parts of the brain, nerves, or muscles. This produces an actual change in the conditions of the tissue, regardless of whatever body it be, physical, causal, etc. Therefore, it is only necessary to have a certain number of thoughts combined with feeling on a given idea such as love, in order to bring about a complete change in the organization of man.

"Thoughts of the highest ideal take root in the individual and the physical tissue is changed and the individual's attitude is changed and he sees life in a new attitude. Old things pass away, all things become new. He is born again of the spirit; life has a new meaning for him, and he is reconstructed and filled with joy, confidence, hope, and energy.

"Now we come to the subject of love. This word is used wrongly. It is that power or higher expression which you possess in common with me.

"It is the ECK Power seeking equilibrium in the union of the masculine and feminine expressions of the divine self.

"When the true polarity is attained, all is in perfect harmony with the positive pole of divine love, and the negative pole of human love reaches up unwaveringly and merges itself into that love and all the forces in all the inner planes interact in perfect rhythm from pole to pole.

"Divine love and human love are often thought of as being quite separate, while in reality they are the same, only opposite poles of the one force called the Master — or that which is God Itself. This being true, you can now grasp the meaning of God in love.

"A careful analysis of love will show that love as man

114

worships the Divine Mother in his own beloved (and vice versa, the God in man) the consciousness of man and woman will eventually be polarized to divine love.

"Now love is actually Light, or what you see in contemplation as the stream of shining atoms whirling about you in a positive radiance. By polarizing yourself to this radiant stream you become a part of it and flow back to the God center, or return to the true home.

"The whole problem of polarization rests upon man's ability to purify his thoughts concerning all forces and functions of his body. He must know that there is no natural function of his body that is not normal and right if put to its proper use and governed by pure thought.

"This divine creative force of God, or Love, which is the link that unites you with God, finds its greatest earth plane expression in the sex force. It also has a corresponding expression on all planes, spiritual, mental and otherwise. The sex urge is creative always and cannot be brought into operation without a definite creation on all planes, their aspects creating upon the higher planes, their lower manifesting on the physical plane. But in all it is the spiritual power working through man into the objective world.

"Now for the part of union between man and woman. Unless this union has been made on the higher planes through pure thought, the physical union cannot bring about peace and happiness, for like all true sacraments it must be entered into and registered upon all planes.

"The law of divine love will bring to each Soul Its true marriage and union in perfect purity on all planes. This true marriage is that of Soul with the ECK—the polarization of each Soul—not two Souls or man and woman coming together. And, as it is, each Soul will be guided through repeated experience by divine guidance until It finds this true love, the love of ECK through the Mahanta. You can be spiritually as well as physically married to a mate only when the old accounts of both have been balanced, and old complications set up through mistakes of the past have been worked out.

"In reality sexual desire is but the effort of Soul to express divine love through the physical vehicle, and should be looked upon as sacred. For in the union of man and woman as two perfectly affinitized Souls there is a force brought into action which is greater than the physical senses can express.

"The senses are transcended and Souls are lifted from the human into divine love. This is the point where divine love touches and overlaps human love, but only where human love is so pure and sacred and holy that nothing human can express it, because it transcends the power of the human mind to grasp. Only then is a new force brought into manifestation, a force which is the vehicle for a direct manifestation of the divine. This force at one end unites the twain, and at the other end unites them into the Godhead, or their mutual spiritual ideal, thus making the perfect triangle. In such a union God is manifested through perfected and purified human love.

"Now here is where unconditional love begins. First, one must love his beloved for everything he or she is, in the divine sense. Unless one has such a love for another, one cannot love God. This is only the sensible approach. The warm love that lovers have for one another offsets the impersonal love they have for God. Now I say impersonal love, for the love of God must be a pure love!

"As lovers, man and woman dwell in a love of deep affection and warmth, sometimes so deep that it becomes painful when one's love or attention drifts away from the other. Often words fly hotly between them, but this is only a part of God's forces working out difficulties and problems on the lower planes to help them rise to the higher. True lovers usually end in an agreement of love — a kiss, or love-making, which is only an expression of God-power becoming positive again.

"This is based upon ignorance and especially do we think that it is good to endure the sufferings received from the hands of those whom we are supposed to love. If you desire to have a life filled with havoc and error just try this.

What I mean to say is this: have a friendly, open-minded attitude towards all, but let experience tell you where it is right to give love or friendliness to those whom you desire to be close to you. Let the divine instinct tell you where to place your love.

"Now do you see where unconditional love has its part in the universal order?

"Now a few more words before closing. You are overeating and need to do some fasting to straighten out some karmic conditions in your body. I will tell you when to fast.

"Think more; contemplate more; sleep less; eat less; and love the ECK strongly, should be your motto.

"All my promises have borne fruit. You often do not see them in the right attitude. Awaken more, think of me more and then you will see what I tell you.

"Goodnight!"

# PRACTICAL WISDOM

Rebazar Tarzs appeared a little later than usual tonight. It was almost 1:30 a.m., before he came into the bedroom and started pacing up and down the floor with both hands behind his back. Finally he started speaking.

"R.T.: "There is so much to do. The world is making another step toward the spiritual side, and needs help everywhere. The Sat Guru must be everywhere and helping all who call for him."

P.: "I know there is much to be done. But where can I start?"

R.T.: "Be patient. Your time will come. At the present you must take down my dictation for the world to read. Be direct with what I say — never leave any doubt in the reader's mind!

"Ah, there is a point. You are a complex person and your mind (like that of many in high circles) works in indirection. You are different from most people. You can cut right to the heart of a problem but most people will not believe you — therefore, you always need complex companionship. It is because of the inner working of your mind that you were chosen to help get out my message to the world.

"Now let me talk about tonight's discussion, 'Practical Wisdom.'

"Man's difficulties are due largely to confused ideas and ignorance of his true self or interests.

"The great task of man is to discover the law of God to which he is to adjust himself. Clear thinking and moral insight are, therefore, of incalculable value. All processes, even those of thought, rest upon solid foundations.

"The keener the sensibilities, the more delicate the tastes,

119

the more acute the judgement, the more refined the feelings, and the more subtle the intelligence, the loftier the aspiration. Therefore, the purer and more intense are the gratifications which existence yields. Hence it is that the study of the best that has been thought in the world gives supreme pleasure.

"God is thought on the mental plane, within man. Thus active thought is active energy and concentrated thought is concentrated energy. So thought concentrated on a definite purpose (such as union with God) becomes God.

"He who thinks to illuminate the whole range of mental action by the light of his own consciousness is not unlike one who would go about to illuminate the universe with a floodlight.

"Soul, like a benevolent stranger, works and makes provisions for our benefit, pouring only the mature fruit into our consciousness. Thus, ultimate analysis of thought processes shows that the subconscious is the theatre of the most important phenomena.

"It was through Soul that Shakespeare perceived, without effort, great truths which are hidden from the conscious mind; that Raphael painted madonnas; and Beethoven composed symphonies.

"Ease and perfection rest entirely upon the degree in which we cease to depend upon the consciousness and make use of Soul power.

"We are aware of how dependent we are upon Soul; the greater, the nobler, the more brilliant our thoughts, the move obvious it is to us that the origin lies beyond our ken. We find ourselves endowed with tact, instinct, and the sense of beauty in art and music, of whose origin or dwelling place we are totally unconscious.

"The objective self is the responsible ruler and guardian of Soul only when in the Master's hands. It is through this high function one can completely reverse conditions in man's life.

"A mind trained in God-thought can prevent any unguarded action by the negative self entirely through its

120

vigilant protection. It may be properly called the watchman at the gate of the great subjective domain.

"The objective mind is reasonable will. Subjective mind is instinctive desire, the result of God-Power.

"Receiving any suggestions as truth, the subjective mind proceeds to act there in the whole domain of its tremendous field of action, even though what the objective mind has suggested may be either truth or error. If the latter, it acts at the cost of wide-reaching peril to the whole being of the individual.

"The ECK Master is on duty during every minute of the hour in man's life. However, the conscious or objective mind is on duty only during the waking hours. When the latter is off guard, or when its calm judgment is suspended, the subjective mind is unguarded and left open to suggestions from all sources, unless the Master's radiant form has been implanted there.

"During a wild excitement or panic, or during the heights of anger or unrestrained passion, conditions are the most dangerous. The subjective mind is then open to the suggestion of fear, selfishness, greed, depreciation and other negative forces derived from surrounding persons or circumstances.

"The result is usually unwholesome in the extreme (with effects that may endure to distress the subjective mind for a long time) unless the Master is called upon for help.

"The subjective mind perceives by intuition. Hence its processes are rapid. It does not wait for the slow methods of objective reasoning. In fact, it cannot employ them.

"It has been found that once you ask the Master for specific desires which will be for the benefit of the whole, forces are set into operation that lead to the hoped-for results. Hence, there is a source of power which places man in touch with the Omnipotence. Herein is a deep principle well worth man's most earnest study.

"The operation of this law is interesting. Those who put it into operation find that when they go out to meet a person with whom they anticipate a difficult interview,

121

something has dissolved the difficulty. In fact, those who have learned to trust the Master's radiant form find that they have infinite resources at their command.

"The subjective is the seat of man's artistic and altruistic ideals. They can be overthrown only by an elaborate and gradual process of undermining the innate principles.

"If the subjective self has received the wrong order, the use of the charged word, or steadily gazing at my radiant form within the spiritual eye, can reverse all conditions and bring back a healthy attitude. Peace returns once again.

"The subjective can change conditions because it is a part of the universal mind and a part must be the same as the creative power of the ECK Power. This (as everything else) is governed by God Law, and this Law is the Law of Love, which is that God-Power in creation, which automatically correlates with its object and brings it into manifestation.

"I am the living ECK Master. I can do all things. You are a part of the Divine Universal Body, and are in God's hands. IT cares for all of ITS children, as a loving father looks after his child.

# THE EXPERIENCE OF SPIRITUAL WEALTH

The Tibetan was waiting when I got home tonight. He left the room while I briefly undressed and showered and got ready for his dictation. Then he came back and started talking while he paced the floor.

R.T.:"I am going to debate for you this evening the subject of 'The Experience of Spiritual Wealth.'

"As the spiritual traveler I know there are some questions which you have wanted answered for a long time. First, if you desire to bring the God-Power into your life what do you do? Of course, you must become conscious of the power. To have what you want you must live by the spirit of these things until they become yours by right. It is then impossible to keep them from you. The spiritual nature of God and the things of the lower worlds are fluid to the cosmic power, so man can, by right, rule them.

"You do not need to acquire control of the spiritual force, for you have it already. But you need to understand it, use it, control it and impregnate yourself with it, so that you can go forward daily and carry the world before you.

"Every minute that you spend in contemplation gives you momentum and your inspiration deepens, your plans crystallize, you gain understanding and come to realize that the world is a living thing made up of the beating hearts of humanity. It is a world of life and beauty to love.

"Remember this — 'Much gathers more' is true on every plane of existence; and that 'loss leads to greater loss' is equally true. The human mind is creative, and conditions, environments and all experiences are the result of our habitual or predominant mental attitude.

"The attitude of the mind, of course, necessarily depends

123

upon what man thinks. Therefore, I say the secret of all power, all achievement and all possessions depends upon the attitude of mind.

"Man cannot express the spiritual power if he does not possess it. The only way he may secure possession of the power is to become conscious of power, and he can never become conscious of the ECK Power until he realizes that everyone can be an instrument for it.

"Therefore, I tell you this. The world without is but a reflection of the world within — but I am speaking of those worlds below the Second Grand Division which man normally reflects outwardly. There is an old saying, 'What appears without is what has been found within.' Inside at the Tisra Til is the answer to all seekers of infinite wisdom, infinite power, infinite supply of all that is necessary; awaiting unfoldment, development and expression. If you sit in silence, gazing sweetly into the spiritual eye, I will come and give you ALL help. Only ask for me.

"If you recognize the potentialities in the world within they will take form within the world without.

"Harmony in the world within will be reflected in the world without by harmonious conditions, agreeable surroundings, the best of everything. It is the foundation of health and a necessary essential to all greatness, all power, all achievement and God-union.

"Harmony within means the ability to let the Master take charge to guide your thoughts, and to determine for you how any experience is to affect you.

"The world without reflects the circumstances and conditions of the consciousness within. Just relax and let the Master take charge.

"As you become conscious of the wisdom in the world within, you mentally take possession of this wisdom, and by taking mental possession you come into actual possession of the power and wisdom necessary to bring into manifestation the essentials necessary for your most complete and harmonious development.

"All spiritual possessions are based on consciousness.

All gain is the result of an accumulative consciousness, be it spiritual or material. All loss at any stage of the spiritual path is based upon the result of a scattering of consciousness.

"Mental efficiency is, therefore, contingent upon harmony, discord is confusion; thus, he who would acquire the cosmic power must be in harmony with the Spiritual Law.

"Man is related to the world without by the objective mind. The brain is the organ of the mind and the cerebrospinal system of nerves puts man in conscious communication with every part of his body. This set of nerves is responsible to every objective sensation, and man lives in a world of senses.

"Now, I tell you this. That when you think upon my radiant form or love me sincerely, the thoughts sent through the cerebrospinal nervous system to the body are constructive and the sensations are pleasant and harmonious.

"Thus, it is through the inner worlds that man builds the constructive forces into his life, but the outer world brings him the destructive forces.

"Man is related to the inner world through the subconscious mind. The solar plexus is the organ of the mind where dwells the seat of the sympathetic nervous system that presides over all subjective sensations of joy, fear, love, imagination and all other subjective emotions. In Yoga this is called the heart center. It is through this center that we are connected with the ECK Power and brought into relationship with the cosmic power.

"A mystic has coordination of these two centers, and the understanding of their functions, which is the great secret of the spiritual life. With this knowledge man turns all over to Spirit, to bring to conscious cooperation and coordination the finite and infinite, and then he gains control of his own destiny — including karma, past and future!

"You agree that there is but one power pervading the entire space of the cosmic worlds, and being essentially the same in kind at every point of its presence. It is all-powerful, all-wise and all-present. All thoughts and all things are within this power. It is All in All!

"This is what ECKANKAR calls the ECK power, or Sound Current, and what is known to the Western world as God.

"God is the only power in the cosmic worlds. IT is able to think, and when IT thinks ITS thoughts become objective things to IT. As this power is Omnipresent, IT must be present in every individual, and each individual is the manifestation of this Omnipotent, Omniscient and Omnipresent power.

"As there is only one power in the universe that is able to think, it necessarily follows that your consciousness is identified with this power, or, in other words, man is that power ITSELF. This is saying that 'I am God and God is I'. This is what you realize upon reaching the Fifth Plane.

"Thus, the power that is focused in your brain cells is the same power which is formed in the brain cells of all men. Each is but the individualization of that power in the highest world.

"The ECK Power is a potential energy, and it manifests through all beings and all beings manifest only through this power. They are one!

"As the sum of all my attributes are contained in my universal body which is Omniscient, Omnipotent, and Omnipresent, these attributes are present at all times in their potential form in all men and all things. Therefore, when man thinks, the thought is compelled by its nature to embody itself in an objectivity or condition which will correspond with its origin.

"Every thought follows out the principle of cause and effect, so for this reason it is absolutely essential that you control your thoughts so as to bring forth only desirable conditions. All power is within and is under your control if you want it to be. It comes through exact knowledge and by the voluntary exercise of exact principles.

"When you gain a thorough knowledge and understanding of these words you will be able to control your thought processes and can apply them to any condition. In other words, you will have come into conscious cooperation with the Omnipotent Law, the All-powerful nature of the Master, which is the fundamental basis of all things.

"The power is the life principle of every atom which is in existence; every atom is striving continually to manifest more life; all are intelligent, and all are seeking to carry out the purpose for which they are created.

"Therefore, you see, to change the effect one must first change the cause, and this is true on every plane of existence. Man fails to see that if he fails to follow out the principle, he simply exchanges one form of distress for another. To remove discord we must remove the cause, and this is found always within the individual.

"From the highest cosmic world comes the universal fountain of ECK Power, and the objective world regardless of its plane is the outlet to this stream. Man's ability to receive depends upon his recognition of this universal fountain, this divine stream, this infinite energy of which each man is an outlet, and so is one with every other individual.

"Recognition is a mental process, mental action, and is, therefore, the interaction of the individual, of the ECK Power working on the Third Plane, and the ECK Power is the intelligence which pervades all space and animates all living things; this mental action and reaction is the Law of Causation. The principle of causation does not begin in the individual but in the cosmic power. It is not an objective faculty but a subjective process, and the results are seen in an infinite variety of conditions and experiences.

"In order to express life there must be the power. Nothing can exist without the cosmic power. Everything which exists is some manifestation of this basic power from which and by which all things have been created and continually are being recreated.

"Man lives in a fathomless sea of this plastic ether called the ECK Power; and this substance is ever alive and active. It is sensitive to the highest degree. Thought form takes mould or matrix from that which the substance expresses.

"Remember this — that it is the application alone that the value consists of, and that a practical understanding of my Divine Law will substitute abundance for poverty, wisdom for ignorance, harmony for discord, and freedom for tyranny, and certainly there can be no greater blessing than my love for you! This is only the beginning of your wisdom and love. You must stretch your understanding to vision, knowledge and faith in my living word.

"This is all on this subject. Goodnight!"

# THE HEART CENTER

Rebazar Tarzs came tonight about 10:30 p.m. and sat on the side of my bed talking while emphasizing each point with his square hands.

R.T.: "Now you must eliminate any possible tendency to complain of conditions as they have been, or as they are, because it rests with you to change them and make them what you would have them. Direct your efforts to a realization of the mental resources and God-resources at your command, from which all real and lasting power comes.

"Persist in knowing that the teacher is with you always; my radiant form is always with you.

"Each function of life and each action is the result of conscious thought. Habitual actions become automatic and the thought that controls them passes into the realm of the subconscious, carrying my radiant form with it. But the effort must be made.

"It is necessary that every thought becomes automatic in order that the objective mind may attend to other things.

"The new actions will, however, in turn become habitual, then subconscious in nature, in order that the mind may be freed from this detail and advance to still other activities. When you realize this, you have found a source of power which will enable you to cope with any situation in life.

"The cerebrospinal system is the organ of conscious mind, and the sympathetic system is the organ of the subconscious.

"The cerebrospinal system is the channel through which we receive conscious perception from the physical senses and exercise control over the movements of the body. This system of nerves has its center in the brain.

"The sympathetic system has its center in a ganglionic mass at the back of the stomach known as the solar plexus, and is the channel of that mental action which consciously supports the vital functions of the body.

"The connection between the two systems is made by the vagus nerve, which passes out of the cerebral region as a portion of the voluntary system to the thorax, sending out branches to the heart and lungs, and finally passing through the diaphragm it loses its outer coating and becomes identified with the nerves of the sympathetic system, so forming a connecting link between the two and making man physically a single entity.

"Every thought is received by the brain, which is the organ of the conscious. It is here subjected to our power of reasoning. When the conscious or objective mind has been satisfied that the thought is true, it is sent to the solar plexus, or the brain of the subjective mind, to be made into flesh, to be brought into the world as reality. It is then no longer susceptible to any argument whatever. The subconscious self cannot argue, it only acts. It accepts the conclusions of the objective as final.

"The solar plexus has been likened to the sun of the body, because it is a central point of distribution for the energy which the body is generating constantly. This energy is very real energy; this sun is very real, and the energy is being distributed by very real nerves to all parts of the body and is thrown off in an atmosphere which envelopes the body.

"If this radiation is sufficiently strong, the person is called magnetic; he is said to be filled with personal magnetism. Such a person may wield an immense power for good. His presence alone will often bring comfort to troubled minds with which he comes in contact.

"Physical illness comes because the sun of the solar plexus or heart center is no longer generating sufficient energy to vitalize some parts of the body; mental illness comes because the conscious mind is dependent upon the subconscious mind for the vitality necessary to support its thoughts, and environment, and the connection between the subconscious mind and God-power is being interrupted.

"The solar plexus, or heart center, is the point at which the part meets with the whole; where the finite becomes

130

infinite, where the uncreated becomes the created, where the universal becomes individualized; the invisible becomes the visible. It is the point at which life appears and there is no limit to the amount of life an individual may generate from the solar center.

"This center is energy that is Omnipotent because it is the point of contact with all life and all intelligence. It can accomplish, therefore, whatever it is directed to accomplish. Here lies the power of the conscious mind; the subconscious can and will carry out such plans and ideas as may be suggested to it by the conscious mind.

"Conscious thought, then, is master of this center from which all life and energy of the entire body flows, and which this center will radiate, thus determining the nature of the experience man has in the objective world.

"It is evident then that all we have to do is to let the Light of this center shine. The more energy we can radiate, the more rapidly man can transmute all indescribable conditions into a source of spiritual joy. The important question then is how to let this Light shine and how to generate this energy.

"Non-resistant thought expands the heart center, resistant thoughts contract it. Pleasant thoughts expand it, unpleasant thoughts contract it. Thoughts of courage, hope, power, confidence, etc. produce a corresponding state. But the arch enemy of the heart is fear.

"When you have destroyed fear, you find you are really one with the ECK and when you consciously can realize this power by a practical demonstration of your ability to overcome any adverse condition by this power you have nothing to fear.

"It is man's attitude of mind which determines the experience he is to meet. If he expects much he shall receive the greater reward.

"But the man who knows that he has a heart center will not fear criticism nor anything else. He is too busy radiating courage, confidence and power. He will anticipate love by his mental attitude. Acknowledgement of man's ability

131

toward peace and harmony will bring him to a realization that there is nothing to fear because he is in touch with the ECK.

"The most natural way of making the desired impression is to put your mind to the Nuri Sarup; then you are impressing the heart center on love. This is the direct way and the way in which best results are secured for joy and peace of the mind and Soul.

"The subconscious mind is a part of the universal mind. The universal mind is the negative principle, or force, of the universe. A part must be the same in kind or quality as the whole. This means that the creative force is absolutely unlimited; it is not bound by precedent of any kind and consequently has no prior existing pattern by which to apply its constructive principle in the Third and Fourth Grand Divisions.

"You have found that the subconscious is responsive to man's conscious will, which means that the unlimited creative power of the universal mind is within the control of the conscious mind of the individual. It is up to his judgement and free will to use it properly!

"Always it is well to keep in mind that it is not necessary to outline the method by which the subconscious will produce the results desired. The finite cannot inform the cosmic power. You are simply to act in accordance to the ECK's desire, and not ask how you are going to obtain it.

"You are the channel by which the nondifferentiated is being differentiated, and the differentiation is being accomplished by appropriation. It only requires recognition to set causes in motion which will bring about results in accordance with ECK's desire for your welfare. This is accomplished because the universal mind must first act only upon and through the individual's wish, and the individual can act only through the universal. They are one.

"This is all for the present—but now you must recognize that this is the teaching of the world plane only and not of the higher ones.

"Goodnight."

# THE WILL POWER

The Tibetan appeared at his usual hour tonight and started talking without salutation.

R.T.: "Let's get down to the discussion for tonight. I want to talk about the will of man, one of the most important aspects of God attributes.

"Everything is but a reflection of the inner cosmic worlds. The past is but a thought, the present a reflection, and the future a dream. The world is but a changing scene of conditions, situations and circumstances created by man. Everything, every thought and deed is but the reflection on this earth plane of the world within man. Only the world within is real; all else is illusion.

"What has this to do with will power? Everything. For much depends upon the will as to which way we go from the inside outward. Everything man thinks goes inward and returns to the outer world; therefore, his conscious mind should be pure (in order to help itself be pure). All that comes from contemplation should be pure. But it depends upon the will power to hold the thought on the ECK long enough for the ECK to start working through us consciously.

"Now as to the will. It is the same whether it be human or divine. The only difference being that in the divine it is the whole; and in the human it is a part; in the whole, it is the Almighty or ECK Power, and in the individual it is a limited power.

"Now I tell you this. The difference between the divine and human will is like the difference between the stem of the rose and its branches, and the branches have twigs springing from them. So it is a symbol of the ECK being the trunk and the saints the branches, and humanity the twigs.

"The will of the ECK Masters is God's will; their word is God's word, and yet they are the branches, because the Truth is the will of God.

133

"Now I say this — the example of having a desire fulfilled is the working of the individual upon the Absolute Will. Sometimes it is due to the strength of one's own will, and sometimes it is Soul working in harmony with the Divine Will.

"One only knows when it is in harmony with the Divine Will and when not by the results that he may have, and the one who knows beforehand is called a psychic or a prophet.

"When man is in harmony with the Divine Will it is like a dream; no effort is needed to fulfill the requests of his life. Problems are solved and actions are achieved without effort. On the other hand, those who use the human will struggle for achievement of their goal and accomplish nothing (or at least very little).

"When man strives for the fulfillment of his spiritual desires, even though he has all the necessary materials at hand, that is when his will is constant to My Will, or what you call the Divine Will. Man's success or failure depends upon the harmony or disharmony of his individual will with the Divine Will. Now, if the individual will is but a source of the Divine Will, how can it get out of harmony?

"This I tell you. It is possible to act contrary to the Divine Will, even though a part of it.

"Saints have taught the part played by harmony. The scriptures say, 'Resist not evil' and yet many will partake of evil such as hating when hated, or being angry when another is angry. The law of vibration is a part of this study.

"When a man's emotions are deeply stirred, be it in hatred, danger, or love, he normally touches those closest unless the spectator, or one to whom the emotions are being directed has the power to hold his own vibrations intact, in peace and harmony.

"The technique is the cultivation of the habit of patience. It is like the eye of the hurricane which is calm and peaceful while all around it havoc is being created. Apply this to the makeup of the human individual and see where the secret place will be within him. Does it look complicated now?

"Within this secret place must be held the conditions of harmony and peace, for it is here where the contact with My Divine Will is made. Those atoms or molecules within this abode of man can be changed within the twinkling of an eye if man desires, or can be held intact while keeping contact with My Divine Self. Then the Intelligence of the Power flowing through this center will direct man to do what is in the best interest of the universal cause. However, if the human will has changed them the resulting action most likely will be selfish.

"And remember this — all selfish desires and thoughts defeat their own purposes. We must become the conscious co-worker of the universe in order to gain the greatest that God can give!

"Therefore, man cannot regard his own will to be the universal will unless his will is harmonious with the Will of the SUGMAD. Thus man must practice harmonizing his will with that of his fellow man by developing the traits of tolerance, patience, and endurance, because every ego is working for the lower self.

"The ego of man thinks, 'What can I make another person do for me?' The ego wants everybody to be in harmony with its own way in life. That is why there is a world of rebellion.

"If one desires to conquer he must turn his life to letting the Divine Will rule — to learning what to do in the best interest of all. The way of resistance never wins; it is the way of humility or watchful awareness within and watching that center to keep the continued contact with God.

"The first teaching in the development of will power is through developing the traits with love. For love alone can keep the heart center free from the rule of negative qualities.

"Secondly, I tell you that self-control is the next step towards harmonizing one's self with the Divine Will. This is the greatest step. It may be fast or slow, depending upon the individual, but when we pause to think of the difference between man and animals, we see the greatness in this simple idea of yielding the will to My Divine Desire.

"Man's selfishness shows itself in wanting to get the better of his fellow man. If man develops love, he acts, sees and understands differently. The heart can be satisfied only by knowing that the other person is happy. True pleasure lies in the sharing of joy with another.

"You can become one with My Divine Will at any moment you make up your mind to do so. The difficulty is to make up your mind. The next thing is carrying out the decision. Only peace and harmony open up the harmonious feeling and bring the Divine Will into harmony with man's own. Man's blessings become divine blessings, his words divine words, his atmosphere the divine atmosphere, although he seems to be limited for his will becomes absorbed into the whole, and so his will becomes the Will of God.

"That is all for the discussion.

"Goodnight."

# THE TRUE REALITY

The Tibetan took his seat in the chair as usual tonight and started talking.

R.T.: "This is to tell you that one of the greatest ways to realize the power within you and to transcend all time and space, is to realize all of your past lives and how much power you attained to reach this point on the path to God.

"You must become obsessed with the idea if you desire the true wisdom. For it is only the Divine Self, within Spirit, that can give you the love you need. By your love for God you are losing that mental block which made you criticize people, hesitate, and stumble over words. You no longer fear the ridicule of others, nor do they secretly scorn you. You feel adequate, for you are fulfilling your special mission on earth.

"Very shortly you will be able to free Soul of the conscious mind, at will, and go beyond space and time to the knowledge of all things dwelling in God. You know that knowledge is infinite and manifests through all Souls that have lived in the earth plane and continue to live after having lived on earth, and all Souls that shall live on earth.

"All material substance is available to you as Soul now. All that we call substance is due to the limitation of space and consciousness of space exists only in the limitations of conscious mind; but to the freed Soul there are no such limitations.

"All substance that we call matter is not solid substance at all; in fact and truth, it is nothing but empty space and energy.

"Now as Soul transcends Its limited perception of things in form and time, you shall begin to know all life in all time. The past still exists; the future already exists.

"This reveals the mystic truth that you can now have

whatever Soul desires in the spiritual world, for whatever you want already exists for you.

"So whatever you desire spiritually is already prepared for you, but as long as you bind yourself by your conscious mind's limitation, you will fail to get beyond these limitations. True time is eternal and all that exists is ever present.

"Soul never needs to make a striving effort in order to expand Its consciousness anywhere. Soul never needs to struggle to unfold all of Its wants. It has within Itself whatever is needed in the spiritual world.

"Imagination is true reality. Not the imagination mortal man thinks about, but true imagination in the other worlds. This is anchoring your mind upon my Nuri Sarup, and thinking around this point. Think of Me as love — then use your imagination of tenderness, kindness and happiness.

"Have you any idea of what I am trying to say?

"Then look at it this way. The awakening of knowledge within one is essential, like the awakening of that which has been evolved into an acorn, so that it may come forth in magnificence as the oak tree.

"The secret of spiritual attainment then lies in the knowledge of spiritual power. If you know the truth in doing good then you are working towards the reality of God. This comes in training your imagination (within the mind) always to keep looking to the good; keep looking to Me — I, your Master, who can take care of you in all circumstances spiritual or otherwise.

"You have a great spiritual talent and can use it easily and readily. This gift God has given you. Furthermore, you can fill your mind with great love and vibrations. You have this ability which can be used in my work on the earth plane.

"I will be back soon.

"Goodnight!"

# THE DESIRE OF SOUL

Rebazar Tarzs came tonight and stayed for a longer time than ever. He sat silently for a long time. After a while he started talking.

R.T.: "I have come to you tonight, Paul, for the purpose of telling you a few things which should be known to you in secret.

"I am changing your attitude upon life completely. You are now imbued with love, and it draws to you great love. Just imagine the great love that God has for you, then you can imagine to a small degree the love I have for you, and that others have for you.

"Frankly, love is desire, and desire is feeling. Therefore, when you have a deep feeling you have a desire for something.

"I ask you this. What is this desire for? Is it to injure your fellow man or to bring him misery or trouble; or is it to give him good wishes for his spiritual and material welfare?

"This is your free will choice. If you take the negative approach, then your life becomes confused and erratic, but if you send out love vibrations then love is returned and your life becomes harmonious and runs with the ease of a machine.

"Now I tell you this. Love is absolute, but the conception of love varies with the individual consciousness. Therefore, no one can say when the individual consciousness has developed to the point where further development is impossible. On the other hand, love is not a matter of belief. It is a matter of demonstration. It is not a question of authority, but a question of perception and action.

"The inexorable requirements of growth demand that we exert the greatest degree of love for what is perfectly in accord with us. Man's highest happiness will be best attained through his understanding of, and conscious cooperation with, the Divine Law.

"In order to possess vitality, man's own thought processes must be impregnated with love. Love is the product of the emotions. It is therefore essential that the emotions be controlled and guided by the intellect and reason.

"It is love that imparts vitality to man's mind and heart, and thus enables love to germinate. The law of love will bring to you the necessary materials for your spiritual growth and maturity.

"Therefore, if you require love, try to realize that the only way to get love is by giving it, that the more you give the more you get, and the only way in which you can give it is to fill yourself with it until you become a magnet of love.

"Simplified, the mechanics of love is this: Thought is a channel of emotions and is carried by the law of vibration, the same as light or electricity. It is given vitality by the emotions through the law of love; it takes form and expression by the law of growth; it is a product of Soul, and hence it is divine, spiritual and creative in nature.

"Now I tell you this. That the principle which gives thought the dynamic power to correlate with its object, and, therefore, to master every adverse human experience, is love. This is an eternal and fundamental principle, inherent in all things, in every system of philosophy, in every religion, and in every science. There is no getting away from love. It is feeling that imparts vitality to thought. Feeling is desire and desire is love.

"If you are impregnated with love you become invincible.

"Thus I say that the way to develop love is to educate your desire for love. Educated desire is the potent means of bringing into action the law of love.

"Now for the sake of going on record let me say this — that there are people who have by solid inaction allowed the delicate brain matter to harden and ossify until their whole life is barren and fruitless.

"We find this truth emphasized wherever the power of love is understood. The divine ethers are not only intelligence, but substance, and this substance is the attracting force which brings electrons together by love so that they form atoms.

140

The atoms in turn are brought together by the same law and form molecules. Molecules take objective forms, and so love is the creative force behind every manifestation, not only of atoms but of the worlds of the whole creation of spiritual life, of everything, of all of that which the imagination can form any concept.

"It is the operation of this marvelous law of love which has caused man in all ages and all times to believe that there must be some personal being who responds to their petitions and desires, and manipulates events to comply with their requirements.

"It is the combination of thought and love which forms the irresistible laws of gravitation, or electricity, or any other law operating with mathematical exactitude. There is no vacillating — it is only the channel of distribution which may be imperfect.

"If the law of love seems imperfectly demonstrated by an inexperienced or uninformed person, man cannot conclude that the greatest and most infallible law upon which the entire system of creation depends has been suspended. He rather should conclude that a little more understanding of God is required, for the same reason that a correct solution of a difficult problem in mathematics is not always readily and easily obtained.

"Man manifests more and more life as his thought, or inner self, becomes clarified and takes higher planes. This is obtained with greater facility and he uses word pictures that are defined clearly, and is relieved of the concepts attached to them on the lower planes of thought in the Astral worlds.

"It is with words that he must express his thoughts, and if he is to make use of higher forms of truth, he must use only such materials as have been selected carefully and intelligently for the purpose in mind.

"This wonderful power of clothing thoughts in the form of words is what makes man different from the animal kingdom.

"We know that God-thought has for its goal the creation

of form and we know that the individual thought is likewise forever attempting to express itself in form. We know that a word is a thought form, and a sentence is a combination of thought forms. Therefore, if one wishes his ideal to be beautiful and strong he must see that the words out of which this temple is to be created eventually, are exact and that they are put together carefully. Accuracy in building words and sentences is the highest form of architecture in civilization and is a passport to the spiritual kingdom.

"Believe in the SUGMAD. Believe in the ECK Master, for I am the ECK Master, and no one else but He. That is all that I ask of you.

"I will leave off here for tonight! Goodnight!"

# THE PURE MIND

Rebazar Tarzs came tonight. He took a seat on the edge of the bed and talked on small points for several minutes. He seemed to be preparing me for something.

R.T.: "You must have complete faith in my word, for I, only I, can give you that of the ECK."

I nodded in agreement.

He rose from the bed saying, "Come now I want you to go with me."

Taking my hand he pulled me off the bed. The walls suddenly disappeared into nothingness. We seemed to be standing in a green field covered with a blanket of strange flowers. I have never seen anything like them.

We walked up a sloping path where tall trees made a cathedral aisle, and the light and shade were a sweet pattern against the earth. I noticed it was strange that neither the Master nor I made shadows against the ground from the bright sun.

We entered a small vale where stood a brown stone monastery. A solid looking man in a maroon robe, bald head, dark eyes, swarthy skin and a wide mouth sat on the lawn in an easy chair. Several people were seated before him upon the grass. Rebazar Tarzs smiled as he made a low bow. I realized we were in the presence of the great ECK Master Yaubl Sacabi, in the spiritual city of Agam Des.

R.T.: "We have arrived, Master."

Yaubl Sacabi smiled, "Be seated please. My discourse is about to begin."

The great ECK Master spoke again.

"The SUGMAD alone is real!

"You must abandon your seeking for everything, but the SUGMAD. Until you come to the true reality all else is vanity.

"You must know and understand that God, alone, is found by the halting of all seeking, and by leaving behind all the dissecting tools of the mind.

143

"The mind is only an instrument given to the body in the worlds below the Atma region, in order to give certain outer protection to Soul and to work with the Divine Law of ECK in acting as the instrument to guide Soul back to Its true home.

"Those who come to this spiritual city known as the Agam Des, in the wilds of the Himalayas must come in their true spiritual body, which is the Tazu, or Soul. The mind and the other bodies are not allowed in this wondrous City of Light. Before you can pass into our fair land you must behold yourself as pure spirit stripped of all mind. This is the land of spirit where only the purer Souls dwell, where the cosmos is achieved in a flash of sudden awakening and Soul experiences Itself in a world where mind is not needed.

"Here is a place where dwells many of the honored ones of the ancient Order of the Vairagi.

"All, therefore, become intuitive and Soul is guided by the hand of the SUGMAD to enter upon the path that will take It to Its true home.

"The SHARIYAT-KI-SUGMAD says, 'Emptiness is within, emptiness is without, emptiness is in the worlds below and above'.

"So we must know that Soul is emptied of Its emptiness and has become filled with the SUGMAD.

"Mind of itself and Its illusions are self-contradictory. The truth of the SUGMAD is beyond any kind of human thought. It is beyond all verbal expression!

"Masters are aware of the teachings of the lower worlds on these matters, but in our compassion we can only communicate a little understanding here and there, for the true purpose of the Master is to lead his devotees to the step on the path whereby they can grasp this in a sudden awakening!

"Words will answer the questions on the true nature of the SUGMAD. But you are gradually lifted into that state of awareness so that the real difficulty lies not so much in your unanswered questions but the continuation of that unfoldment that leads out of this state of confidence in the power of analytic reasoning, into true spirituality.

"As high as you set your goal, so high do you unfold and it is by raising the standard of spirituality that Soul rises up into the highest heaven, says Lai Tsi, the ECK Master of the Etheric world.

"When we find the place where true spirituality begins, all the holy ones and all beings are nothing but the ECK Power, for nothing exists but the universal body of the SUGMAD in ITS pure element. What you see that appears to be a brilliant sun, in the strength of twelve suns, is only the reflection of the great ruler of this plane. And the sound of the violin, or the flute is heard, and you may bathe in the lake of nectar which washes away all sins, and become pure in Spirit. Then you will no longer hanker after material things but yearn for the divine and the downward pull is lost!

"The spirit self of man there is inborn and indestructible. It has no age, no classification in accordance to earthly measures, and can transcend time and space.

"This self is the substance you see before you and if you reason or analyze it you at once fall into error. It is like the boundless void of time which cannot be fathomed or measured.

"This universal self is ECK and there is no distinction between ECK and man except that man is attached to forms and so seeks ECK in the sensory world, in a sensory way.

"By his very seeking for ECK, he produces the opposite effect of losing IT, for that is using ECK to seek for God, and using mind to grasp mind.

"You do not know how to stop the thoughts and forget your anxiety. God is directly before you, for this very power —the ECK Power, is God; and God is in all living things. God manifests in the lowliest as well as the highest.

"What good does it do you to practice any spiritual exercise since you are fundamentally complete in every respect, and it takes only self-surrender to the Mahanta, the living ECK Master, to become quiescent and realize your divinity.

"If you are not convinced that the power itself is God, and willing to be attached to forms, practices and performances then you must stay in the lower worlds until your realization is achieved, be it a million years according to

145

your earth time. But you are the Chosen One, as was I in my little world of ancient Egypt when my Master came for me.

"The power is God, and the way is God's way, and there is no other power nor any other way. God is that which is like the void, having no form or appearance whatsover.

"To make use of God so to speak, in the ordinary sense, is to use God to become attached to forms. God which has always existed does not attach itself to any form or appearance whatsoever.

"So I say awaken to the ECK Power, and realize that there is nothing to attain. This is God. God and man are the ECK Power and nothing else.

"The power is not a mind, and is completely detached from form. If you detach yourself from reasoning and questioning you will accomplish everything. Then you will have God when you no longer need God. This is what might be called in the physical world reacting to facts.

"Respond to a fact and you are at once in sympathy to it. Respond to worry brings fresh cause for worry! So the great law is that neither seek it, nor be against it for the struggle for and against it is man's worst fault.

"Therefore, God-Realization is, in all truth, nothing which can be apprehended with senses. It is void, omnipresent, silent, pure, and strangely peaceful, and that is final. You must be awakened to it; fathom its depths. All paths leading to it, and all contemplation to achieve it are but dreams, for when you are suddenly awakened to it you will merely regard the struggle to achieve nothing but unreal action.

"God, the Source of all, shines on everything with the brilliance of ITS own perfection. But man fails to perceive the spiritual brilliance of God. If you could eliminate all intellect then God would manifest ITSELF like the sun, illuminating the Whole in such Light and Sound that all mankind would swoon.

"In man's existence upon earth he must use his sense of perception. He need not cut off his right hand because it does not lead him to God. No, I say that reasoning of God will not bring you to God.

"Do not abandon your senses in reaching for God, yet do not cling to them, nor dwell in them, but exist independently of them, and of all that is about you. The way does not lie below, or above you, nor to the left or the right of you. It lies within you.

"You must look inwardly. Be independent of the external way. Practice the spiritual exercises of ECK. Listen to the sounds of ECK. This is the way to reach God! This is the way into the Nameless Void, and to be one with that Nameless One who lives in the pure region of the SUGMAD, when man becomes identical with the ultimate transcendental Absolute. This is the infinite and eternal dream of reality and spirituality.

"If man seeks the Godhood there is nothing he can do except follow the path of the ECK. Seek the Holy Light, watch for the Holy One only, and listen to the Holy Sound. Practice Zikar. If nothing else is sought, the mind will remain in its childlike state; and if nothing else is clung to, the mind will not go through the progress of negativism for that which is neither born nor destroyed is God.

"Ordinary man seeks that which is in his outer world, while the seekers look into themselves, but the real way to God is for man to forget both the external and internal selves.

"Man is afraid to forget his mind, fearing to fall into the Void with nothing he can cling to. That is why the Nuri Sarup (the radiant form) of the Master is always with his disciple, until the devotee is able to stand alone. But man does not know that the Void is not an empty space, but the very real realm of God alone.

"It is the nature of ECK to be without beginning or end, as old as space, neither subject to birth nor destruction, neither existing nor non-existing, neither pure nor unpure, both ageless and youth. Without color, but still colored, silent and noisy. It is, but still it is not.

"Who can explain God's glory with words?

"But man must learn that his mind and the objects of his sense perceptions are nothing. That he must leave this world of fantasy someday and return to his true home in the name-less region, where dwells the Absolute.

"No human words can compass or disclose enlightenment, and the man who gains it does not say he knows, for it comes not as reward for achievement but as the result of stilling the senses, and giving up to the ECK Master.

"If you can eliminate the use of the reasoning or analyzing faculty within the brain; if you can concentrate on the eli-mination of analytical thinking, you soon discover the truth of God.

"The cosmic body of God is real. His human bodies are phenomenal and shaped as they are needed in the physical worlds. To him who sees this, all illusions on the earth planes are vanished and he lives in bliss, in the city of Agam Des, always ready to be taken higher into above worlds.

"So I tell you this that the more man seeks God in the outer worlds, the more God flees from him. The more man talks about God, or thinks about God, the further God recedes from him. To pursue the Light is to lose the Light.

"The secret of having God in your life is to stop talking, stop thinking, stop pursuing and there will be nothing you will not understand. Remember that wisdom neither seeks nor desires.

"I will leave you with this riddle to solve.
The centipede was happy, while the frog in fun
Said, 'Which leg, please, comes after which?'
This raised her doubts to such a pitch,
She fell confounded in the ditch,
Not knowing how to run."

My eyes opened to find Rebazar Tarzs standing at my side in the bedroom. He smiled hugely as if he had a secret joke.

R.T.: "Now, dear one do you understand the ways of God? Do you know that I can take you to any place, any-where, at my own desire?

"This is the beginning of many journeys you will have in the inner worlds — and I promise that your future will be interesting and busy."

148

# BECOMING GOD

Rebazar Tarzs: "Each time you give away something old, you gain spiritually and I put in your way something to replace it.

"You are me, and I am you. How can you ever be without anything. God takes care of you-me. Grasp that you-me. God-me. God and Self, or God and Soul.

"Now take this a little further. What is Soul but only that part of God which is a ray of pure power. Therefore, it is no longer God the Absolute. See now, God is all. God the over-all.

"That self you call you is not true. It is maya. Instead it is God!

"So henceforth, you understand that you are God, the divine. The self of the universe. Since I am God, then I am you. You operate upon this physical plane a separate body than this physical body because of maya. But in truth that entity is only myself as an extension of God.

"You are simply a part of me, moving at my own discretion when and where I desire to move. Understand?

"I want to go further than this. The teachings of the ECK Masters give you the basic truth that man cannot be without a living Master at anytime in this world.

"Without the true Godman, nothing could exist. All the worlds exist in Him. The macrocosm of the universe is He. Therefore, man as the microcosm is only the little world in movement whose divine self can travel at will throughout the

149

body of the Mahanta's world, or the universal self of God.

"The Master gives this privilege to those who deserve it. Or seek it most earnestly. The secret being based upon the heart of the seeker. What is there which draws the Mahanta to him. Or he to the Mahanta?

"Is it love?

"Rather. But not in the sense that those of the religious systems or philosophies are teaching. It is in higher terms, the divine consciousness of the seeker. Yes, divine consciousness, a phase. I use it to describe the state of the heart or Soul for greater evolvement. Thus man thinks in the terms of cosmic consciousness which is only the first phase of awareness toward reaching Soul and arousing the tremendous desires in man to seek the highest. To seek God, or Sat Nam, the true manifested symbols of the divine reality.

"When Soul reaches the fifth region and becomes One with God, then his consciousness has reached the last stage before going into that glorious state called God-consciousness. Past the fifth region into the region above and finally to Anami, the Nameless place, Soul is fully aware of Its identity with God — or what is known as God-Realization.

"You may call this the God-Consciousness.

"To reach this state the royal highway is long, sometimes difficult and other times filled with joyous undertaking.

"Soul which leaves this home to seek Its way through the worlds below is described in the parables about the prodigal son. Let us compare the wandering of Soul with the bee which has lost its way home!

"The farther away from its true home the little creature flies, the more confused and bewildered it becomes until it reaches the screen door of a home in a big city, and amidst all confusion and great activity loses its strength and finally dies.

"Soul is similar to this illustration for It descends into the

150

worlds below through the following bodies; the mind or causal body; the astral or subtle body and the physical or material body.

"By now It is in the lowest world plane, in this universe and on this earth. This is the house of darkness where only the light of the true devotee shines lighting the night for those who seek.

"Now ruled by the senses Soul seeks outwardly to find God in the pleasures of the flesh, not even knowing that a true home exists. Now Its processes of existence have reversed and the mind has control perhaps for centuries through the incarnations of Soul. It carries through many lives the same problems, for the mind enjoys its sense-pleasures.

"God will not let Soul remember any of Its past; each incarnation is hidden so It will have almost a new start in each life, an opportunity to find Itself. Often Soul struggles against the negative forces in this lower world, until It does not have the inspiration to continue. Then It wonders if something else contains this life and then, for the first time, a spark of Its divinity flashes into Its awareness; and for the first time during Its earthly sojourn, Soul realizes that Its destiny is guided by a super-power.

"This is what we call awareness of Soul, and thereafter Soul in like the Hound of Heaven. There is no relenting in Its pursuit to find the path back to Its true home.

"The progress on the path is not always the same with each Soul, but one of individual travel. It may be hard and tedious, but again it could be swift, depending upon the karma collected and dispensed; the spiritual earnings It has in store, or whether the hierarchy decides to use the Soul as a channel for a spiritual mission.

"Regardless, Soul will sooner or later reach the stage where teachers are put in Its path; and later, at the proper moment, the Mahanta appears.

151

"Perhaps Soul has flashes of cosmic consciousness, or perhaps it takes the Mahanta to tear away the veil and let the devotee peep into the inner worlds — see the Light and hear the Sound Current.

"Thus, Soul has found the living Mahanta. The true God-man who can give It the instruction and take the devotee in hand.

"Next, the devotee must take his own discipline in hand and practice the teachings of the Master, the spiritual exercises of ECKANKAR. For only by regulated periods of contemplation which includes the Sound, can Soul hope to reach Its true home again.

"And third, Soul must make constant contact with the Mahanta inwardly, who will begin to take It across the far borders of those inner cosmic worlds to teach It the secret of entering the higher regions after death of the physical body.

"Soul will, of course, have Its awakening in the following process: (1) Through arousing It, first, by a spark of awakening and (2) on meeting the Mahanta, usually It has a taste of the cosmic consciousness of the planes below the second grand divine consciousness, which is the state of awareness of the fourth and fifth planes; and finally, the God-Consciousness which is the state of awareness of the fifth region and above to the nameless world. This is what one in metaphysical terms calls complete and conscious union with God.

"To those whose eyes have not yet been completely opened, the difference in the states of awareness are jumbled and cannot be fully comprehended, but after one has traveled the inner planes, they are aware that this is one of the first secrets revealed by God so Soul will know, understand and appreciate each state. It is a measuring stick for Soul to judge Its fellow Souls by.

"The Mahanta offers the definite solution to salvation. I tell you it is true that you may have the same spiritual experiences as my self. But you must listen to my word and do as I say, not as I do.

"You call me an Adept, because my ways are not understood, however, there is no mystery shrouding my life or my teachings.

"Man as well as all other living entities is endowed with Soul and mind, beside the physical body.

"The origin or the creator in myself is called the SUGMAD, Lord, God, or any name you desire to call IT. I am Omnipresent and Omnipotent and all forms reflect and emanate from my universal and absolute form.

"The individual Soul emanates from God, and is designed to merge again into IT. The mind is an instrument, not merely the sum total of thought and feelings, through which the individual Soul establishes contact with, and works in the universe through the universal mind called Brahm or Kala. Man is the complete microcosm reflecting the macrocosm. He is in the macrocosm and the macrocosm is in him. As I said before, God is in him and he is God.

"The Supreme Soul is in the individual Soul and the individual Soul is in the Supreme.

"God pervades throughout the macrocosm by Name and Word, or ECK or the great Sound Current. God similarly is present in the microcosm.

"The Sound Current, or ECK though all pervading cannot be experienced by the physical senses of man.

"The path of God is the audible Life Current, or ECK. It is the vital teachings which distinguishes ECKANKAR from all other philosophical sciences. It is the Voice of God calling his flock back to his feet, and those who can hear are indeed fortunate, for it represents the royal highway to the gates of Paradise. The Light and the Sound are the essential of this faith.

"The road is not like a river, as the scriptures would have us believe, but more like radio waves flowing out into every direction from a central broadcasting station. It comes from God, the Supreme center of the universe of universes!

"Now the Sound Current or wave has two aspects, an outward or centrifugal flow and an inward or centripetal flow. Moving out from God and returning to God again. Moving upon that Current, all power and all life appears to flow outward to the uttermost bounds of the universes, and upon it, all life must return to its source.

"However, we are concerned only with its centripetal aspect, for upon that wave we have to depend for Soul's return to Its true home.

"Goodnight."

# THE DIVINE CONSCIOUSNESS

Rebazar Tarzs: "There is much to tell you.

"Impatience sets up counter vibrations and you are set back. You can never hurry anything in which Soul has control for It is never in a hurry. It has all of eternity in which to do Its work.

"Every thought you think is a creation of a force or entity. As you think and send out good thoughts to every person, they return; but ladened a thousand fold with good towards you, and for you, and remain in you to be sent out again on these errands of good.

"Now do not allow your vibrations to be disturbed, for remember — you are holding the omnipotent power of God within you. To throw that mighty force at anything with anything but love, or toward any person, is more than likely to cause them pain and perhaps instant death. Think peace, love, happiness and plenty to all. You see?

"What am I trying to tell you?"

P.: "I am not certain."

R.T.: "I am going to speak to you about the Light. That which comes to you and gives you understanding. With it I speak also of the Sound. You see?

"Who are the God-Realized?

"They who have seen the face of God, the ECK Masters, are the God-Realized. You ask what is the Face of God?

"I tell you the Face of God is the Light of Lights, that Light which pours out of the feet of God. What can words tell you? I have none to praise the glory of God.

"I can show you. Stand here in the center of the great Light. Tell me what do you see?" ·

"P.T.: "At last!

"I am the Absolute!

"Everything is in Me, and I am in everything!

155

"All existence begins in Me, and all existence ends in Me!

"The secret of love, wisdom and understanding is unlocked and that self encased in the clay temple is swifter than thought. It overtakes all others who are running. It is I, Soul, now God, the Absolute!

"The Light comes from within, a blinding sheet of pure ray. The music is that of the spheres of the seven heavens. I can see all and hear all!

"I stand at the top of the worlds, with two great deities at my side. One whom I know, but the other is a divine being of shining countenance.

"Below in the world, history takes its stand like a cinemascope and new creation unfolds within me to evolve into universes not yet seen by man.

"Love flows out of My body in a wave of streaming atoms to envelope All. Man is but an iota in this limitless ocean. He seeks to come to me in his struggle, not knowing that sincerity is the path to My heart. That his thoughtlessness leads only to the way of death.

"Man wars against Me, but only destroys himself. He who seeks to injure Me or My beloved, creates the destruction of his clay temple.

"Souls flow upon the waves of My ocean. Those who have My divine love are the ocean itself, but those who struggle against Me do so in agony. To love Me is to love the highest, for I am He who penetrates all life.

"Sweet is the light, loving is the bliss, and tender is the sound of this world where I look down upon all. What words can I use to tell you of My bliss, My joy, or glory? It is a flash in the darkness that comes to light the night. I tell you nay, for error is in man. Not I, God. For My Light is always there. Man must seek IT, and yet not be in vain for grasping for IT.

"Man cannot seek IT like he does things of the earth plane. The Light is not a manifestation, but the power of Myself pouring life into the worlds. Man evolves into nothingness for I am nothing, yet everything permeating the divine vacuum. I am beyond time, reality and space.

"Man cannot find Me unless he gives up himself.

"Books, teachers and scriptures have no place in My kingdom. I can give man all. I can lift him into the Kingdom of Heaven, and make him like My Light for he too is the Light, if only he would look inwardly for it!

"The secret is within Me, Alone, beyond and below, the secret is contained and no man shall find it less he comes to Me in love.

"If man will seek for My secret then he will find it. The joyous knowledge is hidden within his heart. Yet his heart is My heart.

"The secret of reaching Me is not love, nor joy, nor bliss nor any of those ideals which all scriptures tell you. It cannot possibly be of the occult, esoteric or spiritual knowledge which man has taught men — it is beyond all this knowledge of the self — called in the lower worlds, the Laws of Nature.

"I tell you this. The Voice of God is that which reveals the secret to you. That is My voice. I can whisper it in your ears should you listen closely.

"The secret of all secrets which man seeks for and never learns, is because it is concealed by illusion and self-delusion.

"Until man learns the true transcendental knowledge of My teachings which show how to be liberated from mind and matter — to come in contact with My divine spirit, he will never know this secret.

"Come closely. I will whisper into your ear, O man of the earth. The secret of the realization of my divine spirit is simply power!

"The Absolute Power!

"Man does not know that power is the way to his true home. That space within My heart. Yet this is not the power which he knows in the Earth plane.

"It is that transcendental self, the divine knowledge, the use of Soul for my power to become his power; the unity with my divine self; the absolute state of Godhood. Who can explain in words what this divine power is for man's understanding.

"In the simplest terms I tell you that divine power is that which flows out of My universal body to sustain all the worlds. Call it Light and Sound.

"Man is sustained by IT. ECK is ITS name for IT represents both the Light and Sound. Man must seek this and contain IT, master IT, subdue IT and make IT his servant along with the rest of his united, individual self.

"I know the secret, and tell man of it. For neither does religion nor metaphysics nor any of the mystics yet realize the true worth of the Mastership of ECK.

"Believe in it for it is the way I speak to man, yet it is no more supernatural than your other senses. Therefore, I say refuse to give it unlimited sway, and never allow it to be the tyrant of the other senses. Let the divine consciousness live in harmony with the old self.

"Love My worlds, My creatures, and all, even though they are to be pitied. Take not refuge in the world of sympathy. Live in the full consciousness of righteous power.

"He who has realized the SUGMAD cannot be touched by harm. Water cannot drown him; bullets nor knives cannot pierce him. Fire will not burn his flesh, and no man can destroy him by slander nor disturb him by anger. Nothing can injure his flesh or break his bones, bring him death, ill health or disease.

"No creature of man's world or the denizens of the cosmic planes can, in any way, stand before ITs Light and Power.

"The Soul who has realized the power of God has God-Realization. He is a true Soul. He has become a part of My divine, universal body. He needs nothing in his worlds for I give him all.

"The scriptures are but man made laws, rewritten so many times by the priestcraft. They are moral codes, and rules for the clergy's protection against man.

"He who has not studied the scriptures of great religions nor the philosophical system is closer to me. He does not have to forget. Many of those who went to earth to preach have not been Masters sent by My divine commission.

"They have been misguided Souls who believe the Astral

plane is the true home upon which the lower wisdoms have been taught. They only believed that their knowledge was of the highest.

"Listen to My Voice. Seekers of My Light know that I can give My power to any who seek IT. But beware how IT is sought and what is done with IT.

"Once My power is bestowed upon the individual his responsibility to the divine cause becomes absolute. He cannot escape his destiny. To do so will only create chaos in his universe.

"When man has gained the power through the way of Soul then he loses his own consciousness of the physical body, or self-consciousness; and he has a trio-nature of infinite power, knowledge and bliss, but conscious of his world outside.

"But as God, I am fully conscious in the sense that my divine consciousness is absorbed in no-thingness. This state of being is manifested through My full consciousness as clear and defined realistic gross states, as My worlds of creations and the life upon them.

"I have finished!"

R.T.: "I can give you the God-Realization at anytime but this is not the true divine realization, only a reflection of that from the above planes. You stood at the top of the lower worlds with Omkar and me to behold the light of the three worlds.

"You became as the ECK and observed all. Now you can see and hear, and know the wisdom of the inner worlds.

"When you are ready for the Fifth Plane I will take you there. I can take you anywhere at anytime, but not until Soul is conditioned for it."

P.T.: "Was that the cosmic consciousness?"

R.T.: "Yes. The cosmic consciousness is only the realization of the Light on the lower planes, especially the Astral.

"Many receive it, and believe they have the full consciousness of God. Many of the ancient mystics went no further than the Astral but left great writings telling us of its glory. Yet the world glorifies them in the greatest light.

"I tell you that man in his ignorance has little conception

159

of the worlds beyond, or the true glory of God in the worlds of the unknown regions!

"Someday I will give you an experience from the higher planes where God dwells in Spirit only. Then you will truly know God.

"Only a few on earth today have actually had this experience. You can count them on one hand."

# WHAT IS LIFE?

Rebazar Tarzs: "Now let us begin our discussion for tonight. I am not going to talk about spiritual psychoanalysis but on another subject. What is life?

"Man seeks God through religions.

"He asks ever of the skies to vision out what lies behind them. It is fear for the end, a subtler form of selfishness. It is this that breeds the vast number of occult organizations and many so-called religions.

"Mark my word, each religion claims the future for its followers, or at least, the good thereof. The evil is for those benighted ones who will have none of it; they are seeing the Light, which the true believer worships, as the fishes see the stars, but dimly.

"Religion comes and religion passes, and civilization comes and goes and none endure the world and human nature. If man would see that hope is from within, and not from without. That he, himself, must work out his own salvation.

"He is there, and within him is the breath of life, and a knowledge of God as God is to him. Thereon let him build and stand erect, and not cast himself before the image of some unknown God, modeled like his poor self, but with a larger brain to think the negative thing, and a longer arm to do it.

"Man is faithful to God so long as temptations pass him by. If the temptation be but strong enough then will man yield. Every man, except the strong seeker of God — like every rope, has his breaking strain, and passion is to man what gold and power are to woman. The weight upon their weakness.

"Man can be bought with woman's beauty, if it be but beautiful enough. And woman's beauty can be bought with gold, if only there be gold enough.

"The world is a great mart where all material things are for sale to him who bids the highest in the currency of man's desires.

"Who can say what is the weight or the measure of love?

"There is only one fixed light in the mists of our wanderings. That light is love. There is only one hope in man's lonely night. That hope is love. All else is false. All else is shadows. All else is wind and vanity. Love is born of the spirit, and often dwells in the flesh. From it man draws his comfort. For beauty is as a star. Many are its shapes, but all are beautiful and none know whence that star rose, or the horizon where it shall set.

"Yes, there is love. Love which makes all things beautiful, and breathes divinity into the very dust we tread. With love the Soul enters into eternity, gloriously, with God's Voice like some great music that has power to hold the Soul on eagle wings.

"Nay, and again I ask you, is there no man that will draw the veil and look upon the face of God? For it is very beautiful. Unto him who draws the veil God will be and give him peace, and the sweet children of knowledge and good words.

"Now, I tell you this that God says, 'Though all those who seek after me desire me, behold, I remain sacred throughout eternity. There is no son born of woman who can draw my veil and love, nor shall be. Only by death daily can my veil be drawn, O truth.'

"Man can never be contacted with that which his hand may pluck. If a lamp shines for him to light his way through the darkness, straightaway he casts it down because it is no star. Happiness dances ever a pace before his feet, like a marsh fire in the swamps, and he must catch the fire, and he must win the star.

"Beauty is naught to him, because there is more than he can hold. Wealth is poverty, because others weigh him down with heavier coins; and a sphere is emptiness because there have been greater men than he.

"Then what is life? It is a feather; it is the seed of the grass, blowing hither and yon; sometimes multiplying itself

162

and dying in the acts, sometimes carried away into the heavens. But if the seed be good and heavy it may travel a little on the road toward its source. It is well to try and journey back to the true home of God. Man must die. At the worst he can die a little sooner than expected.

"Again I ask you what is life? Tell me man, who is earthly wise, who knows the secrets of the world of stars, and the world that lies above and around the stars, who flash their words from afar without a voice. Tell me man, the secret of life — where it goes and whence it came.

"Ah, but you cannot answer. Listen I will tell you. Out of the dark you come and into the dark you go. Like a storm driven but at night you fly out of the invisible planes, or nowhere; for a moment your wings are seen in the light of the fire, and lo, you are again gone into the other worlds. Life here is nothing. Life is all. It is the hand with which you hold off death. It is the glow worm that shines in the night time and is black in the morning; it is the white breath of the oxen in the winter; it is the little shadow that runs across the grass and loses itself at sunset.

"Now you are aware that life underlines all — even that of matter, which is actually necessary for spirit life in the First and Second Grand Divisions of the cosmic planes. But for matter, the Supreme Being would be one huge ocean filling all space. Before creation, spirits lay at the feet of God in unmanifested masses.

"They need life mixed with matter in order to be of service to God. Hence God started creation for the self-improvement of his own beings.

"Many professed to be the seekers of Truth, but there are only a few who try and persist to ascertain it, and fewer still, who sincerely work at any sacrifice to attain it. By truth, is meant the essence, spirit, Soul and life of everything that exists or appears to exist, Itself unchangeable, and immortal.

"Again, I might define truth as the essence of essences, spirit of spirits, Soul of Souls, omniscient, omnipotent, formless, boundless, and unapproachable, unchangeable, the source and beginning of life, an unlimited ocean of love and wisdom. It is concealed in various coatings except in one place — that of the highest region where it can be observed by the spirits' visionary power.

"It should be clearly understood that instead of Sound being the results of vibratory motion, it is really the prime cause and everything in the universe is also of vibratory motion, which is instrumental in furthering the work of creation in the material regions.

"In the lower regions, various Sound Currents originate from vibratory motions and serve the purpose of carrying on the work of creation in various directions below. But the original Sound, or Spirit Current is the father of all motions and forces as well as Light, Sound, elements, etc., that come, subsequently, into existence in the Second and Third Grand Divisions."

# A TALK WITH RAMI NURI

Rebazar Tarzs: "Let us get to the discourse for tonight. Here is a surprise for you—an old friend who is well known in your world, Rami Nuri, the great ECK Master of the Temple of Golden Wisdom, in the City of Retz, Venus."

There stood before me a stately smiling man whose shining countenance was familiar. He opened his mouth and began to talk.

"The SUGMAD is Supreme!

"The Supreme ECK being the unconditioned; the ultimate ground of all Reality, is that from which all life emanates.

"The Supreme Being as the ECK Power is not the power, but that intelligence which sustains all life within the cosmic worlds. This power comes from God as John says in his Book of Revelations. 'I saw the river of life flowing from the throne of God.' He looked into the heaven of his own world and saw the glories of God. Yes, we are taught by the great ECK Masters that the Kingdom of Heaven lies within and John, among the few, was able to realize this.

"Yes, I say that every ECK Master is the Light of the world. Yaubl Sacabi came forth as a Light. Each Master brings with him the Light of the Eternal One. If anyone centers his attention upon the Master and walks in his Light, there can be no darkness in him.

"The river flowing out of the throne of God is the great power called love, or dayal; Prit, God or Sat Purusha the positive force; dayal, the merciful, because it is grace and mercy of the highest. It sustains the infinite universe through its radiant atoms. It flows down from the nameless region and takes form in the first Being in the Fifth Plane, whom you call Sat Nam.

"This majestic Being rules the whole of creation from the positive pole of all the universes of universes. While he himself is not the highest manifestation of the Supreme One, yet he is regarded by the Saints as Our Supreme Father and Creator.

"Hence, this is the reason that we regard the Power as the Reality. The Supreme Power being that of the highest force manifesting itself first in what man thinks of as the neuter being—the reason is, that the great power being that force which carries the properties normally making up the true self. This is what you call the ECK power. This is the highest power — this is what we call God, or sometimes love. But this is misnamed. In fact it is SUGMAD, the creator to us. It is significant that below the Soul plane no member of the grand hierarchy has power to create Souls. They have creative power over all, but no power to create Soul and to destroy Soul.

"In Sat Nam, Lord of the Soul plane, the Supreme creative energy comes into manifestation for the first time in all the upper worlds. In the Sixth and Seventh Plane, the power is so close to God, so slightly differentiated that Sat Nam is considered the first actual or complete personification of the Supreme One. He then becomes manifest as the supreme executive power of the God creation, and its region, known to you as Sach Khand or to others as the bliss plane, may be known as the governing center of the entire system of universes.

"Sat Nam is the sovereign lord with whom Masters have to deal in carrying out their sacred mission of returning Souls to their final home.

"He is the great Father, the Supreme Guru, the Light Giver. He is truly the Heavenly Father. All gods or rulers below Him, we may love and honor, but our supreme devotion belongs to Him, for He is the real Lord God of all existing worlds.

"All rulers above Him, and the Nameless One, the Universal are so utterly incomprehensible, so fathomless and impersonal, that we cannot approach them even in thought. But Sat Nam stands midway between the infinite light and the created universes; so in time when Soul is purged of all imperfections we can approach him as the Father with

166

the spiritual eye and receive his gracious welcome back home. This is the true meaning of the parable of the prodigal son.

"While on Earth man is subject to the laws of the negative power, or what is often termed 'The Laws of Nature.'

"This power arises as the Kal power beginning at the negative pole, which is the top of the three worlds, or what you call the Second Grand Division. This power is the offspring of the great power of God — and has many names. One is Kal which means who is just; who rewards and punishes man for his deeds in this world and who is a reality of the second order. His distinct existence is within the sphere of delusion and relativity. He is known mainly as Jot Niranjan, the King of the negative world.

"This negative power is manifested into the ruler Jot Niranjan. Just as Sat Nam is the positive manifestation of God, so this lower being is the negative manifestation through which the power flows to sustain the lower universes whose vibrations are the coarser nature of matter.

"This being is the creation and lord of the physical worlds. He is the Lord God of the Bible; the Jehovah of the Jews and Christians; the Allah of the Moslems. He is the Brahm of the Vedantists, the Parabrahm of the Sihks and the God of practically all religions.

"None but the ECK Master knows of any God other than the negative being. Yet He is exalted and universally worshipped as the Supreme Lord, but is only a humble subordinate in the grand hierarchy of the universe. He is not free from imperfection and although full of Light, Wisdom and Power, is only small in comparison with the great Sat Nam.

"Under the great negative power are the three lower powers called in Hinduism, Brahma, Vishnu and Shiva. They are the Sons of Brahm, the negative power. The female counterpart of Brahm is Shakti which is another minor creative stream. Often Brahm is thought of as the Divine Mother, and sometimes is given that honor.

"Out of the union of Brahm and Shakti, the three sub-

167

streams flow into the lower worlds, and to these are attributed the creation of all lower planes. These three became creators, lords and governors of the lower worlds under their parent streams, Brahm and Shakti, but more under the supervision of their mother.

"Each performs a certain function in carrying on the work of the world in producing human bodies, and keeping the bodies functioning. They are not gods to be worshipped, but only servants to the great Sat Nam.

"Still lower than these three is another current we call Ganesh, at the foot of the hierarchy, whose business is to serve mankind and carry on the work of the world. Below these are great hosts of beings called angels, but often known as devas, delas, bhuts, prets, etc. They are beings about man, and help serve him in many ways. Of course humanity is at the foot of the hierarchy.

"The great Sound Current in these planes is AUM — the music of Brahm or what you call Omkar.

"To give the truth is to tell you, dear one, more than your Soul might accept. There is the old saying, 'None are so blind as those who refuse to see.' And this is the case of mankind.

"By the grace of the ECK Masters I have been permitted to travel into the beyond to see for myself. But there are many who will neither believe nor desire to do so. Each thinks that his own world is the highest and, therefore, they are halted there.

"All prophets, yoghiswars, yogis, rishis, sages, incarnations of saviors and many others come from the region of Brahm and work with negative powers, which is only another name for the creative power. Their object is to improve the state of affairs in the world of Kala, or Karma but not to take Souls out of their illusion. The mystics of the highest order come from the bliss plane or the highest one, and here I pause to tell you that many of the Christian saints and mystics so highly exalted have hardly gotten beyond the top of the Astral or the First Plane.

"Those mystics who have come from the higher worlds

do not attempt to reform the world as do the saints of the negative world. They desire to take man out of this sphere to his true home of pure and lasting bliss, absolute knowledge and divine love.

"So you see the world of Karma, that of all below in the Second Grand Division; the three worlds are a big prison with many rooms and cells. The warden is Brahm and man is the prisoner. His true home is in the nameless region above, but Brahm does not desire that, although he wishes perpetual reform going on constantly within his prison. So he sends his saints, prophets, moral, social and political reformers, who are to try to set his world right. But as his agents they act with his power, and do his reform work in his prison. They do not even tell that man's real home is in the Absolute; they hardly know of it themselves. The Godmen, however, come from outside the prison and liberate those willing ones from Brahm's power with grace and mercy to reach their home.

"Within this world of Brahm the yugas go on like a great wheel, then all is wiped out and then starts again, without true peace. As stated in the Vedas and other religious scriptures man comes back even from his salvation although after the duration of a vastly extended period, and man's lot could be either a wretched cell or a luxurious mansion.

"The illusions given man by the agents of the negative power is fantastic. However, their work is a waste of energy — they deceive man by making him think they have come to take him to the Father in the highest realm, instead they bind tighter the chains. They come to promote good and root out evil — their sphere of activity is within cause and effect, or relativity and delusion. Even Lord Krishna told the world of his work as an agent of the negative power. Says he: 'Wherever there is decay of righteousness, O Bharata, and there is exaltation of unrighteousness, then I myself come forth.'

"Also he says: 'For the protection of good, for the destruction of evildoers; for the sake of family establishing righteousness, am I born from age to age.'

169

"Thus the incarnations of saviors come into the world from time to time for establishing righteousness, protecting the good and destroying the wicked. Their reform is within the sphere of morality as that of Buddha, Krishna, and hundreds of others; they do not take us to the Absolute, who neither rewards nor punishes, who sees neither good nor evil, for good and evil being relative do not exist there. The Absolute is beyond all relativity and delusion. Krishna was an incarnation of the Kal power for he says so himself.

"God, the Absolute, in the nameless region never manifests himself to destroy and slay mankind; he is merciful to all. He is an Ocean of Mercy and Love. Only those who come from his world have the power to take the Soul of every man back to that region.

"Just as the incarnated ones are the agents of the negative power, so do the sacred scriptures reveal the laws of this prison world. Free men are beyond the laws of the three worlds. The revelations of the Holy Books want man to give up bad actions and embrace good ones, but so few of them tell how to go beyond good and evil, how to transcend the bounds of morality and the Law of Karma. So I tell you that if bad actions are iron shackles, then good actions are gold chains and still both are fetters that bind man to his prison.

"It is difficult to get out of the clutches of maya and karma, but there is always hope if you can take shelter in the shadow of the living ECK Master. Then karma can do nothing and maya cannot deceive you.

"Yet this brings up the issues of what is good conduct? What constitutes bad actions? I can only say that whatever hinders or delays Soul in Its progress toward spiritual freedom is wrong, and vice versa.

"Man is told to do the will of God. What constitutes the will of God? Do you know? I doubt it, for your knowledge is only what the sacred books have given you or that which the priest, clergy, the teacher have said. Maybe you listen to your inner voice, and that again may be the illusion of the negative power speaking. So I tell you listen to only what the Godman says. He knows the will of God.

170

"God is reality, all else is illusion, for without God, Light and Sound, everything is without cause.

"I leave you dear ones with this thought. 'I must always lean upon the mercy of God. I am not worthy of thee, my Lord; but I am thine!'"

P.: "I wish to ask a question of you, Lord."

R.N.: "I am not your Lord, but ask."

P.: "Is there such a being as MAHANTA?"

R.N.: "Only as the manifested power. The same as Rebazar Tarzs and I. The God-Power can take any shape it desires. Usually, the Godman takes the shape of others in the inner cosmic worlds to appear to certain teachers, and devotees to give them the true Light."

P.: "If he appeared in his own form then they would either know him, or perhaps would not believe."

R.N.: "He appears to all ECK chelas as the Mahanta, the living ECK Master and the Master to any of his disciples.

"He is in as many forms as he desires to be. He could appear to one or many in contemplation. He can appear as a thousand or even a million different forms to a million different people in contemplation at the same time. He is the Godman and nothing is impossible.

"However, let us say this — those who do not see him in his true form as the Godman, Himself, will see him only as their teacher or guru, and to them he gives the inner teachings as only they, the disciples, can accept."

P.: "In other words they cannot accept the highest teachings of the living ECK Master. So He arranges for them to get what they can comprehend."

R.N.: "No. It is not that. It is only a preparatory step to the highest teachings. You were compelled to pass through this phase to the higher. However, should you have opened your eyes sooner, it wouldn't have been necessary."

P.: "I have seen many who have accepted the higher teachings, but have only a light opinion of their spiritual achievements."

R.N.: "The higher one goes, the greater he must fall, once his feet are pulled off the path. Even the Godman can

171

fall if He so permitted himself. But it's hardly possible. The Master usually sends them back into the world or places them where best fitted until time to take them home again."

P.: "What of the true teachings of ECKANKAR?"

R.N.: "The true essence of the ECK is pure. Most of the teachers have been too busy trying to please the seekers whose demands cause them to put their energies into organizations and buildings, and emphasize the personality. Remember this that those who demand respect and love of others to themselves are only exercising the negative or attracting power. The true teachings do not discipline in anyway; do not set up duties or difficulties or tasks for teaching their disciples lessons or developing traits or good character, are not bothered with good or evil, neither will they care too much about the love of their disciple. They only ask that their word be heard and obeyed. Their mission on earth is to gather up Souls to be taken home again.

"I tell you this, dear one, for the purpose of confirming the Master's word. You have a great mission on earth. You are in the midst of it now. Keep progressing and very shortly it will show results. You will someday become the MAHANTA.

"The world will make its path to your door. We who are watching over your destiny will see that all that is God's will takes shape in this life. So, do not doubt it. Take courage.

"Now this is all. Perhaps I will come again sometime. Farewell!"

His body faded away like a gray mist and left the Master and I alone. After a while the Master spoke very softly. "The wisdom of God comes in such wonderful ways. God helps those who wish to be helped. You are indeed a fortunate person!"

P.: "Yes, indeed!"

# THE LORD SOHANG SPEAKS

Rebazar Tarzs: "I am going to take you on a long journey tonight. This time into the world beyond the worlds, which you have known before. I am going to give you a grand experience of which you've never had the likes before. The world where you are completely spirit, without the body — it will be your first journey into the Fourth World — the world of Sohang, called the first of the regions of pure spirit where only the atoms of perfected quality dwell. It is the entry into the Kingdom of God.

"Are you ready?"

He took my hand and closed my eyes with gentle fingers. When I opened them we were standing in the center of a strange land where the beauty was magnificent. The light of this world begged words of description. It was beauty of a nature which only a poet could describe in sublime language or that of a Beethoven pastoral.

We passed to the gates of a wonderful city, probably the one described by St. John in his revelations. Many of the ECK Masters whom I recognized hailed Rebazar Tarzs. He returned their greetings with hearty salutations.

Then we moved into a marvelous palace which looked similar to those in ancient pictures with mosaics on the walls. And we were greeted by beings in great Light wearing white robes. We were led into the presence of a Soul whose beauty was so extraordinary that words cannot describe His Light. Every particle of light danced and dazzled its countenance.

Rebazar Tarzs bowed humbly. "O great Sohang, we come to greet thee in the name of that mighty Soul called God, the Almighty Father!"

There was a long silence, then the escorting angel spoke, "The Lord of the Fourth World will speak to thee. Listen closely!"

A voice like the rushing winds spoke. It filled the chamber

with a solemn sound of whirling vibrations that shook Soul.

"Man is a spiritual being.

"The source of this spiritual Omniscience, you may not, in your finite intelligence, fully cognize, because full cognition would preclude the possibility of finite expression.

"The destiny of man is to dwell in his true home.

"His true home is that nameless world where dwells the true Lord of all infinity.

"The argument of the saviors of the three worlds is that man's destiny is perfection.

"Man perfected becomes a God, they say.

"To become a god in the land of Daswan Dwar is to become immortal.

"Let me consider what this means, supposing it to be an axiom of truth.

"Mortality is subject to change and death. Mortality is the manifest — the stage upon which man in his life plays many parts.

"Immortality is what the word implies, Godhood, and recognized in the mortal "I am" or "Om", the charged word of the Brahman of the world of Brahm. It stands for the changeless, birthless, deathless, unnameable power that holds the worlds in space, and puts intelligence into man.

"Yet this power is the Kal or negative power as you know it.

"The lord of the three worlds Kal Niranjan, Parambrahm, or whatever name you desire to call Him, does not have the power to hold Soul immortal. As the sacred books tell us, these worlds are wiped out after a millennium of time, and replaced again. The cycle goes on and on into eternity.

"This power is not pure spirit. It has its roots in matter, yet it is not able to create Soul, only the form or manifestation of flesh, mineral, plant or other matter.

"Yet to the beings of the three worlds it is the unknowable-the Absolute.

"Om, therefore, is the Sound Current, expressing the Omniscient, Omnipotent and Omnipresent power of the worlds below the Second Grand Division.

"The lower cosmic man says that the compound immortal applied to the individual man, stands for one who has made himself at-one-ment with Om, and who has, while standing in the mortal body recognized himself as one with Om.

"This is what they mean, or hope to escape in the second death, to which all Souls of the three worlds are subjected. These worlds are held together by Karma, the Maya of time.

"Thus their saviors tell them — and again I tell you this is delusion or Maya speaking — the above means to them that it is the goal of every human life, the essence, the substance of all religious systems and all philosophies.

"The only chance for disputation among the theologians and philosophies, lies in the way of accomplishing this at-one-ment. so they believe. There is not the slightest opportunity for a difference of opinion as to what they wish to accomplish. Yet, they disagree among themselves, and are at odds on which path to take.

"Neither, do they see nor wish to see when a Godman like the living ECK Master appears among them and gives the highest truth. They will destroy him without the slightest regret.

"Admitting, then, the goal of Soul is the same immortality, we come to a consideration of the evidence we may find in support of this axiom. The evidence does find satisfaction in spirit communication; in psychic experience; in hypnotic phenomena, and astral trips; important and reliable, these many psychic research phenomena are found to be true.

"These are not satisfactory, or convincing evidence of the at-one-ment with Kal Niranjan because they do not preclude the true probability of the second death, but on the contrary verify it to themselves. They do not know anything beyond these worlds — unless while in these worlds, they meet with experiences similar to those on the earth plane. That is, to eventually be drawn to the Master, or the Godman, and get the true essence of teachings which eventually lead them back to their true home.

"Aside from the psychic phenomena there is a phase of human experience that transcends phenomena of every kind.

175

The western world gives it the term 'cosmic consciousness', which is self-explanatory.

"All races have long known of this goal and have terms to express this with varying experiences with the many types of thought but all with the same meaning. However, it means liberation, signifying to be set free from the limitations of sense and self-consciousness that takes in the very cosmos.

"Yet I tell you of what purpose is it to grasp this great consciousness? It is of course an advancement in the life of the human Soul. But until you pass the top of the three worlds and enter into the Fourth Plane, the experience is only a step along the path, great or small, whatever it might be. The true Light is known when the experiencer receives it.

"The experience is accomplished by great Light in most cases — in some it has the Sound Current whether the Light is manifested as spiritual, or as intellectual power determines it.

"When you reach the Third World, then immortality becomes whole. No one can become by any possibility, an immortal in that world in, of, and by himself; no one can become complete without the other half. This is why the teachings of certain religious systems that either of the species must remain unmarried in order to become immortal, are wrong. The true Godman is often a married man, usually has a family, and keeps a household.

"Each and every Soul, therefore, in the lower worlds has its spiritual counterpart — its other half with which it unites on the spiritual plane, when the time comes for the attainment of the highest goal of the world of Brahm and that counterpart is the ECK Spirit.

"Love is an eternal verity. The entire cosmos, below the Second Grand Division is the whole. Everything in the visible universe, in the manifest, is the result of the universal principle, 'As above so below.' Yet, I tell you that this principle does not apply in the Fourth Region.

"Perfection does not apply to any of the worlds above Daswan Dwar—for goodness and evil do not have their place with us. We dwell in perfect harmony, and seeking only

176

to gain the inner strength, knowledge and spiritual courage to take the step into the worlds above.

"Spiritual courage is the essence of all God-seekers. Without it you gain not. The majority of seekers wish but do not have the courage to seize God, hold God, to become God. Here you begin to learn that.

"Male and female created he them — the single principle. This being true, male and female must then return to the source from which they sprang, completing the circle, and gaining what? Consciousness of Godhood, of completeness in counterpart union. Not absorption of consciousness, but union which is quite a different idea. The Kal saviors or savants tell us that out of this counterpart union a race of gods will be born, and these supermen, shall inherit the earth making it a fit dwelling place for the gods.

"It can never be as long as karma holds the worlds together; for the reformers and teachers cannot cope with karma — it deludes them.

"Yet they feel, and there is a substantial reason for this, that this is not too far a distant hope, judging from the eye of the seer, but its proof lies in the emancipation of woman. Its evidences are many and varied, but the awakening of woman is the cause. This awakening of woman constitutes the first ray of dawn which has become a literal truth. The fact that woman is being given her rightful place in the sense-conscious life proves the earth will be a fit dwelling place for a higher order of beings than have hitherto constituted the majority.

"The numerous instances of illumination or cosmic consciousness which is forcing attention at the present time, prove that there is a race-awakening to the realization of unity with the Sound Current of Om.

"The so-called revelation is neither a personal discovery nor any special act of a divine power. 'GOD spake thus, and so to me,' is a phrase which the self-conscious initiated employs because he has lost sight of the cosmic light or because he finds it expedient to use that phraseology in delivering the message of the cosmic consciousness.

"If the term initiation is substituted for the term revelation you will have a clearer idea of the truth. This is why the Mahanta uses the term initiation when he gives you the cosmic light to bring you onto the path.

"A broader concept given means He accepts the responsibility of taking Soul back to Its true home.

"For the most part, the word revelation used in religious systems implies that the plan of the cosmos was unfinished and that the creator having found some person suitable to convey the latest decision to mankind, natural laws were suspended and the revelations made. It is to correct this view that I emphasize the destruction between the two words.

"The cosmos of the three worlds is complete. 'As in the beginning, it is now and ever shall be worlds without end.' A circle is neither with beginning nor end. Man in his individual consciousness may traverse this circle, but his failure to realize its completeness does not change the fact it is finished. Man cannot add to the universal consciousness of his negative world, nor take away therefrom. But he can extend his own area of consciousness from the narrow limits of the personal self into the heights and depths of the World Soul. Who shall set limitations to the power of His God, the higher self, when it has attained at-one-ment with His Om Sound Current? He knows not of the worlds beyond so here he stays until his knowledge through initiation becomes greater and knowledge is gained of the other worlds.

"The awakening of Soul to Its true home in the nameless worlds, and Its needs, which include the welfare of all living things as an absolute necessity to individual happiness, is the purpose of any revelation.

"Therefore, in your worlds, O man, altruism is not a virtue, but a means of self-preservation; without this degree of initiation into the boundless area of the cosmic worlds, you may never escape the karmic law.

"The revelations, therefore, upon which are founded the numerous religious systems, are comparable with the many and various degrees of initiation. They represent the degree which the initiate has taken in a lodge.

178

"This fact of individual initiation into the ever-present truth of Being, as into a lodge, offers no proof that the three worlds will ultimately become the heaven, as many of the so-called Masters have learned after passing into the land of Brahm. It may be best said that they represent the outer lodge rooms, and there will never be a sufficient number of initiates to make the earth a fit dwelling place for a higher order of beings than now inhabit it. All hope tends toward the fact that it is coming under the regenerating power of God, or illumination.

"All lower world prophecies embody this promise; what the materialists call evolution, and occultists name the uncovering of consciousness — all of which points to the time when 'God's will shall be done on earth as it is in Heaven.'

"All who have attained to cosmic consciousness in whatever degree, have prophecied a time when this blessing would descend upon everyone; but the difficulty in adequately explaining this great gift seems also to have been the burden of their outcry.

"I ask why do you desire to live in a world where darkness dwells? The truth of the statement above does not ring true. For the Master's purpose is to take all Souls out of it and return them to the nameless region.

"Many have sought repeatedly to describe the cosmic wonders to his audience, but they had not the breadth of mind to listen. A number of disciples were capable of receiving the Light and Sound, and a larger number are capable of attainment now.

"But your religions and science point to a time when your earth planet will know freedom from strife and suffering. But how can this be as long as karma exists, and as long as man inhabits that world, there shall be karma, unless the ECK Master receives him.

"Until God takes it upon ITS mercy to give cosmic consciousness to the worlds below, it will never be and we who live in this land have not that foresight.

"If IT did, indeed the earth would become a heaven, like that world of great Light, Sound and Love. For here all

179

problems of Soul are dropped; there is an elimination of all negative attributes for we have only universal happiness and well being far beyond the concepts of man's mind."

He finished and Rebazar Tarzs led me away. Then we were standing in the bedroom at the house. He smiled and bid me goodnight.

# A DISCOURSE BY GOPAL DAS

Rebazar Tarzs: "Before we get into the discourse for the evening I want to tell you that your mind is becoming completely alert. You've now a fine alert mind with penetrating power — the ability to see deep into life.

"This mind is opened by the ECK Power and it goes far into the depths of every issue that lies before man in the mental and spiritual world. The ECK Power is working through you at all times.

"Your mind has developed a deep penetrating power which can move swiftly to the source of the question at hand—which can pierce the veil of anything which comes before you, at anytime. You are freed of all negative loads which have been on your shoulders.

"Now let us move along tonight into the Astral world to meet with an old friend of the western world. Come."

Rebazar Tarzs closed my eyes with his fingers, then took my hand, and when I opened my eyes I saw a strange bright land of the inner region. We were standing in a beautiful garden where a tall, slim man stood watching us. He had such a dazzling countenance, I could hardly look at him. His eyes were flaming swords and his beard and hair of deep molten gold. His beauty was radiant, and beyond the essence of words. Who can explain the beauty of this Soul?

Swiftly, he moved forward and embraced the Master, like a long lost brother. The Master shook Gopal Das' hand. Gopal Das looked compassionately at me, but I could not face him, so great was the light and beauty which poured from him.

"He is here to learn." said Rebazar Tarzs.

"I will teach thee," Gopal Das said motioning us under a tree where the shade was sweet. The greensward was a bright color, and the tall boxwood hedge surrounded the lovely garden, and a thousand birds twittered sweetly among the trees. Above the hedge, to one side, peered the elegant steeples of a Gothic styled church. Its roof gleamed in the golden light.

Church-bells were ringing out sweet chimes. The joy was majestic, and the sublime power from Gopal Das sitting in a contemplative posture brought a noble peace.

He folded slender, brown hands and laid them in the lap of his snow white robe. His head lifted as his wondrous voice spoke in prayer.

"Oh SUGMAD, thou great Lord of all, bless this gathering with thy Divine Grace. Send thy love to enter my tongue so it speaks only the highest praise of thy glories and the truth of thy sweet mercy!"

The softest expression filled his beautiful eyes and his lips opened to speak. A golden Light fell like raindrops around his majestic head, swirling in a mist. It became brighter until it formed a cloak, almost too dense to see anything, but his face was surrounded by an aura. His melodious voice floated out of the Light.

"The lofty heights of this divine world is staggering to the journeying Soul that steps across the boundary into the first true land of the spirit.

"The majestic experience of glimpsing for the first time the face of the Almighty is glorious adventure. No word can describe this.

"Only under the guidance of a true Godman, can thou stand in the dazzling light of the cosmic sun and see for thyself the sublime beauty of the Father.

"Soul comes to this world naked and poor. Without senses, body or mind It must stand before the throne of the great deity of this world, who gazes upon It with compassion and mercy, and passes judgment of Its worth in continuing the journey to God, the Supreme REALITY of all.

"Soul has now experienced and become the Knower. The

182

only expression It retains of the human elements is feeling. It wears for the first time, since leaving God, Its true body, made from the divine substance of our Holy Father.

"The divine essence of God is love. Love is the power of the Absolute. This power is the pure, spiritual ether flowing from out of the feet of God, in the unnamed heights in to the true spirit world.

"All Souls in the true spiritual worlds subsist upon the spiritual ether. It is the nectar of our almighty power.

"Below the lower pole of the true spirit world, the great love current divides into another stream, becoming mixed with the material essences, and thereupon is impure. The lowest pole of this division is the physical universe.

"Thou art aware that this love, of which I speak, is the face of God. I spoke of it in ancient earth times that man has yet to see the face of the SUGMAD. Ye, knowing the sublime wisdom, are aware that I speak not of virtues, nor of morals, that make man grow toward perfection.

"Of this I speak. The love which permeates all the true spiritual worlds is that great, sublime, mystic, intelligence which every saint has experienced in the cosmic worlds.

"Man's highest ideal of love is an unlimited self-giving compassion flowing freely toward all creatures. Yet if thee put love in the category of growth toward such an experience of cosmic nature, man expresses at each stage as much of this ideal compassion as his spiritual progress permits.

"The divine challenge to man's belief is to tell thee directly that pure love is the great spiritual force of the SUGMAD in ITS true kingdom. Surely this will settle the question, for that love is that majestic, white Light and the tender music of God. This is the power and the way of truth. This is the sublime stream of nectar pouring out of the feet of God.

"Then good brothers, it is relatively simple to state that when man believes truth is untruth, and sees untruth in truth, he never arrives at truth but will follow blindly through the darkness, like the bridegroom who seeketh the bride's house in the storm.

"So Soul seeks liberation and salvation. Ah, there my

brothers is the basic essence of the path which is established upon Love, Light and Sound. Yes gentle Souls you will find liberation in the Light, and salvation in the Sound. Thus, in order to give further clarification, I mean to say, Soul becomes liberated by becoming one with the God-power or love force, and salvation by becoming God, ITSELF. Nay, doest thou see the issues at stake in seeking true righteousness?

"I stand upon this doctrine as that of the void of nothingness, for its roots are in the body of the great Majestic Creator of all, who is both unconcerned and unaware of ITS multitude of lifeforms through the vast limits of ITS creation. IT knows that all is in its place and, therefore, will at the proper time reach ITS side again, as the prodigal son returned to his father's home.

"Therefore, I tell thee, there is no liberation without conscious contact with the Word, and this thee cannot get without the teacher. Nothing can be accomplished after death in the means of spiritual liberation, unless it is at least begun in thy life in the flesh. For this reason when man has not been given the power to hear the Word, he must return to earth, for another chance to meet the living teacher who gives him that opportunity. This is the Divine Law.

"And this ye must know. No ECK Master can give the Word to a seeker unless He can lead them through the inner planes to God. Most religions have lost contact with the living Word, the sublime contact with the SUGMAD.

"Ye must fasten thy attention upon the Word, which is not of the sense-world, for it is imperishable — something which, instead of bonding man, liberates him from his bondage and brings him to liberty and immortality.

"Thereupon dear ones, the salvation lies in the Word and the teacher. This is liberation from the wheel of sorrow and ills. And the freedom to live forever in a heaven of bliss of thy choice. But without the help of the true living Godman, man cannot gain permanent relief from thy wheel of birth and death.

"Complete surrender to the noble Godman is the path to

complete liberation. To give — never once thinking of the rewards, is the beginning of immortality, holy ones.

"The spiritual word, or the holy stream of love is the only liberation to thee, man. It is the noble way for thee to enter into it, and flow with it back to God. To have spiritual freedom here and now.

"Then my holy friends ye must know that prana or the breath current is a subordinate agent to the ECK or Word Current. The functions of prana are limited to certain automatic actions of the clay temple. If ye dealt with this practice it takes thee little further than the summer region of the Astral plane.

"In some instances the individual Soul has violated the beauty of the Holy Spirit. He has gone to the extreme and identified himself with the boundless sources of spirit, and lost all regard and consideration for it. He has become extremely selfish and proud of his existence which is a mere drop from the Ocean of Spirit and Love — a ray from the supreme sun, the life and Light giver of the whole creation. These have become so infatuated with this thought of being God, they adore nothing. In their ignorance shall they stay in the flesh temple until the true Godman appears to help them.

"The Word was the first manifestation of the SUGMAD and the rest of creation, including ethers and other elements, was created by the Holy Word. It is the Life and Soul of everything that followed ITS first manifestation.

"Again I tell ye that the Holy Word of the ECK Current is the prime mover and the first impulse which came from the SUGMAD — the first cause of motion, color and form.

"The vibratory motion of the Word is confined to the spheres where matter exists in subtle, or pure, or less pure, and coarse form. It is the result of contact of spirit with matter. A simpler explanation is that it is the manifestation of an effort on the part of the Holy Word, descending from the highest heavens to remove the carnal coating of the Word in the lower heavens.

"Know ye clearly that instead of Sound being the result of

vibratory motion, it is really the prime mover of all in the infinite heavens, which again is instrumental in furthering the work of creation in the carnal heavens.

"In the lower heavens, various Sound Currents originate from vibratory motion and serve the purpose of carrying on the work of creation in various diverse ways. But the original Holy Word Current is the father of all motion and forces, Light, Sound and elements that subsequently came into existence in the Third Heaven and below it.

"Thou art curious of true sensation? The attainment of Soul's goal is the highest heavenly house in the truth of truths. As a ray of the Father existing somewhere in this creation of heavens, Soul is covered with carnal sheathings, but they must be severed to give Soul the opportunity for returning home.

"The spirit rays, or Souls, are residing in God's millennium of form throughout all heavens. They exist in apparent bodies forming the creations in various spheres in space and giving them the power of motion, thought, reason, or life.

"In more simplified words the whole creation extending from the highest to the lowest sphere is sustained by the spirit rays, or Souls from the SUGMAD, and disappears or is dissolved upon the separation of spirits from the coatings or bodies in which they reside.

"The whole creation which man, plant, creature or mineral feels, sees and observes, owes its origin and growth to the Word, or Spirit, and is sustained throughout by spirit, and disappears or is dissolved when spirit is separated or withdrawn thereupon.

"To approach the SUGMAD, man must first approach and catch Its ray or Spirit Current and then follow and trace Its course back to God. Man must first know himself (the spirit within him) and then know God, the source of the spirit. Thereupon, I say boldly, that the highway to reach spirit and thence its Source, the Almighty Father, lies within the microcosm, or man's own body.

"The Spirit Current, and its agent currents are flowing downward or outward toward the carnal objects; and to approach their centers, man must change the direction of these currents upward or backward to their eternal sources. This means giving up certain desires in order to proceed on the journey to thy true home. Live in the world, but confine the use of the current to that which is useful to thy life there.

"So then, the splendor of true salvation lies in the attainment of God in his higher mansion. This is true and perfect salvation. Many stop on their way to God's mansion in one of the other lower heavens below the Third World, and regard it as the mansion of God.

"Yet each of these lower heavens is a mansion of comparative truth and in the absence of guidance from the God-man, Soul is apt to believe apparent or comparative truths as real and pure. They unwittingly remain there to die; to be reborn after long periods.

"The sincere seeker of God should never stop at any stage where there is both Light and darkness, but should continue the journey until the regions of pure, eternal, mysteriousLight where there is no darkness. This is the House of God, or pure Supreme ECK.

"God loves and takes great care of those who love him full-heartedly. He draws them to himself, the grand center of pure Light and Word. Those whose hearts are filled with carnal love recede from this center, and fly toward the circumference of darkness and untruth.

"Love knows no boundary, knows no restrictions, and is not limited by conditions and, like its source, is extensive and far reaching in its noble actions.

"Scientists say that matter and motion are the principle factors in creation. This is true so far as the lower worlds are concerned. But they do not or cannot say how, or whence, their motion originated. Motion needs a motor and this motor is the same Spirit or Word issuing forth like rays from the sun, from various centers or spiritual material suns and diffused over all space comprised in the worlds below the third heaven.

"An Energy atom is in itself a ray or current issued from a center and is endowed with Spirit Power which is called energy by the scientists. Unmanifested power is called latent or potential and that brought into action or full play, kinetic energy. Both names apply to the impulses from the spirit force which is the origin and beginning of all.

"The atoms playing their part in the earth world — for example, issue forth from the sun, or the suns above the earth. They are manifested in the sun orb before they issue forth as rays or currents and are thus fitted for the work of creation, or form parts of the bodies they combine to form or give existence to. The Spirit Current, latent in these atoms, is just steeped in the matter of the lower spheres and it requires impulse from a higher Current or Word, appertaining to and descending from, the higher sphere to awaken its energy or actuate it into action.

"Thus ye see that the Spirit Power or force is all in all, or it is the principal factor, or prime action in the whole creation. It is the Life and Soul of everything.

"The true riddle of God and Spirit is dissolved in this statement. The Supreme SUGMAD is a vast ocean of spirit and love and joy that lies in the highest heaven, called the Nameless World. From IT the original Spirit or Word Current emanated. The Spirit or Word and Sound, the prime mover, creator, nourisher and sustainer of the whole creation is the original spirit that emanated from God.

"It is the link between the Almighty and the son, or disciple, and leads and helps the son in returning to the Father's highest mansion.

"The next, is the Supreme Son, or Godman, who is the representative of the Almighty in human form on the earth plane. He appears now and then in that world for the purpose of saving Souls from going down to the lower spheres and raising them to the higher spheres, and finally to the Father's house.

"The next in the chain of the riddle is the chela, the human Soul, or ray or drop, descended from the great boundless ocean of spirit, love and joy, who, directed by mind and matter toward the carnal creation, lost all knowledge of his true divinity.

188

"Only when he finds the Godman, who awakens the disciple to the worship of God through the connecting Spirit and Sound Current will he be taken back again.

"In time I will give thee knowledge of my holy journeys to India and other countries in my youth."

Rebazar Tarzs took my hand and we came back to earth again. He bade me goodnight in the bedroom and left.

# THE FACE OF GOD

Rebazar Tarzs: "Bliss-eternal bliss is for every man, and nothing can keep you from this great inner harmony of life. I give thee bliss, complete bliss to stand forth in your life. This is completely yours — nothing can keep it from you. I have said the word so now you understand.

"Prepare yourself for one of the greatest and most magnificent experiences of life. Now is the time to take thee into the far reaches of the true home and see God. Actually God!"

Rebazar Tarzs took my hand and gradually lifted me. Then, within the brief pause of a moment he bade me to look around.

The shock of fear was too great to tell you. But the deep waves rolled away from this strange body of light which I was wearing. It really wasn't a light but a strange robe of dazzling white, like a cloak. Even my feet were clad in it. Rebazar Tarzs was clad in a similar cloak, like a great, white shining aura.

A million — two million and possibly a billion similar lights were moving in a brilliantly lighted void, so completely blinding I could hardly look at it. It was like standing on the edge of a mighty precipice ready to lead to a bottomless world. I clutched at the Master, but he smiled and waved his hand.

"You are in the nameless world. The light you see is the light of God so vastly brilliant in all its glory that human eyes could not look upon it. You are now the perfect atom, for this is the Ocean of Love and Mercy, the true home of the SUGMAD where all Souls return in time.

191

"Everywhere ye look, see the great rain of transparent drops. It is not the true rain as you know it, but the rain of the perfect atoms, the rain of Souls upon the mighty Ocean of ECK, brilliant, majestic and awe-inspiring in the sight of God. No man looks upon the face of God and stays the same. Thereafter, he is Soul, complete Soul of God for he has seen and heard. Look ye yonder and see!"

I saw a river, a great white river that seemed to flow out of the heavens, and moving, ever widening like a gigantic avalanche, covering all space, and then disappearing or evaporating into the millennium of brilliant lights or atoms.

"The river of God," he explained. "A river which pervades all the universes, for it is the great spiritual Current flowing out of the throne of God. Listen!"

The terrifying flowing light had a singing, a musical sound, strangely penetrating — forever moving and singing. It was the word of the spiritual Current. And then a strange cloud hovering over the flowing light seemed to dissolve and a face which filled all space seemed to hang there with eyes gazing upon all. Yet seeing nothing. And then suddenly I was caught up in a sheet of the white flowing light and the singing sound, moving toward that terrifying face. Yet with the ECK Master at my side.

And then we came to the gigantic heights of a great precipice, which seemed to lie on the very edge of the world, where the great stream flowed swiftly from the far beyond. Rebazar Tarzs pointed.

"Beyond the face of God is God. Look behind the Mask of God, and see God. If this is terrifying and awe-inspiring then you must gird up thy loins for a great sight. For you must go on and on into the very heart of God.

"See the sight of the river of Light is illusionary for it flows not in one single stream, but in a great circular wave, like beams from a radio tower and from out of the center of the eye of God. Look and see, from whence comes the river of Light and Sound!"

I could not look for the sight was too great. Millions upon millions of colors exploded in the great forehead of that gigantic face before us. But then, they seemed to dim, and I saw a tiny circle, the round eye within the forehead of the Deity and from out of that passed a continual stream of light — the great spiritual Current flowing to all the worlds upon worlds. A gigantic spirit sun that manufactured its own spiritual atoms and electrons pouring them into that continuous stream of light.

"I will take you into the sun of light — into the truth of truths," he said. "We can go by becoming one with this current upon which we now ride."

Then suddenly there was nothing of ourselves, except the consciousness of joy, light and bliss. No light-body, nothing except the craving of a drowning man for air, and the feeling of great movement toward that gigantic spiritual eye, and then within the moment of featherly floating we seemed to shoot into another world — a world of extreme light, inside a vast reaching electrical ring from which the light itself poured out a Niagara of indescribable sound. And there was a contingent of light, where the stream began from a pair of feet so large that I cannot describe them. They seemed to be attached to a body which I cannot give words as to its glory of colors, that flashed continuously, and the features of the face were beyond description and glory. It was the cosmic body of the Nameless One, and around him were multitudes of angels so dazzling in color that no eyes could look upon them.

I prostrated myself beside him upon the mystic flooring, face down.

A melody of trumpets blared and silence followed. A great Voice spake from out of the blinding light. It was a Voice so mighty that it filled all space, and made the heavens tremble with the vibrations from its force. Yet IT spoke in a whisper, gradually rising in tone until IT became a mighty roar!

"Look ye, I am the Lord who speaketh to ye courageous sons of heaven!

"Ye are in the House of the SUGMAD. The abode of abodes. The highest of heavens. Ye cannot go higher, and here ye, Soul, having become at-one-ment with my divine self,

193

returns to Its true self, ever ready with Its work in the divine cause!

"Ye are perfect, O Supreme Son. Ye are the messenger in the worlds below. Thy duty is to return Soul to Its true home again, so It can be put into service again for my creation!

"Pilgrims, look ye upon my face. Thy limbs tremble and thy hearts quake. Be not fearful of the Lord, thy Father, for I look upon all creation with divine and merciful love!

"Ye are the atoms of my universal body. Therefore, ye must serve thy place in the divine cause!

"As the perfected atom, ye can become the angel that worships at my feet, or serve in the hierarchy of the spiritual spheres. Ye may become the incarnation of the Supreme Soul who leads Souls back to the true kingdom. Or ye may become the atom in the stream of light. All my creations have free will. They alone must choose!

"Pilgrim, ye must be of the Light and of the Word. Let nothing deter ye from it. Only the way of the Word will bring ye home again. Every Soul belongs to IT, the REALITY, of all creation, and no Soul can escape my call. Time has no place within the heaven of heavens. Therefore, what if the creatures dissect their worlds for knowledge only to find their ignorance. Man in his sensory understanding can find only the sensory answers to his endless quest. Thy mystics find the true solutions, for the truth always seeks truth. The son of the sky is greater than the son of the earth!

"The ECK Saints who deserve my bliss, of perfect attainment, never enjoy it, because they turn back and share the suffering of those Souls still caught in the snares of the earth worlds, in loving concern for their salvation. Their glory in my kingdom shall be greater. All others attain a little bliss!

"I will give ye three precepts to live by. First, love Me, thy Lord, fully. Love Me through my supreme son, and then love Me through thy fellow man, and through all my creations.

"The second precept is to be humble before thy maker, and humble before my son, and all thy fellow men and my creations.

"The third precept is to serve my cause without reward, throughout the seven spheres of heavens!

"All life begins in my heart, and all life ends in my heart, and nothing can escape living within the heart of thy creator, O blessed ones.

"Listen! Serve the cause above all things. Look to the flaming love in the heart of thy beloved and find me there!

"Ye shall find peace and rest only in my being, and seek not elsewhere. Ye are my being, and ye shall serve with thy pen. Thee deserves not anything, for here Soul does not have punishment or rewards. We have nothing but love, the highest love, and standing there in the pure Light ye are love! So man, ye must understand!

"When I want to show the world my highest grace and mercy, I send ye the supreme son. This is my greatest gift and boon. He is the sole Master and absolute lord over all; his will is supreme, his word is ultimate, and his decree final for he represents my power in the seven lower worlds.

"O man, ye shall return to the world to do my bidding. I say worship me, the lord, with a leaf, a stone, or a flower, but worship me.

"Ye will take up this commission and begin thy work. Ye will obey my commands and the commands of my supreme son.

"Go now for I have exalted thee in my name! Ye are commissioned by my word!

"I have spoken!"

The voice died away in a low whisper and I stood frozen in a trance, staring at the gigantic figure hanging in the sky. The Master's hand guided me away and we became one again with the golden, white stream flowing ever and ever out into the unknown, beyond all time and space.

The light became blinding, terrifying and so all-embracing

that I clung to the Master. We seemed to shoot out of the light into a darkness, and into a dawn where the light became gradually day, and then the ECK Master pressed me forward, and I looked down through the wall at the body sitting in the bedroom.

I disliked to return to that body, but Rebazar Tarzs pushed forward and insisted. Then I entered the dark, clay temple, and opened my eyes.

He smiled and held up his right hand. With that he vanished.

# THE SUGMAD SPEAKS

Rebazar Tarzs: "I have returned tonight to take you again into the far reaches of the worlds beyond into the Absolute for you to hear and know the truth of truths from the lips of the Almighty SUGMAD. So you will then know for yourself.

"Do you feel capable of the trip again into the unknown world?"

P.: "Yes, Master!"

R.T.: "Then you shall step from your body into the robe of Soul and follow. I will take you into the realm of God where the Ocean of Love and Mercy abides. Now take my hand!"

I felt a sucking whirl of the body and there was a pop like a cork and there we stood together with that strange white, brilliant light of Soul shining.

Suddenly we were in the midst of a world the likes of which I had never seen before. It was a place of fiery light, which swirled and flared upward into the heights which I could not even imagine.

It seemed as if we were standing in the complete midst of a volcanic action where the red molten lava poured in confusion, through a fiery land.

I held to him, trembling, but he smiled, and said. "We are on the planet Ataras. This is only a stop to the realm of the unknown. The planet will become a sun in time, and be one in the chain of cosmic suns. This is the evolution of creation, and the way that planets are created. Let us journey onward!"

Then we proceeded upward like angels flying to the far skies, through the five worlds into that nameless realm, the infinite ocean, a limitless area, where all is all, and Soul is only an iota in this ocean—only a bubble in the mighty waves.

It was a golden sea of light without an end, a shoreless

ocean which we seemed to be a part of, a drop with the light, like fishes within the sea.

We stood there within the depths of the gigantic sea of light where the very air was so rarified that not even the Soul was conscious of Its breath. Yet perhaps there was no breath. Or does Soul breathe? This I cannot say.

The Master moved forward through the dazzling light until he came to a tremendous gate, opened by a tall, magnificent man in a white robe, and who wore a wreath of holly around his head. He had brown hair and beard and dark eyes.

He greeted Rebazar Tarzs with an embrace, and was introduced as Apollonius of Tyana, the great mystic of ancient times.

"Where do ye travel, cosmic pilgrims?" asked Apollonius.

"To the land of all, to the top of the world of all creation."

"Proceed and ye will find the way, my Lord."

We went through the strange land of marvelous continents and worlds, that seemed to be a wavering light of shadowy substances. Then Rebazar Tarzs pointed at the tiny white shining ball in the sky. "There is the destiny of our journey. There we will go and you shall touch the robe of God."

We were lifted up and suddenly shot into great heights, and came to rest in a strange area of blinding lights, which encircled us, as though we were trapped inside a mystic blaze of white flames that reached beyond any concept of the imagination. There a lotus flower larger than any building of any proportions I had seen, floated upon a pond of brightly glistening waters, and in the center stood a being beyond description, so rare was his beauty. So wondrous in his attire of light. And from everywhere came the murmuring sounds of delicate music, which sent chills of bliss through my Soul.

The being had eyes of stabbing fire, long sparkling hair and wonderful features. And then I saw that the pool was a vibratory center, sending off waves of light like radio waves.

A Voice spoke so rich in quality, so magnificent in tone that I could hardly bear it. The Voice said.

"I will speak to thee, O Soul to tell ye of My wishes for thee.

"I will speak to thee, O Soul, to tell ye of thy purpose in the cosmic worlds and throughout all eternity.

"Listen ye, my worthy one. I, thy God, and Creator, speak to give ye the message of thy work. Ye are among the Holy Ones. Ye are the highest and must serve to take the message of the divine to all my creations throughout the seven spheres.

"Listen, again, O My Soul, and hark to My words. Thou art the most blessed of all My creatures. Thou art Holy, and filled with My mighty power.

"I give thee grace to take up the work. Take up thy pen and write and I will tell thee what to write. Ye must give to the world My love, through thy talent.

"I grant thee mercy and love, O Soul, and the greatness that comes from thy pen. With this I grant thee the devoted love of all Souls. All will go with thee into the realms of eternity.

"I will grant thee the grace of sainthood — but thee must labor for the qualities of this divine state.

"Ye must become ruler over thyself, and also ruler over all things. I will speak through thee to the Earth world, through thy pen, and through thy voice, thy very countenance and actions. Ye are myself, the Divine Power and I am ye.

"All knowledge of the divine wisdom is at thy command, ye have the understanding to grasp all knowledge within the spiritual spheres.

"I give thee privilege to take up the ministry of My cause, and in reaching sainthood lead Souls back to their true home. The element of thy advancement in time is exceedingly small. So make haste slowly.

"I speak to thee again, and say look to thy Creator only. Look neither left, nor right, below or above, but inwardly to thy Creator, at all times.

"To reach thy Creator ye must travel inwardly, to go outwardly, into the cosmic worlds, to reach thy true home. The only way is through the Tenth door, the Single Eye. Keep this eye filled with Light and the inner ear with Sound!

"If ye seek for miracles ye will not find them. Ye are the grand miracle itself. This and nothing more. Look to it

199

for thyself. Soul is My greatest achievement in all the cosmic creations.

"The existence of Soul throughout eternity is the second of My miracles. I speak of Its love for the divine self. All Souls love and seek the Creator. This is My divine law unto Itself.

"The third divine miracle is the elevation of Soul to Its highest glory. None can escape this noble achievement, even though it may take cycles of time.

"The divine riddle of all seekers of My Holy Heart look in amazement upon whether I existed first, or creation was before Me. I was before creation for I created creation, and created Myself to become the Holy of the Holies. None can deny this.

"I slept within My heart, before creation existed and all through the heavenly spheres the divine seed lay dormant until my will was projected.

"My true reality is in the Ocean of Love and Mercy existing within the true kingdom. Here I lived throughout eternity with My creation until My mercy gave grace to creation in the other worlds below.

"I created in succession each world from the highest plane to the physical world. Populating each with its own unique creation until each was satisfied to live as it is within Itself.

"I made each creation, and creature first with its own counterpart, in the worlds below the Second Grand Division, so there would always be creation, among the plants, animals and mankind.

"When Soul goes above the top of the Third World It becomes one, and creation is of Its own volition out of one source. Man has become God, ITSELF, and thereupon can create without the union of the two selves.

"As the Absolute Father of all, the Ocean of Mercy and Love, I create through projection of My divine will.

"O Soul as ye see this form upon the lotus blossom, ye are given only an illusionary vision, for as God I must assume a form, be it in this true heaven or upon the physical plane so each Soul can see me.

"My entirety is too great for even the greatest. Only the Masters can see Me in All — All in All, and they alone can know the truth of all truths, the reality of all reality, the divine of the divine. No Soul can see Me until it comes into the true realization and abides there. This is so little done in the physical body on earth.

"Then I tell thee, My son of heaven, ye must abide by My law and the word of My supreme son. Look ye forward to entering into the kingdom, and the getting along with thy divine work.

"Ye must know and ye must not tell the true secrets of the heart, except to the heart!

"No man can deceive ye, for ye are wise and filled with divine understanding. Ye are the thrice-born!

"Proceed today with thy divine mission.

"Establish the mission of God's house where it can be found, and take thy stand from it.

"Twice I have spake to thee, O Son of My Heart!

"Hark and look below thy feet!"

The voice died away and we rose from our kneeling positions. There was nothing before us, no being, no lotus flower, only the vast sea of dazzling light, within the circle, and we stood upon what appeared to be a vast glass through which we saw billions upon billions of worlds whirling through the magnificent void of light, spinning, weaving and whirling in great speed. Multitudes of colors flashed through the void, from each spinning world, and then I saw that in all, each represented the divine cosmic planes of the Holy creations.

"God has made an illusionary symbol of the spheres of the heavens so thy eyes can see and understand. Look again!"

"The worlds became stationary and dissolved into flat horizontal planes, transparent for the eyes to see through. Each was thickly populated with wonderful creatures moving busily upon some duty, and millions of floral life growing there. I cannot describe the wonders of them.

"This is enough," said Rebazar Tarzs, and he took my arm. We seemed to drop straight through the worlds without seeing them until a darkness suddenly enveloped us and fear came upon me again. But the great ECK Master held me tight and again we stood above the room where my body was resting in a chair.

I dreaded going back to it, but Rebazar Tarzs pushed me forward. My eyes opened and saw his radiant form. He said. "You have received the wisdom of God. Now you know thy purpose in life. Don't hesitate but go forward in life and do it with your heart and greatest strength."

# THE PROCESS OF DEATH

Rebazar Tarzs: "Tonight's discourse is on the process of death. It is a most extraordinary experience.

"I am going to take you through the art of dying in order to show how Soul leaves the body and enters into the next life. You will be able to watch this process of the physical dying.

"Lie on the bed while I talk briefly. Soul usually leaves the body, in death, through the pineal gland, at the top of the head, not always but usually.

"In the case of a man with a lower consciousness Soul can leave by any chakra. This is the case of most of mankind today.

"I show you again how to leave the body. It is a simple process, by letting the spirit move out of it, through the thousand petalled lotus. Now I am going to let you die. Be still."

I laid very still, wondering at what was going to happen. A numbness began to creep up the feet, gradually higher along my body until it reached the heart center and then stopped. It began again and moved on upward and there was a sensation of something moving out of me, and then I was flying like a bird. I realized that it was the astral body which had moved out of the physical.

I stood with Rebazar Tarzs in the radiant body looking at the clay temple on the bed. It neither breathed nor moved from reflexes. The color of the face was a dun-gray. The eyes were wide open, staring lifelessly, and the radiation or aura was gradually fading.

"You see," said R.T. "The temple of man is being forsakened by all. The only growing thing left in it are the nails and hair. They will grow for a length of time and not being nourished will die, too. That was you in the physical life.

"In leaving the body you experienced a strange feeling of being sucked upwardly. This is normal, for the process of leaving the body is normal, provided that one lets it leave at the top of the head in the manner which I have prescribed in the spiritual exercise.

"Man is all animal in the physical world. That is, he has a physical body called by the Orientals, Isthul Sharir. Inside this clay temple is the astral body, called Sukhshan Sharir, the subtle body, called Nuri Sarup or light body.

"When seen it appears to sparkle with millions of little particles resembling star dust. It is lighter and finer than the physical body. This astral body will take shape in harmony with the character of the individual. In other words no deception is possible in this body. It has five senses, and three sets of chakras as does the physical body. It goes to the astral world upon the death of the physical body, and acts as an instrument of expression upon that higher plane of life.

"Inside the astral body is another body, quite distinctive from the astral. It is called the Karan Sharir, which means the causal or mental body. It is here that the real cause or seeds of all things that are ever to take place in the individual's life are found. It is also called Bij Sharir, meaning seed body. This body is much finer than the astral, as the astral is finer than the physical.

"It may be divided into two or more stratas, each of which is given a different name.

"It is a portion of the mind acting as a sort of sheath around Soul, very sensitive to impressions from Soul or spirit.

"Its functions are to receive and transmit impressions between the mind and Soul, on one side, and between mind and astral body on the other side.

"A perfect record of every experience of man throughout all his existence in life is recorded here. Out of these experiences character is formed and from that character all actions flow.

"The causal body or Karan Sharir, also has five senses and the ten chakras in the causal body is man's highest and finest instrument of action, except the mind itself. Here, I pause to tell you that there are twenty-two spiritual valves or openings in the brain which man has not yet been given complete knowledge about for he knows so little about the other bodies.

"It is through the mind that Soul controls all the lower levels of life working through the other bodies. It is hard to distinguish between the two mind bodies. The mind itself lies closest to Soul, a sheath covering Soul. Both are the same only each have a slight difference of function from the other. Both are derived from the universal mind in Tirkuti, the top of the Third World. Both belong to and are taken from the universal mind, and both must eventually return to the universal mind. Both have extremely high vibrations, and both are full of light, and endowed with great power which is taken from Soul.

"The mind is the fourth sheath, or body in man, more subtle and finer than the mind body, endowed with the greatest of powers for it is closest to Soul.

"When the physical body dies, and Soul passes the Angel of Death, It goes upward discarding each body, and finally leaves the mind, or causal body on the causal plane, in the lower part of the Third World. Then in the region above, called Daswan Dwar, It beholds Itself as pure spirit and knows all things, rejoices in all things by direct perception without the bodies of communication or contemplation.

"Soul does not need the mind or material bodies. It knows by direct perception. All knowledge is opened before it without the need of material bodies.

"I will not take up the mind study here, but will do so in a later discourse.

"The last of the bodies which the individual being comes to is that of Soul. This is the divine spark from heaven which has been sent to earth to receive experience and return to God. All power and consciousness resides in Soul. All below it, even the mind, is unconscious, automatic and mechanical in action.

"Soul is so extremely fine, that it cannot contact the lower

205

worlds without the protective sheaths. And it is for this very reason that the Supreme Being Itself cannot manifest in these material worlds for instruction to man. This is the reason a living ECK Master is necessary. It is the only way that God can manifest himself to man in the earth-world.

"Death, as you see, is not the end of man's life, but another chapter in his existence upon earth. As long as he owes one penny to the earth he must return to pay it. The story of Abraham Lincoln, who walked seven miles after the close of his store at night to give back a few pennies for overcharging a customer, is an example of how this law should be respected.

"The physical body will return to decaying carbon, calcium and $H_2O$.

"After death, the individual is taken to the astral region where Dharam Raya, the Judge of Karma, is throned and judges all according to their reward for good or evil. He is often called the Angel of Death and there is nothing but the judgment handed down and the penalty paid.

"However, under the Master, the disciple's future is in the hands of the Godman. The negative power has no control over him, and the agent of death cannot approach him. The Master will administer the disciple's karma as He thinks best.

"In the mental plane death much resembles sleep and its actual arrival imperceptible, but in the deeper realm of the mind, there are often signs of a great awakening. An expression of ecstasy often overspreads the dying one's face; sometimes there are recognitions of friends who have already passed out into the astral or other planes. In some cases there is a great extension of memory and frequently the dying one will express the thought that his Soul is flying upward which is true, for Soul is really leaving the body as you, often do in contemplation.

"The path which Soul is to start upon is the only path to God. The experience is enormously interesting. The inner body, now encased in its sensitive astral body is often seen leaving the body and going through the walls. There are wonderful visions and voices calling to it to come—but if under the Master nothing can affect it.

"Death consists of chiefly getting rid of or shedding off a worn-out husk which is simply left behind much in the same way as the chrysalis sheath of a moth or other insect is left behind, or as the husks of the growing bud of a bulb are peeled off.

"Many initiates die this way. The body has little or no disturbance, or conflicts, but simply withers up, and the spiritual body, which is in the act of leaving the physical self, grows luminous and shining. There is no painful rendering apart, but the spirit returns to the heart center in the initiate, then withdraws upward to the skull, and peacefully retires.

"The same process starts in the body of the dying uninitiated, but at the same time the unit of the self is torn apart by the physical becoming rebellious and introduces serious conflicts into the body. In the case of aging, diseases spring up in the mind, violent passions, greeds, anxieties, and rigid habits. Thus forming independent centers, they fight through a period of time and rend the body and mind until death supervenes, not as a voluntary withdrawal of the spirit to the other worlds, but simply through the destruction of the organism in which the person functions. This is likely to be painful, undignified and repulsive.

"These Souls often leave the body in the lower chakra of the spine, instead of the natural means, through the spiritual eye, as taught you in contemplation. Normally to the individual, death should be no more painful than birth.

"The art of dying can be practiced daily as you already do, by passing the gates of death on the inner planes by voluntary effort.

"To die is a wonderful experience for you awaken on the other side to find Soul. The real self pervades the mountains, heights and stars, and is a part of your body, and you are in touch with the Souls of all creatures. It is to be assured that you are immortal, and can sit with God in paradise. You are now learning what real freedom is. Yet not too soon for you are still in your astral body and unless the Master desires that you shed it, you will stay in the astral world for rebirth or to study there until the Master believes you are ready for the higher planes.

"Through death each Soul has a gradual rising to the consciousness of the God-Soul, a gradual liberation and self-discovery of the divine germ within itself.

"When Soul is ready to enter into the fourth region, all links with the physical, astral and mental bodies are dropped, and everything with the lower worlds is suddenly broken off.

"Physical death is simply an insignificant thing, about as significant as the breaking of a string. Ordinarily at the instant of death the body and the vital astral force are separated completely from the physical body. But the mind maintains the connection with the physical body for the first five days after death and to a slighter degree for seven days after that. In the final annihilation, however, the separation is not between body and mind, it is the astral annihilation of mind and all the mind impressions.

"There is a liberation of Soul, somewhat of a lesser nature achieved after death of the physical body, for the average man. This comes from three to five days after Soul has left the body. This bliss is of the first world and if the Soul is a truth loving one, it will not reincarnate except at the discretion of the Master for work in this world.

"Other Souls, operating on higher planes, can emerge into the bliss of those planes within days after their physical death. They, also, must wait until the Master decides if they will return to earth again, or not.

"Of course, a few Souls reach the Fourth Plane, after death, and maybe some will go on to the fifth region or above where they may enjoy the divine sport of creation.

"One point further is that the silver cord applies to each body, running like a rope, attached to one another, from the physical to the astral, the astral to the causal, etc. Each is snapped off as the singular, particular body is dropped for Soul to rise higher.

"You see what holds Soul down is the weight of the sheaths, and their baggage.

"This is all for death at the present except you have passed through all the processes of it, seeing the beautiful prototype of yourself in the astral body.

"Incidentally, after man dissolves his astral body it may remain in the vicinity for a number of years, like a worn out shell and those who see it think of it as a ghost of its former owner. Entities from the astral world often enter and use it, playing tricks on the former owner's relatives and friends.

"This is all."

# GENERATING POWER

Rebazar Tarzs: "Let us digress briefly on a point which you are now discovering. You cannot seem to make anything click within yourself. There is a reason for this, inwardly you have emotional drive unless it's over an agitation. Fear is an impelling force which drives one into something negative and this fear is a destructive power, yet by its very nature it can be a negative force used for the purpose of generating a positive action. So there. I am giving you one of the deep secrets of nature. Did not Buddha say that hatred begets hatred? All right, now I tell you this. Hatred can beget love, or in another way of putting it, hatred can beget the product of love. You see?

"What arouses the power within you? Or gets you upset mostly? What starts you talking to yourself on some point? What makes you the most angry? Think of what does. One can really get steamed up over such an issue, or anything another proclaims that you disagree with, but can't say openly. Then you get to talking to yourself and really build up inward pressure and sometimes it comes out orally without you thinking and you are in for an evening of battle.

"I tell you this. I would call this the law of reversed effort. If you want money, it being neither negative nor positive, then don't chase money, but reverse the process which you have had heretofore.

"Build up a genuine hatred for whatever you need in life. Your hatred for it will give you a strong feeling against it, and whatever you hate will certainly become yours for the simple reason that it is drawn to you by your intense dislike.

"Hate begets hate, but the law also means that whatever you hate, you can't get rid of because it attaches itself to you. Ignore it, dislike it, or repel it, and that thing will follow you, haunt you and chase you.

"The actual terror and intense fear of something draws

211

it to you. It makes men crazy with the idea, and by being that it haunts them, chases them and actually manifests into their lives. So if you have the same emotional feelings about something, then you can actually know it's going to happen to you. Live in dread of it, fear it, hate it, and by its very being that thing will come to you. That is the reverse law of God. That is the Kal power in operation. Hate being rich, absolutely be in constant fear of it; yet it becomes a terror for you, with all its crazy ways and lo, suddenly you are rich, for the very thing you feared is upon you.

"Now, furthermore, anger which is a form of fear will also help in drawing money to you, for it forms a thought pattern in your mind against something and that the very thought of being against it will throw the thought pattern into reverse to draw it to you. It is like this. What you are violently against is that which is going to become yours. It's like having a problem which you try to get rid of but hug it to your breast just that much more, and all the while it becomes bigger.

"The Kal power manifests quicker in this earth plane, than the Akal, because it is more powerful with most people, they being negative. The negative manifestation is the result of negative electrical charges in the brain which sets the pattern in the mind, and the attracting thoughts are put into action.

"The way of visualization as taught by the metaphysicians is wrong for they try to teach that all is brought to man because of his visualization patterns in the use of positive power. True but it doesn't work. There is another group which teaches that the purity of character is going to be an asset in the attainment of material and spiritual things. True, but not complete — and third, is the group which believes that they gain materially by the use of the will power. And this is true also, but not completely.

"Remember this, that victory on the issues of a situation is determined not by the plans of the participator, not by the place where he is stationed, not by the number of his supporters or the moral support he may have, but that imponderable force called the spirit, and if you make use of the force, and direct it, as far as it is in your power, you will win.

"If you have the desire for victory then put yourself in the most advantageous position for victory.

"You must have a positive aura for the matter of creation and maintenance of the operation of the law within you. The positive aura is simply the general personal atmosphere, but directly and positively charged by a concentrated effort of will.

"If you should have your real strength of character marred by abnormal self-consciousness, shyness, timidity and sensitiveness, then you would actually suffer from the positive brutality, rudeness and superficiality of the public. Everybody would have a contempt for you. Your aura would not only be negative, but actually attractively negative — that is to say, it would be so negative that it actually would attract more positive natures who would impose on your weakness. This is not unusual — it is a rule of the psychic as well as of the physical world, among animal and men.

"If you would use a mental command at those people to move out of your way demanding respectful attention, then you would get it. You would adopt a mental attitude and personal atmosphere of a person with great confidence.

"Find out your weak spots of personal atmosphere, and then proceed to build up the opposite qualities of mind and character. Find out your negative points of attraction and then proceed to build up their opposite positive qualities. Overcome any fixed and stubborn points that anything is wrong with your mental makeup and proceed from there.

"Once you have filled yourself with positive courage, your degree of concentrated force will be generated so powerfully you can actually be felt in passing through a room.

"Always be direct and positive in your approach on all things. Put all your spiritual force behind your smile, behind your replies, and behind any mental command and flash it right to the point — squarely into the mentality of the persons you wish to work with.

"Two things I would like to point out at this point; first is that you must always edit your thoughts, and see that the others' feelings are your chief concern. Secondly, do not be led into confusing the possessions of ideas with intelligence.

"This world is the theatre of the intellect. This is the play of the mind. However, there is a vast field beyond the mind in which only the developed Soul can enter. It is beyond this world of light and shadows (positive and negative forces) where lie innumerable worlds of intense light, intense color, beauty, rhythm and joy. This is where you wish to dwell constantly. The Master leaves the limitations of the body and travels in these higher worlds in full consciousness and returns to report what he has seen, heard and experienced. Therefore, death is only an illusion as all this world is. When you leave this world, stepping through death's door you can go on to the higher worlds.

"You must attain mastery over the higher faculties to move freely in the other worlds. Whenever anyone believes that the union with God is to dwell fully in conscious contact with the Light and Sound, with extreme joy, they are putting a limit on their concept. We go completely beyond this — for this is only a symbol of God's Light and Sound in the highest region. I desire for you to become efficient enough to travel upon your own through the inner-worlds in order to gain wisdom, knowledge and love.

"Illusion or maya is the cunning cloud of glamour which the negative power has set to trap Soul and hold it prisoner in his empire. The world of illusion will have a downward pull on the senses of Soul to enslave it. This is all under the law of karma, or cause and effect.

"All you do in this world with physical action is the indifferent pure phenomenal reflexes of the ECK transcendental essence; that is the self not only of yourself but of all things. Do you understand this?

"The one and only self is made to seem multiple by the deluding force of your own inborn ignorance.

"Indeed, in highest truth, an elephant is non-real. Nevertheless, you and I are as non-real as that elephant. Everything is God, the infinite, pure and real, boundless and beyond the pairs of opposites, devoid of differentiating qualities.

"This is the final meaning of all wisdom.

"God is the sole reality. That divine one may be found in everything, unaffected by suffering or any fault. Everyone, including you and me is ITS abode, every form is an obscuring figuration within that acting activator we call the ECK.

"The object of showing you the illusion of life is to give you the difference between the universal principles and limited knowledge.

"The flow of the God-power is a tide and ebb flow. It operates in both directions. If you perceive this great truth you are one with the spirit. You will never recognize your power, force, life or every one as being separate from the source of God's attribute. You are never apart from it in thought or action. You recognize no barriers to the illimitability of your supply. While fully cognizant of your individuality, you do not conceive of yourself as a unit and act in accord with that acceptance.

"Man is a center, the center in the body of God. Where is the center? Everywhere. So as long as you continue to think in unity the center projected into a line of extension is connected with the primal power. When, however, you lose the sense of that connection you admit the appearance if not the fact of duality and the great illusion possesses you.

"You thus picture yourself as cast adrift from your moorings in mind. This is the great illusion. You dimly perceive reality, but at a distance. You live in the reality of Soul abandoned to Its own weak, isolated and detached case. You are helpless in the midst of all power. If you see only the physical world as reality, you deliberately cut yourself off from reality and live in a world of illusion. However true the illusion may be, you are subject to your belief and live in an atmosphere of falsity.

"When the mind is closed to these appearances, when the reflection of things opens to reality, reality at once begins to cooperate for use.

"Illusion springs from false beliefs, thoughts, ideas, fertilized by the emotions and made so real the effects produced are factual to your man's limited interpretation. That emotions play a large part in creating a belief in these three illusions is contributory to the idea the great illusion is factual.

"Now I tell you that all around you, and your own being is the net of entanglement called maya, the world creative power. Maya manifests its force through the rolling universe and evolving forms of individuals. To understand that secret —to know how it works, and to transcend if possible, its cosmic spell breaking outward through layers of tangible and visible appearance and simultaneously inward, through all the intellectual and emotional stratification of the psychic, is the pursuit conceived to be the primary and finally undesirable human task.

"Being of the spirit and God substance which render you higher on the scale toward heaven, you have the power to do anything in this world.

"This is all for now."

# SEVEN PRINCIPLES OF CONSCIOUSNESS

Rebazar Tarzs: "Now, I want to talk with you about the seven principles of consciousness. They are as follows:

1. Appreciation, 2. Sincerity, 3. Unselfishness, 4. Idealism, 5. Devotion, 6. Personal effort, and 7. Attainment.

"These are invisible laws: I will attempt to explain further. For example — 1. Appreciation is — appreciation of the teacher; 2. Sincerity is — to inspire the seeker to seek higher levels of consciousness; 3. Unselfishness — the willingness to sacrifice the individual self to the universe; 4. Idealism — the faculty of perceiving spiritual values through a perfect pattern; 5. Devotion — to fill the mind and Soul with love, aspiration and giving of the self to universal consciousness; 6. Personal effort — spiritual motivating force of intelligence which is within all men; 7. Attainment — the reward for spirit action.

"Negative images close the superconscious — positive images open it. Wandering dissipates superconscious expression, while controlled and focused minds attract it.

"Consciousness is the quality of air. It is the diffusing medium, the controller of emotions, the awareness. It's different from the intelligence, reason and emotions, and develops a high grade of consciousness placing them under our control. Insofar as we can absorb the feelings image in the body do we realize we are in control of environmental influence.

"Intuition is a faculty of consciousness, clarity is another. See things as they are and not as they seem.

"Abstraction from the image allows you to be detached from any influence that is undesirable. You become your own creator and no influence can get you under its sway without your voluntary consent.

"The quality of fire, the principle of heart, light and electricity are the motive force, the medium of attachment, and the indication of attachment of life and the medium of diffusing prana throughout all nerve centers, organs, and vital tissues. It makes blood circulate more freely. Mental equipment is purpose and accomplishment and is derived from mind power.

"Non-resistance is a quality of water and the mental quality of receiving influences and impressions. The ability to relax gives you peace and contentment and reflection.

"Stability is a quality of earth, rigid, unchanging and immobile. It gives you the ability to decide and stick to the decision. It gives mental quality to truth, attaching itself to it and not wavering.

"Here are some of the classifications of the qualities just named:

> Stability and rigidness............................Earth
> Relaxation and flowing .....................Water
> Energy and power ...................................Fire
> Freedom and rhythm..............................Air
> Detachment and control ....................Ether

"Mental pictures are divided into: (1) Receptive (feeling image), the feeling and visual pictures or images.

"2. Reflective — creative ideas and faculties of induction and deduction. Faculty of these two are questions and discrimination; faculty of deduction accepts and applies without question.

"3. Motivating — depicts application or action.

"4. Abstract — portrays knowledge and understanding of principles, ideals and symbols.

"Work divided into principles are mechanisms which are commands (mantras).

"1. Principles are knowledge which when applied become wisdom. Principles can be learned thoroughly, reflected upon and viewed from all angles.

"2. Mechanisms are the applying of a principle through cancellation, contemplation or reflection.

"Mantras are the use of a command to impress a principle upon the subconscious mind. When said aloud they are used

218

to carry the feeling of the principle into action. The feeling factor is the best and easiest link with the subconscious.

"Within the ability to act with the feeling image of the commands lies the whole secret of control over the subconscious faculty.

"It is necessary to acquire feeling back of the command words. By experiencing them aloud and catching the feeling we establish direct connection with the subconscious.

"A mental image is developed by stating a command. The feeling embodied must be applied during concentration and to the degree of positive generated, and to that degree only, do we attract direct action of our superconscious.

"One of the greatest secrets of spontaneous action is to recognize the fringe or first approach of negative moods.

"Next one is recognition of a restriction, and seeking the knowledge whereby the restriction can be removed, understanding and practicing the proper mechanism, and beginning yourself to realize that it is possible to accomplish.

"Reality is approached through illusion. We cannot disregard the world. To seek reality by ignoring the world is to fool ourselves. There must be balance in all things.

"This is all."

# MAYA, THE QUEEN OF ILLUSION

Rebazar Tarzs: "Tonight I want to start a discussion on the subject of Maya and its spiritual relationship based on the theory of relativity.

"Since Einstein formulated his theory of Relativity, almost every book on science and philosophy in the West has given some reference to the principles of Relativity. If you would count the number of books written on the subject, or those giving reference to this, I would safely say they would number about 25,000.

"The gain to philosophy by the theory of Relativity is the famous doctrine of Maya expounded by Shankacharya, which you may find difficult to understand. It is greatly simplified if one can translate Maya as a measure or a measuring instrument.

"The new physical science definitely comes under the Kal Power, or negative teachings. It begins by correcting the instruments of measurement. The subject of study for modern science is not nature itself but our observation of nature. The Law of Nature tells us little or practically nothing about nature but certainly something about man. Assertions about the world are really assertions about ourselves. What man experiences in the ordinary course of life relatively is nothing but the Absolute experienced in a special way.

"Nature knows nothing of space and time separately, being concerned only with the four dimensional continuum. Yes, where space and time are welded together inseparably into the product which we may designate as space-time. Man's views divide this into space and time and introduce a false division between them. The law of Relativity which gives us a relative time has almost replaced the theory of evolution formulated by Darwin, based upon one uniform time. Natural laws do not explain anything in a wide sense of the word, but tell what happens, not how, or why it happens.

"The theory of relativity asserts that the laws of phenomena in the system of physical bodies, for the observer who is connected with it, will be the same whether this system is at rest or is moving uniformly and rectilinearly. If this law is applied to psychology it means we can know only about the existence of subtle or invisible lives similar to our own.

"This theory also points to the synthetic process of unifying different points of view rather than the analytic operations of distinguishing between them. It inquires into the possibility of obtaining statements of facts which hold good when a reference system is exchanged for another. Forces are, in general, artificially induced by any change of coordinates. Therefore, when a man becomes an ECK Initiate, there is a great change in his bodily coordinates and his measures. New forces and new life then begin to be formulated.

"A gravitational field of force is exactly equivalent to a field of force introduced by a transformation of the coordinates of references. This means that as soon as man thinks about Soul, or God, he creates or enters into a new reference system (or life), and his being as man and his former coordinates (or life) begin to change completely. Gravitational forces and the geometrical properties of the regions, planes, places or fields in which these forces occur are but different aspects of the same thing. This means that gravitational fields and fields of forces artificially introduced by change of coordinates (or life) are equivalent. A gravitational field may be compared to the Sarup of the Mahanta. The field or force introduced artificially by his Bhakta-devotion through change of his former life becomes equivalent to the gravitational field.

"The beginner on the path of devotion must remember that a natural gravitational field cannot be transferred away from where attracting matter exists. Therefore, he must give up attraction and repulsion and surrender to God before he can hope to ascend to a higher gravitational field. The theory of Relativity shows that the course of a ray of light depends upon the geometry of the space through which it moves. No space is rigid and no system of reference is rigid.

"The quantities which enter as multipliers into expression for the internal element also specify the gravitional forces in any region. The stars as we see them are not where we see them. Their lights are curved when they pass near the gravitational field of the sun. This fact has been proven in the photographs of stars at the time of the sun in eclipse. The light projected by a broadcasting station is curved where there is an electro-magnetic field created by aerials on the house tops of those who have TV or radio sets. Similarly, the light of Soul is also curved when we are in the company of those whom we like or dislike.

"Matter also has a wave structure. The more matter there is in the universe, the more curved space there will be. Therefore, those who have large families and who are attracted to them get into more curved spaces. This is what Shankacharya calls Vpadhies. The more the space is curved, the more rapidly it will bend back on itself and, as a consequence, the smaller the diverse will be, just as a circle which curves rapidly becomes one which curves more rapidly.

"The tendency of modern physics is to resolve the whole material universe into waves and nothing but waves. These waves are of two kinds, bottled up waves which are called matter or Jiva, and unbottled waves which are the radiation, or light, or Bhagwan. The process of annihilation of matter is merely that of unbottling imprisoned wave-energy and setting it free to travel through space. These concepts reduce the whole universe to a world of radiation or existent. It no longer seems surprising that the fundamental particles of which matter is built up should exhibit many properties of waves. This means that every Jiva has within it the properties of God.

"If we know that an electron is at a certain point in space, we cannot specify exactly the speed with which it is moving. Therefore, a Jiva which is attached to the body does not ordinarily know its power to spread anywhere. In the same way, if we know the exact velocity of an electron, nature refuses to let us discover its exact position in space.

"Therefore, God cannot be located at one place and if you do as is sometimes done in Saguna Upasova* you cannot perceive its infinite motion and Omnipresence at the same time, or you cannot know its Nirgin Sarup† at the same time. Matter and radiation are found equally to resolve themselves into waves. Therefore, the Omnipresent God is more real than God located at one place.

"The relative (jiva or matter) is not present in the Absolute; it is but the Absolute experienced in a different way. Thus, there is no reason for the Relative, no origin or cause of it; it has no purpose and serves no end and in no way does it increase the glory of the Absolute, since it is always the Absolute.

"When you make objective relatives out of things which are but relations to man, then we have created monstrocities which henceforth will ever haunt our philosophical atmosphere. Good and evil are real enough as relations of things to man. To absolutize them is to create insuperable and insoluble problems. The Absolute is truly beyond good and evil.

"Relativity reigns everywhere in the three worlds. What is right for one is wrong for the other. Nothing is right or wrong in itself. Thus that which is the right or duty of the disciple is wrong for the householder, or for the woodsman. No scheme of life or set of rules is right or wrong in itself. The doctrine of non-violence preached by many in Indian sects is good for those who were in the caste but it can't be applied to other men as householders who have to take care of their families. It can't be followed by those who are meat eaters.

"The theory of Relativity states that the universe is non-mechanical. Time, space, causation, motion, duration, mass, force, etc., are relative and have no absolute significance.

---

*Highest understanding one can have.
†The SUGMAD true body—Ocean of Love and Mercy.

They are not attributes of physical realities but are relations whose value changes with the observer's attitude to the object. This is the ultimate and perfect realization which transcends the subject-object relation.

"As change of coordinates produces a gravitational field, our center of interest must be transferred to the system as a whole. The value of the whole is greater than the value of the sum of its parts. Philosophy begins with a sense of totality. Aesthetic pleasures arise when the ECK discovers Itself in the sensible. Therefore, gross objects and unseen Soul are one. Death and decay will exist in our midst, for us, if we ignorantly consider ourselves as human beings, for the Atma (Soul) is all there is ever in immortality, other than God.

"Things are not what they seem. There is an Absolute thing in the world but we must look deeply for it. The things that first present themselves to our notice are, for the most, relative. The beautiful hues which flood our consciousness under stimulation of light waves have no relevance to the objective reality. For a color blind person, the hues are different.

"Man knows nothing about the real nature of the constitution of an atom. All that he knows is only the radiation that comes out of it and never the sources of the radiations. We can never identify an electron at one time with the electron at another, if in the interim the atom has radiated energy. The electron ceases to have the property of a thing as conceived by common sense. It is merely a region from which energy may radiate. Radiation, too, is only a series of events of which the last perceptible ones are occuring in the observer's brain.

"Radiation moves like water but breaks up into grains of photons (light-quanta) and appears as particles as soon as it encounters matter. Therefore, when you see something which is not your true self, that something is changed into matter, and the observer is also changed into jiva. When we see God everywhere, there is no obstacle and radiation is not obstructed.

"Radiation waves are mere mathematical waves. They possess no physical reality. The event of constituting light waves are only known through their effect upon our eyes, optic nerves or brain and these effects are not themselves. They are logical constructions of our mind.

"Nature is honest at heart and she only resorts to these apparent shifts of concealments when we are looking for something which is not there. Separation in standpoint, or in order and level, is knowledge tending to supercede the motion of separation in existence. To turn space into a variable is to make a mental factor enter it. The universe requires re-interpretation. There are as many truths in the physical world as there are possible ways of looking át a thing. To think of objects apart from the men who study them is to think of abstractions. It is like two ends of the same stick. You cannot have one without the other. An object is never independent of the conditions affecting a particular observer. The world known by an ordinary human being is a sense-world. What the five senses tell him constitutes this world. If the earth looks flat and is actually round, seems stationary but is continually rotating, the error is evidently in the observer himself for his senses are at work in moulding and presenting the picture of the earth to him. We carry our world views wherever we go. We make an abstraction from all possible appearances of an object and then proceed to assert that we have seen the object. There is a wide discrepancy between experience and truth of experience. The true view point is the viewpoint of the whole, the false viewpoint is the knowledge from any one point. The first is Absolute and true.

"What is immediately seen as the outside thing is really the mental picture and being purely mental, it is not distant from the mind itself. Mind unconsciously projects perceptions into space and then views the thing of its own making. Our thoughts or observations of these objects really are our experiences of them and these thoughts have no position in space. A blind man who was operated upon and recovered his sight thought at first that all objects touched his eyes.

He could not judge the smallest distance and couldn't understand that the things were outside each other. The reason why we see multiplicity is that out of our experiences, we unconsciously select only that in which we are interested. We may be doing some work and the clock strikes but we don't hear the sound. Consciousness grades down to dimness or even to nothingness when we pay no attention to what we see and it lights up the object where there is good concentration. Therefore, mind makes the world. The images are not produced by experience but they themselves produce experience. Thought has imprisoned us and thought may release us. The science of relativity has exploded the myth of the common-sense conception of a world of reality as some solid tangible mass existing by itself.

"Every thought and act that endeavors to maintain a material existence is a waste of energy and a lost opportunity to spiritual progress. Spirit withdraws when matter holds our attention. A spiritual thinker desires the testimony of the physical senses and translates things back into their original substance through spirit. Eddington says 'The Absolute world is of so different a nature that the relative world with which we are acquainted seems almost like a dream.'

"Therefore, the Absolute consciousness of the whole would be unconscious of anything i.e., it would be the absence of any objective universe. This means in other words that the world is subjective and therefore full of divine substance.

"The Western culture teaches that everyone should be ready to die for his country. It is a philosophy which brings death to millions of men because it is made up of divided national spirit. The divine wisdom teaches that everyone should be ready to live for the good of all God's creatures. It is a philosophy which gives eternal life to those who want it.

"Which is better and gives the fullness of life? The dictator and politician have no wisdom. They will have to give up the relative point of view and sit at the feet of the saints to learn the wisdom of wholeness. Then only, will they be able to solve many of their difficult problems. A higher culture treats all as brothers or as one's own self.

"War can be permanently stopped only by the God-culture and not by paper treaties. In the absence of God, parties and divisions exist and create endless chaos economically and psychologically. The true remedy is to destroy all negativism and try to create the brotherhood of love between men. Unless this is done, then all powerful nations will continue to prey upon the weaker and there will be no end to trouble. Man only removes one kind of selfishness to create another. An act, which in the life of a man is considered cruel, is praised when done in the name of his nation. National cruelty reaps its own karma. Unless youth is properly educated in God-principles the earth will continue in its present way. Man must become a citizen of the world looking after his fellows' needs, not a citizen of a nation.

"However, all affairs in the three worlds below the Second Grand Division are ruled by the negative creative forces and will always be in a state of flux, from good to bad and vice versa.

"The theory of Relativity has clearly proven itself by mathematical equations that space and time are not fixed but relative and that man can increase them as he likes by changing the system of philosophical references of the observer, thus creating his own worldly paradise.

"A man's life is not developed by dying for his cause. He can expand his space time by living for the whole of humanity, that is for the good of all God's creatures."

# THE MIND AND ITS FUNCTIONS

R.T.: "I will disgress for a few minutes while talking about the mind. The human mind has never been taxed to the limit of its ability. Man does not know the full extent of its power and not many use more than a fifth of their brain's potential. But the brain can be likened to a recorder. Anything that makes an impression on the mind, and a good deal that seems to make no impression at all, sinks below the level of the consciousness and is recorded and stored for future use. It becomes part of the total of man's experience. Hence, your encounter became a part of your experience.

"Furthermore, he tried to establish an association of ideas of himself in your mind which stimulates a recall response pattern. It is a complicated, continuous process, hooked up to the activity of your sensory nervous system.

"The response pattern used here and described is to relieve the objective mind of the burden of constantly being aware of all the trivia one picks up during his daily routine. It is largely an automatic or reflex action, and we can be grateful that it is. If it were not, we would never remember anything, nor would we have time to explore new ideas.

"If most of man's subconscious process were not automatic, if things did not become habitual, the simplest act would be an extremely complicated process requiring intense concentration, a conscious tracing out of the intricate motor movements, such as walking.

"An unbalanced person usually indulges in fantasies, or even spontaneously acts out the fantasies, some of which may be of a sexual nature. Secret memories and suppressed desires are revealed. He may have strong feelings of guilt, or shame, or feel exceedingly hostile because of his subjective revelations. This may overtake the personality and weaken the ego, making it unstable to the point whereby it will disintegrate.

"The ability to understand God is one that can be learned when one understands the principles it is based upon. The first principle is the law of suggestion. People vary in their susceptibility to suggestion, but all except the most negative people are influenced by it. Advertisers realize the potency of suggestion and the susceptibility of man to it; hence the constant barrage of communication on radio and television, and advertising on signboards, newspapers and magazines.

"Man's attitude is mostly autosuggestion—but it is the manner in which he uses it that determines its good or bad effect. It would seem that most people have a negative attitude, which is always pouring harmful ideas into the subjective self.

"A negative attitude is insidious and destructive. People who talk of another's severe illness often find themselves feeling badly. Imagination plays an important role in the effects of the attitude good or bad!

"The negative attitude produces inner negative suggestions and this starts a vicious circle, with a state of anxiety producing symptoms, and increasing symptoms usually produce an increased state of anxiety. You produce cycles of courage, and joy as well as the opposite. Too often we are equally aware of the rewards of spiritual failure. Without a negative attitude we could do a better job.

"Will power has little or nothing to do with the success or failure of an appointed task—the emotions of the devotee is the deciding factor. Negative suggestions are emotional responses to stress. People have a greater fear of failing than they do of succeeding, and because of negative suggestion, each spiritual success increases the fear of failing, for the higher a man advances, the more he has to lose if he fails. His imagination brings that fact home to him sharp and clear. The vicious cycle continues.

"But the negative attitude can be controlled by faith in

Christian Science, Divine Science, Mental Science, magnetic healing, sacred shrines and faith cures.

"Take for example the absentee healer. The patient is interviewed by the healer and goes home, convinced he is going to get well. At an appointed hour, arranged between the healer and patient, the latter takes his seat with perhaps the healer being a thousand miles away. Through magnetism or mental telepathy the patient receives the healer's treatment. He may be cured at once, or it may take several treatments. But the truth of the matter is, the healer might be doing anything and the patient, unaware, sitting faithfully at home receives all sorts of vibrations which he is convinced are emanating from the healer.

"Most people claim to have psychic powers but are only deceiving themselves. Those proclaiming occult powers often merely create within themselves auditory or visual hallucinations. The occultists are past masters in the art of self-suggestion.

"Man is misled in his thinking by emotions, rather than by intelligence. The negative attitude within is always ready to set up a conflict within man—a conflict of 'Can I, or can't I?' Therefore, eliminate body consciousness and breath control through the ECK Master, and keep the mind on him at all times.

"The Nuri-Sarup eliminates the 'can't I?' and substitutes faith in the Master. When a negative attitude becomes part of one's routine of thinking it is very difficult to destroy without the Master's help. A person's attitudes are the sums of his experiences. Thus he is more susceptible to negative suggestions if he has suffered much.

"The manner in which a person reacts to early experiences tends to crystallize into a behavior pattern. So, if a person is basically insecure or feels inferior, he will think more or less negatively for his entire life unless taught to use positive thinking.

"Religions and cults consciously use hypnosis, self-hypnosis and auto-suggestion, whether they will admit it or not. It is an established fact that the art of suggestion exists in rhythmic breathing and excessive breath retention which produces a peculiar form of self-intoxication taught in various metaphysical schools.

"They are first taught monism or morsoidism which means to concentrate upon one idea or one thought. From here it is just one step into the samadhi state. The state of meditation, which the Buddhist monks in Tibet go into, is a hypnotic state, brought about by folding their hands and gazing at their thumbs which creates within themselves a dissociation from where they are, and to all intents and purposes, splits them off for a time from the outside world. In this meditative state they are able to center their whole attention upon their various problems until they come up with some kind of a solution.

"Relaxation is the key to the elimination of pain. You can be either a victim of negative suggestion or a master of the positive approach. You can be psychologically prepared to suffer pain.

"Often when we have a tough job to do, the ego will try to lead us away to a more pleasurable subject. If allowed to have its own way, the ego would send the body on an endless search for pleasure. It is governed by the pleasure principle. It cannot weigh pro and con what is best for the individual because it cannot reason.

"The objective mind must do that, and must control the pleasure-seeking ego. With the right attitude toward work, work can be a pleasure that is sought by the ego. Whether or not you get pleasure from work, or are completely bored by it, depends upon your attitude and behavior pattern.

"If, as a child, you were given no incentive to work, you will have a difficult time applying yourself to a task. But bad behavior patterns and wrong mental attitudes can be overcome—by a restraining of the mind. A healthy outlook can be firmly implanted in your mind until it becomes a permanent conditioned reflex.

"A symptom is only the expression of a hidden emotional problem and a severe problem to be dealt with. Often the Master will make you go over your problems so often that

232

you slowly become desensitized to them, reacting to them with less and less energy until the saturation point has been reached.

"You must be continually aware of yourself at all times. You must constantly analyze your actions and motives in the light of what you have learned from the ECK Masters. You do this until the new pattern of behavior becomes a subconscious process and your reactions are automatic.

"When you are in deep samadhi, and the ECK Master has you in hand traveling through the inner worlds, the scene is usually one which appeals to the pleasure principle, seated in the subconscious mind. All suggestions should appeal to this pleasure principle, which is emotional rather than intellectual.

"The subjective is more concerned with the pleasures of life. It is when those pleasures the subjective minds seeks are desired that frustration results. The subjective self is always seeking some way to fulfill its desires. The first pleasure principle one experiences after birth is satisfaction of hunger. When its stomach is filled the babe is contented. He thinks of eating as being a very pleasurable event, for it satisfies the basic desire of life, of keeping its body alive.

"When the babe becomes an adult and other pleasures are denied, the subjective mind may compensate for those desired pleasures by creating a feeling of hunger. The objective mind reacts to this feeling with the thought of food and provides it. It is interesting to see that the food selected is usually sweet, or very rich which further caters to the pleasure principle. Such people are usually too fat and no amount of exercise will reduce them. The only way is to avoid starchy or sweet food, eating between meals, and only enough to satisfy hunger.

"Suggestion works best when it appeals to man's pleasure principle. This is why many so-called teachers of truth will work upon this principle, often known as selfishness, greed or by other names. They appeal to its nature in man.

"Suggestion to it has force and once implanted, these suggestions take the form of energy and this energy must be expressed in action.

"The teacher may lull his devotees into a light trance so they become suggestible, and their minds are narrowed to one thought or idea. The threshold of their consciousness is lowered, allowing access to the uncritical part of the mind—the subjective!

"There is one obstacle that might arise when a seeker, who has no Master, attempts to train himself in samadhi and that is the appearance of a defense mechanism which tends to hinder the hypnotic state.

"This defense mechanism is a sort of resistance the mind creates to defeat the trance effort. It is seen in the form of itching, restlessness, sudden unexplainable anger or dropping off into regular sleep.

"Some seekers, when attempting relaxation, will instead of relaxing become more tense, and the harder they try to relax, the more tense they become, so contemplation is impossible. Or they feel an itch on some part of the body and have the desire to scratch. The more they resist the more intense it becomes, so that it begins to torment the mind. Sometimes contemplation progresses beautifully when there is a sudden surge of anger, or nervousness in the seeker which he can't explain. Other times he may go sound asleep.

"If the seeker is under an ECK Master, these conditions will cease and his spiritual endeavors will be properly corrected.

"During a half-hour radio program, you usually get three commercials expounding a certain commodity. Perhaps, you do not consciously listen to the commercial, and perhaps you even reject it impatiently. But the subconscious mind, nevertheless receives the suggestions, and sometime in the future when you have need for that commodity, you will automatically reach for the brand so named in the commercial you had rejected.

"The power of suggestion lies in its appeal to man's emotional rather than his intellectual natures, for if man were to evaluate a suggestion he would destroy much of its power.

234

"However, man thinks emotionally, and a suggestion, if presented consistently and sincerely, though rejected by the objective mind, passes into the subconscious where it takes root.

"Then, when the objections and resistances to the suggestion are finally broken down, the suggestion rises to the conscious mind and the individual acts upon it, completely unaware that he had at one time rejected the idea, or, if he is aware that he had once rejected the suggestion, he will go through a process of rationalization in which he finds an acceptable reason or excuse for acting upon it.

"Rationalization is the emotional process of thinking. It is designed to protect the ego from feelings of guilt, or to be more specific, it is the process whereby the ego protects itself from guilt by justifying the act which is committed or contemplated.

"Thus a person can think bad thoughts or even do a wrong or unkind act and completely justify his actions by telling himself that in the long run what he is doing, or has done or is about to do is right, though on the surface it may appear wrong. In this way his ego can assure him that he is right after all!

"The prestige factor heightens the power of suggestion. A suggestion coming from a prominent person will more readily impress man than a suggestion coming from one who has no prestige at all.

"Prestige is a single asset of most so-called Holy Men. It is his stock in trade. He convinces you that he is, and will take your affairs in hand, and you are impressed, to such an extent that you fall under his power.

"Most people are hypersuggestible in every way and the so-called Holy Ones know this. And from the minute you enter his aura his will is working upon you. He even has catchlines and slogans in his literature which usually refers to him as the greatest in the world.

"He is even surrounded by his local pitchmen who sing his praises and are trained to move at his command. His personality completely dominates at all times. His movements are flamboyant and well-timed. He is quick and sharp, and always on top of the situation. Confidence exudes from his every movement and he keeps his devotees off balance and confused.

"He is like a stage hypnotist who has many tricks up his sleeve which can be used instantly. But now I am trying to get over the point of prestige

"One of the tests you can tell whereby the teacher is or is not sincere is by two simple statements he often gives his devotees—especially those who do not understand nor successfully follow his technique of meditation. He tells them 'You are resisting. You are not cooperating.' He never admits that his technique is wrong or he himself is at fault. It is always the devotee who is wrong.

"In this same manner when he fails to convince a seeker that he is their teacher, then he assures the seeker in a gentle, indirect way that it is his fault that he is not seeing the truth. That he is subconsciously resisting truth and not co-operating, or concentrating. And he always assures the seeker that if he attends his class just one more time he will know that his is the only path to God.

"One of the most popular misconceptions of a teacher is the belief that he will hypnotize you and that his devotees are either weak-minded or below average in intelligence. Nothing could be further from the truth. The more intelligent a seeker is, the easier it is to take him as a devotee; and usually this is done through appeal to his senses and reasoning.

"It is extremely difficult to give the truths to a normal person, or a skeptic for they have not the grasp of understanding or the staying mental power that others have.

"The belief that unworthy teachers can rob the devotee of his will power is also erroneous. Instead, the unscrupulous neatly turns the seekers' will power to work for his cause and makes use of it in an unscrupulous way. Then it seems that the teacher has complete power over the seeker. Instead, the seeker has been tricked into the use of his stubborn nature, reverted to an ideal which only hinders the teachers' intentions.

"There are several degrees in samadhi; varying from the light state of relaxation to the suspended animation that the Hindus achieve, where the pulse rate and heart beats are slowed until they are almost imperceptible and there is no visible sign of life. This state is virtually impossible for occidentals to obtain; although with training, they can go into a very deep somnambulistic state where there is the cosmic consciousness prevalent.

"While in this state the objective mind is set aside, allowing direct access to the subconscious and the cosmic mind in man. Then he is under control of the Master Power and receives divine wisdom which pours through into the subconscious and is stored up for release into the conscious mind at the proper time; or a light trance is brought out into the conscious mind for immediate release into the world.

"Trance or samadhi is a valuable aid to writers and artists, allowing them freer access to the mass of material stored into the subconscious mind. Actors can profit by being relieved of that tension known as stage fright. Their memories improve so they can remember their lines easily and reduce the true lines from their memorized scripts.

"The relief from the symptom may be only temporary when the emotional conflict causing it has not been dealt with, and there is always the possibility that the symptom will reappear in the matter of days, weeks or months, perhaps in a totally different or exaggerated form. These symptoms can make an invalid of the devotee if they are severe enough.

"The symptom is a crutch upon which the patient leans, and this is considered his karma. The Master knows that if it is removed, as in severe cases, the personality tends to collapse, or disintegrate. Without the crutch the devotee can no longer maintain his balance with society; and unless he is under the Master's care, he could destroy himself or commit aggressive acts against his fellow man.

"The symptom is more bearable to the patient than the underlying problem he is repressing.

"Symptoms manifest themselves symbolically, physiologically or both. The symbolic symptom involves the muscles or senses by crippling them so they cannot be used as in paralysis of an arm or leg. Other symbolic symptoms are convulsions, trembling, loss of sight, hearing, depression, extreme tiredness, and other noticeable physical feelings.

"When physiologically, these symptoms show up as a permanent state of anxiety and tension, the devotee is usually irritable and easily disturbed. He might complain of stomach disorder and all sorts of pain. Anxiety and tension experienced over a long period of time can lead to actual organic illness, mucous colitis, ulcers, migraine headaches, and heart conditions, all of which the Master can take away by eliminating the emotional problems, underlying the tension and anxiety.

"A parent image in others can often have a direct reaction on the devotee's emotional life. Everyone reacts to the stress of life with their particular patterns of behavior. These behavior patterns are learned and tend to remain fixed throughout one's lifetime. Normally, a person's behavior pattern toward stress is that he reacts in a rigid manner, and he reacts in the same way to the same kind of stress every time. His behavior pattern doesn't change because he can't understand what makes him react as he does.

"The Master must take care in removing the emotional trauma so it will gradually lose its power and the devotee gains confidence.

"The feeling of guilt and shame is the greatest problem the Master has to handle in his devotees.

"Remember all that has been told you. You are the next in line for the spiritual mantle, to become the Mahanta, the living ECK Master.

"This is all!"

# INDEX

## A

Adept, 153

Aggression, Purpose of, 63-68

Analytical Thinking, Eliminate, 148

Anami, Nameless Place, 150, 152, 191-196, 197

Angel of Death, 205, 206

Apollonius of Tyana, 198

"Astral World, Influences of" (Chapter), 89-96

Astral
  Body (Sukhsham Sharir), 151, 203-206, 209
  Entities, 209
  Influences, 89-96
  Life Span of the, 25
  Plane, 97-100, 105, 159, 168
  Will Power, 87
  World, 181

Astrology, 111

Ataras (Planet), 197

Atma
  Lok, 111
  Sarup, 64, 70

Atmosphere
  Five Layers of, 97-106
  Of Concentrated Will, 213
  Of Places, 112
  Weaknesses of Personal, 213

Atom(s)
  Constitution of the, 225
  Duality of the, 99
  Endowed With Power, 186, 187
  Law Forms the, 140, 141

Plays Its Part in Creation, 188
  Power, Life-Principle of the, 127
  Rain of Perfect (Souls), 192
  Shining Stream of the, 115
  Spiritual, 193
  Stimulated, 102
  The Perfected, 194
  Universes Sustained Through the, 165

At-One-Ment, 175, 178, 193

Attachment, 31
  Difference Between Detachment and, 95
  Dropped From Mind, 33

Attention, 84, 85

Attitude, 117, 122
  Autosuggestion, 230
  Neutral, 18
  Of Balanced Mind, 30, 95
  Sum of Experiences, 231
  Toward
    Love, 29
    Others Change Situations, 67

Aura
  Man's, 99
  Master Reads, 95
  Of Love For Master, 23
  Positive and Negative, 213

Awakening
  After Death, 206
  Of Knowledge, 138
  Of Soul, 152, 178
  Of Woman, 177

239

# B

Balance
In All Things, 219
Needed In Lower Worlds, 29
Ourselves in Life, 63-65
The Attitudes of Love, 29, 30
"Becoming God" (Chapter),
149-154
Beethoven, 120, 173
Book of Revelations, 165, 173
Brahm (Negative Power), 167-
169, 174, 176, 179
Buddha
Balanced Life, 65
Middle Path, 29
Sayings of, 211

# C

Causal Body (Karan Sharir),
151, 204
Cause and Effect, 60, 126, 127
Centrifugal & Centripetal Flows,
154
Cerebrospinal System of Nerves,
125, 129
Chakras, 43, 108, 109, 203, 204
Child of Light, 54
Chosen One, The, 146
Church
Control of Masses, 13, 14
Moral Code of the, 94
Worship in, 111
Civilization Changing, 13
Colors, Meaning of, 99
"Consciousness, Seven Principles
of" (Chapter), 217-220
"Consciousness, The Divine"
(Chapter), 155-160
Consciousness
Accumulative, 125
Matured Through Soul, 120
Of Godhead, 177

Of God-Soul, 208
Of Great Masters, 29
Of No Body, 193
Of Space, 137
Scattering of, 125
Two Streams of, 29
Universal, 178
Contemplation, 123, 133, 146,
152, 234
Contradiction, Lack of
Understanding, 74
"Cosmic Worlds, The"
(Chapter), 97-106
Cosmic
Body of Nameless One, 193
Catastrophe, 91
Consciousness, 22, 42, 150,
159, 176, 177
Light, 17, 178
Man, Lower, 175
Mind, 237
Planes, 158, 201
Power, 72, 93
Consists of, 39
Control of, 42, 123-125
Development of, 108
Instrument of, 92, 132
Jesus Christ, Name for, 71
Sound Current, 11
Struggle, 90
Cosmic
World
As Real as Physical, 73
Explorers of, 97
First, 32
Inner, 152
Invisible Structure, 72
One Power in, 125, 126
Personification of, 92
Within Man, 11
Vibrations, 17
Cosmos Complete, Plan of, 178
Co-Workers of Universe, 12 39
135
Creation

240

Basis of, 40, 42
Cosmic Planes of, 201
Depends Upon Law of Love,
141
Divine Sport of, 208
Explained, 200
Evolution of, 197
Of Physical Worlds, 167
Positive Aura Necessary for,
212
Principle Factors in, 187
Sat Nam Rules All, 165
Soul, Greatest Cosmic, 200
Started for God's Beings, 163
Top of World of, 198
Unfolds Within, 156
Unmanifested Masses Before,
163
We Have Power of, 34

## D

Daswan Dwar, 101, 174, 176,
205
"Death, The Process of"
(Chapter), 203-210
Death
An Illusion, 214
Hold Off, 162, 163
Of Physical Body, 152, 225
Philosophy of, 227
Second, The, 175
Thoughtlessness Leads to, 156
Desire
Is Feeling, 139
Without Conflict, 67
Detachment From Fears, 79
Dharam Raya (Angel of Death),
206
Disciples of Master, 23
Discrimination
Between Aggression &
Submission, 65
Of Love, 17, 18

Divine
Cause, 194
Challenge, 183
Consciousness, 150, 152, 155-
160
Creative Force of God, 115
Desire, 135
Drama, 10, 34
Ethers, Intelligence, Substance,
140
Goal, 46
Knowledge, 157
Law, 128, 184, 200
Love, 156, 194
Mission, 201
Power, 113, 157, 158, 177, 199
Reality, 107
Riddle, 200
Seed, 200
Self, 108, 149, 157, 193, 200
Spirit, 157
Vacuum, 156
Will, 134-136, 200
Wisdom, 199, 227, 237
Donne, John (Devotion 17), 22
Dying Daily, Art of, 207

## E

ECK
Center of all Expression, 34
Creative Nature of the, 34, 111
Current, 184
Essence, Pure, 172, 214
Initiate, 222
Love the, 117
Marriage of Soul and, 115
Mastership of, 158
Potential Energy, 126
Primal Substance, 40
Procedure of Teachings, 94
Represents Light and Sound,
158
Saints Help Mankind, 194

241

Secrets of, 20
Should Control Our Lives, 9,
54, 94
Spirit, Counterpart of, 176
Will Power Holds Thought on,
133
"ECK Master, Love For The"
(Chapter), 21-26
ECK Master, 167, 173, 184, 231
Believe in the, 142
Explored Cosmic Worlds, 97
ECK Master
Gopal Das, 181-190
Guides Spiritual Rhythm of
Soul, 11
Has Seen Face of God, 155
Lai Tsi, 145
Light of the World, 165
Opens Devotee's Heart, 79
Rami Nuri of Venus, 165-172
Settles in Chela After
Initiation, 48
Sought for Guidance, 29
Spiritual Destiny of, 19, 22
Surrender to the, 148
Teachings of the, 149
Traveling with the, 233, 234
Uses, Awakens Man's Power,
37, 38
Who is the, 74
Word and Will, God's, 133
Yaubl Sacabi, 143-148
ECK Power, 93, 94, 110, 165,
181
Attract the, 109
Channel for the, 38, 94, 108
Control of the, 10, 111
Creative, 122, 166
Essence of the, 40, 57, 127
Force of Love, 113
God and Man are, 146
Is Not God, 72
Masculine-Feminine
Expressions in, 114
Surrender to the, 75

Within Man, 37
ECKANKAR
Goals of, 94
Teachings, 93
A Blessing, 10
Basic Elements in Body of,
28
Distinguished From
Philosophical, 153
Follow Mystery Schools, 15,
16
What are the, 172
Ego
Eliminate, 50
Exposed, 77
Pleasure-Seeking, 232
Protected, 235
Works for Lower Self, 135
Einstein's Theory of Relativity,
221-228
Electro-Magnetic Fields, 41, 42
Emerson, 57, 59
Emotion
Balance of, 79, 134
Controlled, 140
of Aspirant, 77
Spring of, 78
Emotional
Body of Man, 110
Conflict, 237
Problems
Eliminated by Master, 238
Hidden, 232
Process of Thinking, 235
Response to Stress, 230
Energy, 130, 166
Esoteric Philosophy, 14
Etheric Body Attacked, 24
Evolution, 179, 221, 222
"Experience of Spiritual
Wealth, The", (Chapter), 123-
128
Experiences Benefit Growth, 109
Eye of Hurricane, Be Like, 134

242

## F

Faith, Keystone of Spiritual Life, 74
Fear
  An Impelling Force, 211
  Destroy, 38, 131, 132
  Detachment from, 79
  Draws Feared Thing to You, 211
  Enemy of the Heart, 131
  Of Failure, 230
Feeling Combined With Thought, 113, 114
Fifth Plane, 25, 111, 126, 150, 152, 165, 208
First & Second Grand Division, 163
First World, 34, 35, 168
Fountainhead, Divine, 35, 38, 40, 63, 110
Fourth Plane, 152, 159, 176, 208
Free Will, 86, 87, 139
Future, The, 137, 148

## G

"God, Becoming" (Chapter), 149-154
"God, Channels To" (Chapter), 13-16
"God, The Keystone To" (Chapter), 55-62
"God-Realization. A Dialogue On" (Chapter), 9-12
"God, The Face Of" (Chapter), 191-196
"God, The Feeling Of" (Chapter), 107-112
God
  Adjust Ourselves to, 9
  And Soul, You-Me, 149
  Anxiety to Reach, 64

Attributes of, 79, 133
Bliss of, 17, 21, 27, 42
Cause of, 75
Channel for, 11, 107
-Consciousness, 15, 49, 150, 152
-Culture Stops War, 228
Descends to Man, 55
Detachment of, 35
Divine Plan of, 86
Draw Back Veil of, 162
Eye of, 192
Face of, 155, 162, 191-196
Faced Alone, 32
-Feeling, Definition of, 107
Feet of, 155, 183
Follower of, 92
Glory of, 155, 160
Grace of, 25
Guides Soul, 10
Heart of, 192
Highest Teachings of, 14
How to Love, 29
Is Sole Reality, 215
Knowledge of, 111
Law of, 119, 122
Life Directed by, 57, 58
Living Truth of, 54
-Love Not the Highest, 54
Mask of, 192
Meaning of Love and, 114
Messenger of, 10
Music of, 182
Must Assume a Form, 116, 200, 206
Names of, 37, 167
Neither Born or Destroyed, 147
Only Way to Find, 83
Paradoxical Nature of, 41, 44, 45, 84
Path of, 153
Path to, 137
God
  Power, 126, 155, 179

243

Control of, 10, 123-128
Interrupted, 130
-Realization, 90, 92, 94, 111, 146, 158, 159
-Realized, 155
Riddle of, 188
River of, 192
Secret of Gaining, 107, 148
Seen by Paul, 191-196
Thoughts on, 45
Three Aspects of, 71
Throne of, 165, 192
Touch Robe of, 198
True Home of, 163
Understanding of, 141
Union with, 85, 94, 110, 111, 120, 124, 152, 214
Way to Mansion of, 187
Will of, 133, 136, 170
Godhood, 61, 174, 177
Godman, 151, 152, 170, 171, 175, 176, 182, 187-189, 206
Godmen, 169
"Gopal Das. A Discourse By" (Chapter), 181-190
Gravitational Forces, 222-225
Guilt-Feelings, 80-82, 229, 235, 238

**H**

Harmonize, Inwardly, Outwardly, 108
Harmony, 132
In World Within, 124, 128
Of Man's Will, 134
-Peace, Conditions of, 135
Positive-Negative Poles in, 114
Healing by Telepathy, 231
"Heart Center, The" (Chapter), 129-132
Heart
Center, 132, 135, 136

Enemy of the, 131
Knowledge Hidden Within 157
Of the Seeker, 150
Secrets of the, 201
Hegel, 72
Hindu Kush Mountains, 7, 38
Hukikat Lok (Ninth Plane), 111
Human
Love, 116
Mind, 229-238
Will, 135
Humanity, Inspiration & Service to, 12

**I**

I AM
God, 126
That, 103
The Absolute, 155
The Lord, 193
The Soul of Every Man, 31
With You Always, 38, 50
Illumination, 177, 178
Illusion, 133, 157, 169, 171, 214, 215
Imagination, 141
Important in Attitudes, 230
Train Your, 138
True Reality, 138
Immortality, 174, 175, 225
Incarnation of Supreme Soul, 194
India, Philosophy of, 7, 14
Individual
Acts Through Universal, 132
Attitude Changed, 114
Consciousness, 139, 178
Manifestation of Power, 126
Peril to Whole Being of, 121
Responsibility, 159
Self, 158

Vibrations, 11
Will With Divine Will, 134-136
Initiates
  Channels for Master, 23
  Death of, 207
  Limited by Guru, 18
  Of Mystery Schools, 15
Initiation
  Cosmic Light, 178
  Interplay Between Master &
  Chela, 80
Inner
  Assurance, Key to, 11
  Capacities, 94
  Conflicts, 61, 64, 92, 93
  Destruction, 90
  Disharmony, 95
  ECK Master, 85
  Harmony of Life, 191
  Lives, Unorganized, 95
  Master
    Love the, 30, 33
    Takes Over, 50
  Planes, 152
  Powers Lifted, 22
  Rhythmic Attunement, 11
  -Self, 92, 94, 141
  Strength, 177
  Teachings, 171
  Voice, 170
  World, 9, 89-90, 152
    Most Powerful Force in, 113
    Real, All Else Illusion, 133
    Touch Defined, 74
    Wisdom of the, 159
Introduction to "Dialogues With
  The Master", 7
Introspection, Man Analyzes
  Through, 9
Intuition, 121, 217
Invisible
  Becomes Visible, 131
  Most Powerful Force, 113
  Soul, 35, 153, 185
  Thought, 142

J

Jesus
  Light of World, 51
  Meaning of Name, 71, 72
  Quotations of, 19, 65, 85
  Victim of Mistakes, 24

K

Kabir, 104
Kal Force
  Explained, 167
  Greater on Earth, 43
  Incarnation of, 170
  Misunderstood, 44
  Saviours, 177
  Terrorizes, 32
  Truthful to Degree, 61
Karma, 179
  Burn-Off of, 92, 100
  Controlled, 125
  Dharam Raya, Judge of, 206
Karma
  Disciple's, Master
  Administers, 206
  Law of, 170, 178
  National Cruelty Reaps, 228
  Negative, 81
  Pattern of, 80
  World, 168
  Worlds Held Together by,
  175, 177
Karmic
  Conditions, 116, 237, 238
  Effects, 91
Know Yourself, 81
Knowledge
  Awakening of, 138
  Control of Power, 61
  Divine, 157
  -Knowing, Difference
  Between, 57
  Manifests Through Souls, 137

# L

Law
Divine, 128
Invisible, 217
Of Action, 111
Of Causation, 127
Of Earth Plane, 22
Of Gravitation, 141
Of Karma, 170, 178, 214
Of Love, 18, 19, 115, 122, 140-142
Of Manu (India), 14
Of Mind, 47
Of Nature, 70, 79, 157, 167, 221
Of Opposites, 46, 47
Of Physics, 47
Of Relativity, 221
Of Reversed Effort, 211
Of Suggestion, 230
Of Vibration, 134, 140
Omnipotent, 127
Unto Yourself, 93
"Life, What Is?" (Chapter), 161-164
Life
Breath of, 161
Current of, 27-29
Divine Drama of, 10, 34
Expressed by Power, 127
Is a Paradox, 31
Mixed With Matter, 163
Reality of, 10
Stress of, 238
Light, 105, 106, 152, 161, 167, 182, 183
And Sound, 28-30, 33, 43, 46, 51, 59, 73, 110, 153, 158, 171, 179, 214
Origin of the, 192
Conveys Word, 28, 29
Cords of, 76
Experiencer Receives True, 176

From Within SUGMAD, 192, 193
Is Love and Hope, 162
Indifference to the, 68
Liberation in the, 184
Master's, 42, 51
Mental Plane, 59
Of First World Deity, 33
Of God, 191
Of the Three Worlds, 159
Of Lights, 155
Power, Not Manifestation, 156
Pursue and Lose the, 148
Sound and Form, 71
Transformed by the, 96
Like Attracts Like, 50, 211
Living ECK Master
Deity on Each Plane, 35
Destroyed Without Regret, 175
Form of the, 171
I Am The, 122
Instructs for SUGMAD, 206
Lifts Above Cause & Effect, 46
Live in Shadow of, 170
Man Cannot Live Without, 149
Paradox of the, 31
Simplifies Techniques, 10
Struggle for the, 10
Lord
God, Real, 166
Krishna, 169, 170
Of Fifth Plane (Sat Nam), 105, 106, 166
Of First World (Jot Niranjan), 32-35, 98
Of Fourth World (Sohang), 173-180
Of Infinity, True, 174
Of Second World (Omkar), 56, 57
Of the Universe, 40
Of the Worlds, 54, 104
Of Third World (Ramkar), 101, 159
Lotus

246

Flower
  A Being Stood Within, 198
  Form Illusionary, 200
  Thousand-Petalled, 43, 98
  Two-Petalled, 108
"Love, Impersonal" (Chapter),
  17-20
"Love, The True Meaning Of"
  (Chapter), 27-30
"Love, Unconditional"
  (Chapter), 113-117
Love
  Analysis of, 114, 115
  And Hate, 81
  Anticipated by Attitude, 131
  Channel of, 22, 23
  Circle of, 23
  Concentrated for Master, 84
  Contradiction of, 18
  Cord of, 11, 22, 42, 73, 80
  Discriminate Use of, 17-19
  Draws Master to Us, 73
  Fill Mind With, 138
  For the Traveler, 25, 26, 52
  Human and Divine, 114-116
  In Accord With Soul, 109, 139
  Inability to Give, 78
  Infant's Need for, 78
  Is Creative Force, 141
  Is Desire, 139
  Interpretation of, 17, 18
  Law of, 140-142
  Magnet of, 140
  Man Searches for, 81
  Of ECK Through MAHANTA,
  115
  Of Self, 78
  Power to Hold Soul High, 162
  Principle of, 17, 18
  Pure, 19, 27
  Purest, Last Invisible World,
  113
  Question of Perception,
  Action, 139
  Secret of, 17, 156
  Test of God's, 35
  Traits Developed, 135
  Vibrations, 139
  What and Whom to, 28, 29
Lower
  Astral World, 89, 91, 141
  Powers, Three, 167
  Wisdoms, 159
  World
    Plane, 151, 159
    Prophecies, 179
  Worlds, Teachings of, 144

## M

Macaulay Quotation, 46
Macrocosm, 153
MAHANTA
  Appears, 151, 152
  Body of the, 72, 150
  Channels Chela's Life, 42
  Faith in the, 110
  Love of ECK Through, 115
  Offers Salvation, 152
  Paul, Next, 238
  Sarup of the, 222
  See the "Whole" Via, 58
  Surrender to the, 83
  Teachings Given by the, 16
  Turn Problems Over to the, 60
  What Draws the, 150
  Who is the, 72, 171
  World, Body of the, 150
  You Will Become the, 172
Man
  Aggressive, Submissive Nature
  of, 63-68, 92
  An Expression of God, 34
  As Microcosm, 149
  Attitude Determines
  Experience, 131
  Battleground for Good, Evil,
  13, 61
  Born Again of Spirit, 114

Composition of, 42
Controls ECK Power, 40, 41
Creates World, 72
Deceived Prisoner, 169
Destiny of Man, 125, 174
Difficulties of, 119
Directed by Soul, 9
Ethically Different, 76
Evolves into Nothingness, 156
Has Become God Itself, 200
In Harmony With Divine
  Will, 134
Individual Origin of, 81
Is Center in Body of God, 215
Is Cosmic World, 9
Karmic Symptoms of, 237
-Kind Blind to Truth, 168
Lazy in Devotion, 24, 25
Needs Visionary Symbol, 61
Outlet of Infinite Energy, 127
Seeks God Through Religions,
  161
Selfishness of, 135
Success, Failure of, 134
Whole Being of, 110
Will of, 133, 134
-Woman, Love, 115
Works Out Salvation, 161
Marriage, 95, 115
"Master, The Voice Of The"
  (Chapter), 75-82
"Master, Who Is The?"
  (Chapter), 69-74
Master
  Absolute Trust in the, 107, 124
  Anchor Mind on Nuri-Sarup
  of the, 138
  Atma-Sarup of the, 64
  Channel of the, 39
  Conscious Awareness of the,
  11
  Disciples of the, 23
  Embodies Power in Man, 41,
  42
  For Desires, Ask the, 121
  Found by Seeker, 15, 92

Gives Mystical Experience, 92
Greatest Problem for the, 238
Hand, Touch of the, 110
Humility Toward, 77
Lord of All Planes, 56
Mercy of the, 93
Moves Others Toward
  Harmony, 67
Needs Love of Man, 21
Practice Presence of the, 68
Prepares Soul for Purification,
  33
Purpose of the, 179
Radiant Form of the, 95, 96
  108, 110, 121, 122, 125, 147,
  201, 203
Spiritual Duty of, 25, 121
Surrender to the, 11, 35, 39,
  64, 83-88
Takes Chela Karma, 80, 81,
  237
Teachings of the, 11, 152
Thought Instruction of the, 76
Withdraws Love, 18, 23
Masters
  Attributes of the Great, 29
  Cause, 39, 51
  Evolution of the, 29
  Mission of the, 53, 98, 166
  Not by Divine Commission,
  158
  Only Can See SUGMAD, 201
  Word, 172
Matter
  Formed by Thought, 39, 40
  Wave Structure, 223, 224
"Maya, The Queen of Illusion"
  (Chapter), 221-228
Maya, 149, 170, 175, 214, 216
Mental
  Attitude
    Anticipates Love, 131
    Of Confidence, 213
  Baggage, 31
  Body, 204

248

Command of Respect, 213
Mental
  Concept
    Of God, 28
    Of Self-Surrender, 83
  Efficiency, 125
  Equipment, 218
  Illness, 130
  Image Developed, 219
  Pictures, 90, 218
  Plane, 59, 97, 100, 101, 120
  Possession, Take, 124
  Processes, 91, 127
  Vibrations, 112
  World, 57
    Gate Guarded by Master, 48
    Teachings, 55-61
Mentalization, Code of, 76
Microcosm, 149, 153, 186
Middle Path (Buddha), 29
Milarepa, 75
"Mind And Its Functions, The" (Chapter), 229-238
"Mind Control" (Chapter), 45-52
"Mind, The Pure" (Chapter), 143-148
Mind
  Action, Principles of, 108
  An Instrument, 153
  Attitude of, 123, 124
  Balanced, 29, 30
  Build Qualities of, 213
  -Consciousness, 20, 49, 120, 137
  Control, 46, 47, 51, 151
    Of Masses by Priestcraft, 13
    Process of, 50
  Creative Human, 123
  Directed to Soul by Master, 10
  Disorganized, 91
  Free for God, 23, 45, 46
  Gate of the, 46
  Illusion of, 27, 28

Lift of, 80
Of Man, 109
Power
  Deludes, 56
  Needs Education, 41
Raises to God, 55
Release, 50, 146-148
Restrain the, 232
Mind
  Rules Egotistically, 9
  Seat of the, 109
  Views Its Thought, 226
  Waves, 103
Miracles, 102, 199, 200
Mortality, 174
Motion, Vibratory, 185, 187
Mozart's vs Beethoven's Compositions, 58
Music of the Spheres, 156
Mystery
  Of the Universe, 35
  Schools
    Explained, 14, 15
    Lunar Mysteries, 15
    Mystery of Nature, 15
    Solar Mysteries, 15
    Universal Mysteries, 15
Mystics, 97, 98, 101, 104, 125, 158, 159, 168, 194

N

Negative
  Attitude Destructive, 230
  Attributes, Elimination of, 180
  Creative Forces, 228
  Forces
    Attack, 51
    Generate Positive Action, 211
    Subjective Mind Open to, 121
  Points of Attraction, 213
  Power, 174

249

Agents of the, 170
Illusions, Fantastic, 169
Laws of the, 167
Misunderstood, 44
Side of Man, 64
Used by Prophets, 168
Principle of Universe, 132
Qualities
  Free of, 135
  Lose Fear of, 93
Traps Soul, 214
Negativism, Dispel, 108
Ninth Plane, 111
Niranjan
  Jot, 33, 43, 98, 167
  Kal, 174, 175
Nuri-Sarup
  Light Body, 204
  Of Master, 138
  Substitutes Faith, 231


O

Objective
  Forms, 141
  Mind, 121, 130, 232, 235, 237
  Reasoning, 121
  Self, 120
  Sensation, 125
Ocean of Love and Mercy, 106,
  163, 170, 185, 188, 191, 197,
  200, 224
Occidental-Oriental Differences,
  76
Occult
  Empires Ruin Mankind, 56
  Organizations, 161
  Powers, Destructive, 41, 231
  Studies, 111
Occultists, 179, 231
Omkar (Mental Plane Lord), 56,
  57, 100
Omnipresence, 153
  Man in Touch With, 121


P

Pain Eliminated, 232
Paradox of Life, 31-36
Passiveness, Purpose of, 63-68
Past Lives, 137
Patience, Cultivate, 134
Perfectionist, The, 68
Physical
  Body, 204, 206, 208
  Illness, 130
  Transformers, 19
  Violence Causes Karma, 65
Pineal Gland, 109, 203
Planes, Comparison of, 98-106
  Planets, 28, 197
Plato, 73
Pleasure Principle, 232, 233
Polarization of Souls, 115
Positive
  And Negative Stream, 40, 47
  63, 114, 115
  Force, 165
  Stream of Life, 29, 30
"Power, Generating" (Chapter),
  211-216
Power
  Become Conscious of Spiritual,
  123
  Conditioned to, 38
  Defined, 38
  Destructive, 211
  Genius' Used, 41
  Of God, 51
  Of Suggestion, 234
  Names of Spiritual, 37
  Seek Highest, 61
  Splits into Two Streams, 40
Prada-Vidya (God-Knowledge),
  111
Prestige Factor, The, 235
Prodigal Son, Parable of the,
  150, 167
Psychic
  Channels, 89

Destructive Experience of the,
92
Disturbances, 91
Perception Through Thoughts,
67
Research Phenomena, 175
Situation, 90

# R

Radiation, 225, 226
"Rami Nuri, A Talk With"
   (Chapter), 165-172
Raphael, 120
"Reality, The True" (Chapter),
   137-138
Reality
   Is Ocean of Love & Mercy,
   200
   Of God, 138, 171, 194
   Power As, 166
Rebazar Tarzs
   Appeared to Paul, 7
   Dialogues With Paul, 7-238
   Glance of Love of, 77
   Manifested Power, 171
   "Past Is But a Thought...",
   133
   Perfume of, 17
   Took Paul to God, 191-202
Relativity, Theory of, 221-228
Religions
   Buddhism, 57, 170, 232
   Christian Science, 231
   Christianity, 15, 57, 66, 167
   Divine & Mental Science, 231
   Hinduism, 57, 167, 237
   History of, 13-15
   Moslem, 66, 167
   Of India, 66, 167, 224
   Of Orientals, 62, 66, 67
   Sufism, 57

Use Hypnosis, 231
Vedanta, 57, 167
Religious
   Empires Ruin Mankind, 56
   Systems
      Delusions of, 174, 176
      The Revelations of, 178
Respect, Command, 213
Riddle
   Of Frog-Centipede, 148
   Of Life, 34, 36

# S

Sach Khand, 104, 106, 166
Sainthood, Grace of, 199
Saints, 94, 96, 104-106, 134, 165
   166, 168, 173, 183, 227
Salvation
   In the Sound (Word), 184
   Of Souls by ECK Saints, 194
Samadhi, 233, 234, 237
Sat Nam, 43, 104-106, 111, 150,
   165-167
Sat Purusha, 165
Scientists, 97-99, 101, 104
Scriptures, Man-made Laws, 158
Second Grand Division, 29, 35,
   40, 100, 124, 163, 164, 174,
   176, 200, 228
Secret
   Language, 77
   Of All Secrets, 157
Seeker
   Of God, 161
   Of Truth, 163
   Problems Beset, 89
"Self-Surrender" (Chapter), 83-
   88
Self
   Condemnation, 93
   -Consciousness, 159, 176, 213
   -Control, 50, 135

251

-Delusion, 157
-Division, 94
Ignorance of True, 119
-Indulgence, 78
Is Maya, 149
-Knowledge, Wisdom Revealed
    Through, 10, 70
Negative, 120
Objective, 120, 121
-Preservation, 178
-Realization, 111
-Regard of Soul, 61
Spirit, 145
Subconscious, 130
Subjective, 11, 121, 122
-Surrender to Master, 83
Universal, 145
Senses in All Bodies, 73
Sex Urge, Creative, 115
Shakespeare, 120
Shame, Greatest Problem, 238
Shankacharya's Doctrine of
    Maya, 221
Shariyat-Ki-Sugmad, 144
Silver Cord, 208
Sixth, Seventh Planes, 166
"Sohang Speaks, The Lord"
    (Chapter), 173-180
Sohang, 103, 173-180
Solar Plexis, 130
Sorrow and Joy, 79
"Soul, The Desire Of"
    (Chapter), 139-142
Soul
    Anguish of, 10
    Awakening Process of, 151,
    152, 178
    Becomes
        A Saint, 106
    Channel for ECK, 94
Soul
    Bodies of, 34, 101, 186, 203-
    206
    Cataclysmic Experiences of, 93

Dependence Upon, 120
Descends Through Bodies,
    150, 151
Elevation of, 200
Essence of the, 70
Evolution of, 21, 28
Experiences World of No-
    Mind, 144
Expresses Divine Love
    Through Sex, 116
Faculty of, 110
Freed of Conscious Mind, 137
Goal of, 175, 186
Guardian of, 120
Guided by God, 9, 10
Illusion of, 80, 168, 170, 214
In Harmony With Divine Will,
    134
Incarnations of, 151, 194
Individual, 35
Liberation of, 208
Light, 101, 223
Manifests Knowledge, 137
Measuring Stick for, 152
Misguided, 158
No Punishment-Reward of,
    195
Now God, The Absolute, 156
Of Indescribable Light
    (Sohang), 173
Peace of, 11
Perfected, Approach God, 166
Power Through Way of, 159
Riddle of, 188
Seat of the, 109
Self-Regard of, 61
Sick of, 92
Spiritual Counterpart of, 176
Struggles, 138, 151
Submits Self to Master, 84, 85
Subsists on Spiritual Nectar,
    182
Supreme & Individual, 153,
    194
Tests of, 32, 33

True
>Home of, 104, 151, 152, 154, 169, 175, 178, 179, 191, 194
>Marriage of ECK &, 115
>Wandering of, 150, 151

Sound Current, 96, 99-105, 152-154, 155, 176
>Known as God, 126
>Listen to the, 82, 147
>Moves us Homeward, 188, 189
>Of OM, 174, 177, 178
>Of AUM, 57, 100, 101, 168
>Originates From Vibratory Motion, 164
>Teachings of the, 11

Sounds of Various Planes, 99-103, 145

Spirit, Power Possessed by, 113

Spirito-Material Worlds, 100

"Spiritual Conflicts" (Chapter), 63-68

"Spiritual Power, The" (Chapter), 37-44

"Spiritual Wealth, The Experience of" (Chapter), 123-128

Spiritual
>Activity, Polarized, 107
>Attainment, Secret of, 138
>Benefits, 11
>Breath, 21
>Cities
>>Agam Des, Tibet, 143, 144 148
>>Quito, South America, 19
>Conceptions, 81, 114
>Conflicts, Two Main, 63-68
>Courage, 177
>Current, 24, 192
>Duty of ECK Master, 19, 25
>Energy Manifested, 49
>Entity, 109
>Evolution, 13
>Exercises, 145, 147, 152

Eye, 108, 122, 167, 193

Forces
>Balance of, 21
>Control of, 123

Freedom, Progress Toward, 170, 185

Giants, 13, 38

Hand Clasp, 74

Hierarchy, 24, 151, 166, 168, 194

Journey, 7, 32

Kingdom, Passport to, 142

Knowledge, 157

Law, 125
>Of Love, 18, 19, 139-142

Leaders of Mystery Schools, 14, 15

Life, Creation of, 141

Mantle, 14

Mission of Soul, 151

Nature of God, 123

Path, Advancement on, 18

Power, 10, 21, 37-39, 108

Preparation Finished, 138

Process, Reasoning, 114

Rhythm of Self, 11

Searchlights, Questions, 114

Strength, 38-40

Striving Causes Illness, 80

Talent, 138

Truth, 10, 74

Spirit
>Welfare Seeker, 15
>Worlds Within Us, 10

Streams
>Negative, 29-31, 167, 168
>Of Consciousness, 48-50
>Of God-Current, 37, 38
>Of Light, 53
>Of Thought, 48, 49
>Positive, 29, 30

Subconscious
>Attributes of the, 58-61
>Directs Mental Powers, 57
>Eruption of the, 91

First Step to God, 59
Mind, 125, 130, 132, 218, 233, 234, 237
Process, Habitual, 229
Responsive to Conscious Will, 132
Self, 130
Theatre of Phenomena, 120
Subjective
Mind, 121, 233, 234
Self, 122
Sensations, 125
Submissive Nature, Purpose of, 63-68
"SUGMAD Speaks, The" (Chapter), 197-202
SUGMAD
A Living Force, 105, 106
Attributes of, 27
Believe in the, 142
Bring Problems to, 20
Creator Within Called the, 153
Face of the, 183, 191-196
First Manifestation of the, 185
Highest Creator, 166
House of the, 193
Love the, 19, 23, 28, 194
Master is the, 71
Religions Lost Contact With the, 184
Soul Guided by the, 144
Talks to Paul, 193-196
Three-Form Eye Symbol of the, 73
To Approach the, 186
True Home of the, 191
Truth of the, 144
Unharmed, Those Who Realize the, 158
Universal Body of the, 145
Will of the, 135
Supreme
Being, 105, 106, 111, 163, 165, 166, 188, 206
Son, 195, 201

**T**

Tension, Conflicts Released, 86
Tenth Door, 199
Thales, Greek Philosopher, 81
Third
And Fourth Grand Division, 132
Plane, 127, 176, 200, 205
Thought
Active Energy, 120
Atoms, 48
Automatic, 129
Combined With Feeling Brings Change, 114
Creates, 40, 73, 155
Difficult to Express, 77
Edit Your, 213
Forms, Importance of, 141, 142
Imprisons, Releases, 227
Instruction from Master, 76
Kept Pure, 133
Life Result of Conscious, 129-131
Non-Resistant, 131, 218
Others Sense Our Innermost, 67
Pattern, Anger Forms a, 212
Power
Extended, 53
Of Cause & Effect, 41
Processes, Control of, 126-128
Responsibility for, 77
Solidifies into Situation, 50
Threefold Aspects of Deity, 71, 73
"Tiger's Fang, The", 7
Tisra Til, 108, 124
Traveler,
Adheres to Earth's Laws, 22
Buffeted by Negative Force, 23
Is Light & Sound Blended, 30
Is Symbol of Inner Worlds, 48

254

Manifests Elements of
SUGMAD, 28
Needs Love of Man, 21-23
Trinity Explained, 71, 167
Truth
Defined, 163
Is Will of God, 133
Mystic, 137
Of Truths, 193, 197
Truths of God, 55, 56
Twitchell, Paul
Attitude Changed, 139
Commissioned by SUGMAD,
195
Conditioned to Power Quickly,
38, 39
ECK Channel, 54
Granted Sainthood, 199
Incarnation of Supreme Soul,
194
Inner Problem of, 58, 59
Method of Contacting Rebazar
Tarzs, 53
Purpose in Life, 202
Revelation with Milarepa, 75
Special Mission of, 137
Spiritual
Duty of, 26, 201
Goal Discussed, 69, 70
Taken to see God, 191-202
The Mind of, 119
Thrice-Born, 201

U

Uncreated Becomes The
Created, 131
Union of Man & Woman, 116
Universal
Becomes Individualized, 131
Body, 58, 111, 126, 158
Cause, 39, 42, 53, 97
Form, 153

Fountain of ECK-Power, 127
Love Atmosphere, 112
Mind, 100, 122, 131, 132, 153
Plan, 109
Self of God, 150
Spirit, 106
"Universe, The Paradox Of
The" (Chapter), 31-36
Universe
Chaos in, 159
Created, 40
One Power in the, 126
Secret of the, 52
Supreme Center of, 154

V

Vairagi, Ancient Order of the,
144
Vedas, 97, 101, 103, 111
Vibrations
Between Master & Chela, 77
Control of, 107
Cosmic, 17
Counter-, Impatience Sets Up,
155
Drew Rebazar Tarzs, 53
Energy, 65
Established by Master, 51, 138
Law of, 134
Love, 139
Motion is Prime Cause, 164
Pace of Individual, 10, 11
Right Mind, 50
Types of, 63
Vibratory
Channel for God, 11
Control, 49, 50
Motion
Of the Word, 185
Sound Currents Originate
from, 186
Visions, 91, 92

Visualization, 212
Voice of
  God, 52, 153, 162
  Silence, 79

## W

Water Symbol of Rebirth, 81, 82
Wheel of Eighty-Four, 105, 184
Whole, The, 58, 176
"Will Power, The" (Chapter),
  133-136
Will
  Human & Divine, 133-136
  Power, 88, 135, 230
"Wisdom, Practical" (Chapter),
  119-122
Wisdom
  Absorb, 109
  Astral vs Higher, 25
  Final Meaning of all, 214
  In Worlds Within, 125
  Of God, 172, 202
  Of Wholeness, 227
  Revealed Through Self-
  Knowledge, 10
Word, The, 184, 185
Words, Importance of, 141,
  142

World
  First, 33
  Inner, 9, 32, 124, 125, 133,
  148
  Law of the, 79
  Of Rebellion, 135
  Outer, 9, 124, 127, 148
  Subjective, Setbacks in, 32
  Without, Reflection of Within,
  124, 133
Worlds
  Messenger of the, 194
  Ten Million, 78

## Y

Yaubl Sacabi, 143-148, 165
Yoga
  Heart Center, 125
  Mantram, 60
  Pranic, 43
  Raja, 56
  Supreme Being in, 100, 101
  Teachings of, 89

## Z

Zikar, 147

# ECKANKAR Also Offers Spiritual Study Courses

People want to know the secrets of life and death. In response to this need Sri Harold Klemp, today's spiritual leader of Eckankar, and Paul Twitchell, its modern-day founder, have written special monthly discourses which reveal the Spiritual Exercises of ECK—to lead Soul in a direct way to God.

Those who wish to study Eckankar can receive these special monthly discourses which give clear, simple instructions for the spiritual exercises. The first two annual series of discourses are called *Soul Travel 1—The Illuminated Way* and *The ECK Dream Discourses*. Mailed each month, the discourses are designed to lead the individual to the Light and Sound of God.

The exercises in these discourses, when practiced twenty minutes a day, are likely to prove survival beyond death. Many have used them as a direct route to Self-Realization, where one learns his mission in life. The next stage, God Consciousness, is the joyful state wherein Soul becomes the spiritual traveler, an agent for God. The underlying principle one learns is this: Soul exists because God loves It.

## Study of the ECKANKAR discourses includes:

1. Twelve monthly discourse lessons (Some titles from the series *Soul Travel 1—The Illuminated Way:* "The Law of Strength," "Love as the Doorway to Heaven," "The Universality of Soul Travel," and "The Spiritual Cities of This World." From *The ECK Dream Discourses:* "Dreams—The Bridge to Heaven" and "The Dream Master.")
2. The *Mystic World,* a quarterly newsletter with articles about Spirit and a special Wisdom Note and feature article by today's Living ECK Master, Sri Harold Klemp.
3. Special mailings to keep you informed of upcoming seminars and activities around the world, new study materials, tapes from Eckankar, and more.

---

## How to find out more about the monthly ECKANKAR discourses

For more information on how to receive these discourses, use the coupon at the back of this book. Or during business hours, call (612) 544-0066, weekdays. Or write: **ECKANKAR, Att: ECK Study, P.O. Box 27300, Minneapolis, MN 55427 U.S.A.**

# Introductory Books on ECKANKAR
# The Ancient Science of Soul Travel

## The Wind of Change, Sri Harold Klemp

What are the hidden spiritual reasons behind every event in your life? With stories drawn from his own lifelong training, Eckankar's spiritual leader shows you how to use the power of Spirit to discover those reasons. Follow him from the Wisconsin farm of his youth, to a military base in Japan; from a job in Texas, into the realms beyond, as he shares the secrets of Eckankar.

## In My Soul I Am Free, Brad Steiger

Here is the incredible life story of Paul Twitchell—prophet, healer, Soul Traveler—whose spiritual exercises have helped thousands to contact the Light and Sound of God. Brad Steiger lets the famed ECK Master tell you in his own words about Soul Travel, healing in the Soul body, the role of dreams and sleep, and more. Includes a spiritual exercise called "The Easy Way."

## ECKANKAR—The Key to Secret Worlds,
Paul Twitchell

Paul Twitchell, modern-day founder of Eckankar, gives you the basics of this ancient teaching. Includes six specific Soul Travel exercises to see the Light and hear the Sound of God, plus case histories of Soul Travel. Learn to recognize yourself as Soul—and journey into the heavens of the Far Country.

## The Tiger's Fang, Paul Twitchell

Paul Twitchell's teacher, Rebazar Tarzs, takes him on a journey through vast worlds of Light and Sound, to sit at the feet of the spiritual Masters. Their conversations bring out the secret of how to draw closer to God—and awaken Soul to Its spiritual destiny. Many have used this book, with its vivid descriptions of heavenly worlds and citizens, to begin their own spiritual adventures.

For more free information about the books and teachings of Eckankar, please write: **ECKANKAR, Att: Information, P.O. Box 27300, Minneapolis, MN 55427 U.S.A.**

Or look under ECKANKAR in your local phone book for an Eckankar Center near you.

# There May Be an
# ECKANKAR Study Group near You

Eckankar offers a variety of local and international activities for the spiritual seeker. With over three hundred study groups worldwide, Eckankar is near you! Many cities have Eckankar Centers where you can browse through the books in a quiet, unpressured environment, talk with others who share an interest in this ancient teaching, and attend beginning discussion classes on the spiritual principles of ECK.

Around the world, Eckankar study groups offer special one-day or weekend seminars on the basic teachings of Eckankar. **Check your phone book under ECKANKAR, or write ECKANKAR, Att: Information, P.O. Box 27300, Minneapolis, MN 55427 U.S.A. for the Eckankar Center or study group nearest you.**

☐ Please send me information on the nearest Eckankar discussion or study group in my area.

☐ I would like an application form for the twelve-month Eckankar study discourses on the innermost secrets of Soul Travel and spiritual unfoldment.

Please type or print clearly                                    941

Name _____

Street _____ Apt. # _____

City _____ State/Prov. _____

Zip/Postal Code _____ Country _____

(Our policy: Your name and address are held in strict confidence. We do not rent or sell our mailing lists. Nor will anyone call on you. Our purpose is only to show people the ECK way home to God.)

**ECKANKAR**
**Att: Information**
**P.O. Box 27300**
**Minneapolis, MN 55427**
**U.S.A.**